EARLY TRAUMA

Green Balloon Publishing

Professor Dr Franz Ruppert is Professor of Psychology at the University of Applied Science in Munich, Germany. He gained his PhD in Work and Organisational Psychology at the Technical University of Munich in 1985.

Since 1995 he has specialised in psychotherapeutic work, with a particular focus on the aetiology of severe mental disorders. This has led him to an in depth study of attachment processes and trauma, and the resulting impact of early traumatisation on the infant.

His publications include: *Verwirrte Seelen* (2002, Kösel, Munich), (*Confused Souls*, not available in English), followed by four books translated from German into English: *Trauma, Bonding & Family Constellations: Understanding and Healing Injuries of the Soul* (2008), *Splits in the Soul: Integrating Traumatic Experiences* (2011), *Symbiosis & Autonomy: Symbiotic Trauma and Love Beyond Entanglements* (2012), *Trauma, Fear and Love; How the Constellations of the Intention Supports Healthy Autonomy* (2014) all published in English by Green Balloon Publishing, Steyning, UK.

Ruppert teaches in Germany and many other countries including Brazil, Canada, Britain, Ireland, Italy, Russia, Netherlands, Poland, Portugal, Romania, Turkey and Spain, furthering his insights into the deeper transgenerational effects of trauma in different cultures, and researching the methodology of constellations as a means of better understanding the effects and healing of trauma.

About this book

This book is a collection of essays on the topic of pre-, peri- and post-natal issues that are traumatising for the infant. Professor Franz Ruppert is the editor and contributes three essays. Practitioners who work with his theories and method, bringing their own particular interest and expertise to understanding this subject of early trauma, have written the other 16 essays.

The book covers a wide range of issues: the influence of the attitude of the mother and father towards the unborn child, the 'unwanted' child, inability to get pregnant, IVF, miscarriages and stillbirths, abortion, adoption, pre- and post-natal depression, attachment failure, marital violence, and more. As such the book provides a rich resource of thinking, ideas and research. The early life of the infant, from conception on, will be the most important therapeutic exploration and consideration of our time, having far-reaching effect on who we are as individuals and as a species, and how we think about our development into the future. This is an exciting book. Ruppert has drawn together some extraordinary writers, whose writing is informative and compelling.

Vivian Broughton, Editor of the English language version. Translated from the German edition *Frühes Trauma* (2014), Klett-Cotta, Stuttgart

Other books by Franz Ruppert published in English translation by Green Balloon Publishing:
Trauma, Bonding and Family Constellations: Understanding and Healing Injuries of the Soul (2008)
Splits in the Soul: Integrating Traumatic Experiences (2011)
Symbiosis and Autonomy: Symbiotic Trauma and Love Beyond Entanglements (2012)
(Above titles originally published in German by Klett-Cotta, Stuttgart)
Trauma, Fear and Love: How the Constellation of the Intention Supports Healthy Autonomy (2014)
(Originally published in German by Kösel-Verlag, München)

EARLY TRAUMA

Pregnancy, Birth and the First Years of Life

Franz Ruppert

Co-Authors:

Birgit Assel, Doris Brombach, Vivian Broughton,
Annemarie Denk, Christina Freund, Gabriele Hoppe,
Liesel Krüger, Petra Lardschneider, Cordula Schulte,
Alice Schultze-Kraft, Manuela Specht, Andrea Stoffers,
Dagmar Strauss, Marta Thorsheim, Margriet Wentink

Translated by Julia Stuebs
with the assistance of Rick Hosburn

Edited for the English edition by Vivian Broughton

Green Balloon Publishing

First published in the United Kingdom in 2016
by Green Balloon Publishing

German edition first published under the title Frühes Trauma
by Klett-Cotta

All case studies in this book are based on real events. In order to protect
the identity of those concerned, names and, where necessary,
personal details have been altered.

Green Balloon Publishing, Steyning
www.greenballoonbooks.co.uk

ISBN 978-0-9559683-7-2

Book production by The Choir Press, Gloucester
Set in Times

Contents

Preface   ix
English Language Editor's Foreword   xiii

1   Early traumatisation and the 'Constellation of the Intention' *Franz Ruppert*   1

2   Conception as a source of early trauma *Marta Thorsheim*   54

3   Maternal ambivalence during pregnancy *Alice Schultze-Kraft*   66

4   Unfulfilled desire to have children. *Annemarie Denk*   76

5   Abortions and trauma *Gabriele Hoppe*   89

6   Traumatic experiences in the womb *Doris Brombach*   111

7   Pregnancy and giving birth from the perspective of multi-generational psychotraumatology *Birgit Assel*   119

8   Premature birth as the result and cause of traumatisations *Manuela Specht*   148

9   The process of separation and re-bonding: the final birth phase *Dagmar Strauss*   157

10   Miscarriages and stillbirths as trauma *Cordula Schulte*   173

11   'Psychosis' following the birth *Petra Lardschneider*   186

12   Mothers caught between wanting to have a career, having financial difficulties and making time for their children *Christina Freund*   197

13   Growing up with grandparents as an early trauma *Andrea Stoffers*   209

Contents

14 Violence instead of love from the very start
Margriet Wentink   218

15 Early trauma, adoption and foster parents
Liesel Krüger   234

16 Eating disorders as a consequence of early
traumatisation *Andrea Stoffers*   246

17 'Anorexia' and early trauma   *Franz Ruppert*   253

18 Symbiotic trauma in the individual setting
Vivian Broughton   256

19 Healing and prevention of early traumas
Franz Ruppert   267

Glossary of Special Terms   274
The authors   276
References   281
Index   293

Preface

We may be aware of the fact that we are usually nine months old when we arrive in this world, but it is not generally understood that our psychological life begins in the time before we are born. If it were, we would have a different attitude towards nascent life – in our partnerships, families, pre-natal care, midwifery, and in thinking about assisted reproduction.

Unborn children show awareness, feeling and recognition. Their experiences during pregnancy and the birth process shape their subsequent physical and psychological development. These experiences can be good and loving ones that lay a solid foundation for a stable, self-contained personality, or they can be stressful experiences that may negatively influence the person's entire life.

So in the course of psychotherapy, intense consideration should be given to the various experiences that can cause an 'early trauma'. If people suffer from symptoms that could be described as 'anxiety, 'depression', 'personality disorders' or even 'psychosis', then it is possible that the cause may be found before the patient was born.

Early trauma is the continuation of the project of developing a comprehensive theory of trans-generational psychotraumatology. I began this project when I wrote *Verwirrte Seelen* [Confused Souls, not translated into English] (2002, Kösel, Munich). This book was followed by *Trauma, Bonding and Family Constellations; Splits in the Soul;* and *Symbiosis & Autonomy* published in the original German in 2005, 2007 and 2010 by Klett-Cotta, Stuttgart, and in English translation in 2008, 2011 and 2012 by Green Balloon Publishing, Steyning, UK. These were followed by *Trauma, Fear & Love*, which was published in 2012 once again by Kösel, Munich, and in 2014 in English by Green Balloon Publishing.

The 'Constellation of the Intention', based on my theory of trans-generational psychotraumatology, has since become a therapeutic method in its own right for treating trauma. It can be applied to a wide spectrum of psychological and physical symptoms, identifying the cause in depth and developing suitable ways of helping. As the many case studies in this book demonstrate, this method is particularly suitable for gaining insight into the stored wordless memories from the time before the development of speech. From the point of view of a transgenerational trauma therapy it is important that the focus is not only directed at conception, pregnancy, birth and early infancy and childhood, but must include the historic period from the end of the 19th century and the start of the 20th century, because those born around the 1930s also seek psychotherapeutic help, and their parents and grandparents who lived during this period may have experienced very different conditions during pregnancy and giving birth.

Through their training in my theory and method, and their own personal work, some therapists have developed personally and professionally along these lines. So it was not difficult to find authors, all of whom are women who, based on their own personal experiences and their experience as therapists, were able to deal with subjects relevant to "Early Trauma". Their contributions to this book are written primarily from the perspective of practitioners.

I am extremely grateful to Birgit Assel, Doris Brombach, Vivian Broughton, Annemarie Denk, Christina Freund, Gabriele Hoppe, Liesel Krüger, Petra Lardschneider, Cordula Schulte, Alice Schultze-Kraft, Manuela Specht, Andrea Stoffers, Dagmar Strauss, Marta Thorsheim and Margriet Wentink for their spontaneous willingness to contribute their knowledge, their intuition and their therapeutic commitment to this book.

One author, Doris Brombach, died completely unexpectedly on 25th January 2014. We are all deeply saddened by Doris's death and hope that her contribution to this book will show the intensity with which she devoted herself to her therapeutic work. Through her contribution to this book we will have very special memories of her.

I am especially grateful to the employees of the Klett-Cotta publishing company. Dr Christine Treml, as reader, has guided the book with her customary assurance and brought it to publication. And again, my heartfelt thanks to Vivian Broughton for editing the translation into English and also to John Mitchell from Green Balloon for making the book available for English readers.

Also my thanks to Julia Stuebs who has done a wonderful job of translating the manuscript from German, and to Rick Hosburn for his assistance.

Munich, May 2016   Franz Ruppert

Note on text:
I have varied the use of male and female pronouns. All usage always applies to both unless it is a specific person in a case example.

Bibliographical references in the text are to the English edition where one exists.

English Language Editor's Foreword

As the editor of the English language version of this book, and privileged to be a contributor also, I am very excited at its publication. This is such an important topic.

My thanks to Julia Stuebs, the translator, for her excellent translation of the text; her work makes mine easier and I believe our collaboration then offers a book that makes this difficult topic accessible and absorbing for the English reader.

In addition I would mention John McClean for his assiduous proof-reading; Miles Bailey and his colleagues at The Choir Press for their excellent handling of the production of the book; and John Mitchell of Green Balloon Publishing for his co-ordination and management of the project.

Vivian Broughton
English Language Editor

1

Early traumatisation and the 'Constellation of the Intention'

Franz Ruppert

Starting the Motor of Life

Manfred[1] has come to therapy for his third constellation[2]. In the previous two constellations he had been working on heart symptoms that had been troubling him and making him anxious. Amongst other symptoms he had high blood pressure and palpitations. He is forty years old and an only child. He only met his father two years ago because his parents separated when his mother was pregnant with him. He grew up in his mother's family, who had rejected his father as being "unsuitable for their daughter". In his first constellation, in a relatively large group, he chose a woman to represent his intention. In this way his symbiotic entanglement with his mother was plainly visible; by choosing someone of the opposite sex to represent himself, he showed he was still unable to differentiate clearly between himself and her. In his second constellation he again chose a woman to represent his intention. This time it became clear to him how little his mother had been there for him, that she had not been prepared to be a mother to him. At his third constellation (in a private session), apart from me, there was a guest student present. His intention was to find out why so often he has cold hands and feet,

---

[1]   All names have been changed in all the case studies.

[2]   The therapy method used in this case study – the 'Constellation of the Intention' will be described more closely later in this chapter.

and how he could change that. Shortly before this, he had done an ECG test on a bicycle ergometer during which, paradoxically, the more he exerted himself, the colder his hands became. He thought that this might have something to do with an experience of power-lessness. When I asked him what situation he was thinking of, his birth occurred to him, which had been difficult and had taken a very long time. The umbilical cord had been round his neck and he had been delivered by emergency caesarean. When he was born, his face was already turning blue and he was taken immedi-ately to the paediatric clinic where he remained alone for several days, without his mother.

This time he consciously chose me, a man, to represent his intention, which was to discover the cause of his cold hands and feet.

As his intention, my first impression is that I have a clear head and can take in everything around me. I feel very sharp, as if I am completely in control of everything, or at least aware of every-thing. However, I don't feel the rest of my body. It's as if I've just been put there, feet positioned close to one another and the hands hanging down motionless. After a while I notice that I'm unable to move, even if I had wanted to. Instructions from the head don't get through to the body; impulses to move don't arrive lower down. I tell Manfred this and he confirms that he often feels a blockage in the region of his throat, neck and shoulders. Yes, that's what it feels like to me: as if there was a huge, thick block that is isolating the head from the rest of the body.

This makes me think more and more about the birth situation that Manfred had previously described. I feel wide-awake but somehow pushed aside. I feel like I was just laid down after the birth, and now I'm lying there and waiting and I can't do anything. When I tell Manfred my sensations he confirms them, and now he'd like to include his father in the constellation. He says that a few days before he had been walking with him in the mountains and he had felt very good. His hands and feet had also been warm.

As the representative of his intention, I can't understand this suggestion. Obviously the contact with 'our father' had not solved

2

the problem for good; to do that we had had to remain dependent on help from outside, on someone who is there for us, and this did not seem a good idea for me. Instead we have to find the solution to our problem from inside. Manfred thinks about this and then agrees. He now asks me, as his intention, what I need in order to feel better. The impact of this question slowly dawns on me. I feel touched that someone is actually interested in how I feel and what I need so that I can feel better. From deep down in my body I feel an avalanche of sadness rising up which culminates in an intense fit of weeping. Manfred, who till now had stood about half a metre away from me, now comes towards me and I can rest my head on his shoulder. My whole body starts to shiver intensely and suppressed sadness makes its way through me. My right ear is pressed to Manfred's chest and I hear his heart beating furiously. He embraces me, rests his head on my shoulder and begins to weep as well.

After a while I notice that my legs want to move. First I lift one leg and then the other. From the perspective of a baby I experience it as kicking. Manfred spontaneously imitates this leg movement. After a while the kicking exhausts me and I want to rest from this exertion and sleep for a little. The thought then occurs to me that I can't yet stand on these 'baby' legs. This thought activates my arms and I raise them to cling to Manfred's jumper. Now I feel more secure. I can hold on myself.

After a while I notice that I feel agitated. However, it's not that I'm over-excited, as Manfred initially thinks, but it feels like a good form of excitement. I'm excited that something is happening around me and that I'm challenged to react. It's something similar to anticipation, readiness and joie de vivre all at the same time. I feel ready to live!

The contact with Manfred feels pleasantly warm. I feel that I'm becoming more at one with him and I am slowly sinking into him. I can easily imagine, from inside there, being able to function as a driving force from within him.

We end the constellation. Manfred is visibly moved and charged with energy. I have also just had a very profound experience of how it might feel for a new-born baby if he has a complicated birth that makes him split psychologically, with a part of him descending into a passive observer role. It was fascinating to experience how the driving force in such a child can come to life again and how feelings and movement can start flowing again. After allowing the experience of pain and sadness to be expressed, the zest for life has been released.

Some weeks later, Manfred told me that he no longer had any problems with cold hands and feet and that he had discovered that he's going to become a father.

1.1 Trans-generational psychotraumatology

Cold feet and hands – the result of a trauma? In Manfred's case the answer is obviously yes. He had tried to solve the problem in many different ways (thick socks, warm shoes, hot baths, warming creams), none of which had provided lasting help. And physical exercise, which normally stimulates the circulation, had resulted in the exact opposite. The many and diverse physical and psychological symptoms we humans suffer from are specific as well as quite common. We have fears that will not disappear; we suffer from insomnia and nightmares, we feel listless and see little hope for the future, we become stuck in destructive relationships or feel internally empty, lonely or confused. In addition we frequently suffer from physical illnesses that don't improve despite medication, massage or medical operations, and some of these illnesses, such as cancer and autoimmune diseases, can become life threatening.

I am more and more convinced that an apparently 'objective' theoretical construct, such as 'illness', does not do justice to the subjectivity of our human existence. In my view often what manifests in our bodies that we call 'illness' is the result of harmful interpersonal relationships in which we find ourselves helpless, powerless and trapped. My experience has shown that most of the symptoms for which clients seek help are the result of trauma, even if sometimes the symptoms appear quite mundane. The question is then: what particular trauma is reflected in a particular physical or psychological symptom? Finding that out seems to me to be the most important challenge for effective psychotherapy. How does one arrive at the point of the original trauma that caused the symptom and is still generating it? When one has understood that people can be traumatised by more than one event, a further question arises: how can the different traumas be separated from one another and be therapeutically addressed, when in many cases they are superimposed on one another and originate from different periods of the person's life?

The study of trauma, 'psychotraumatology', is a scientific discipline that has seen huge advances in knowledge in the last few years by, amongst others I would like to mention here, Fischer and Riedesser (1998), Levine (2010), Seidler, Freyberger and Maercker (2011), Huber (2013), Heller and Lapierre (2013) and Rauwald (2013). In my opinion the most important criterion for what constitutes a 'trauma' is the fact that the human psyche is unable to process traumatic experiences and integrate them into the individual's life, and so has to split in order to keep the memory of the traumatic experience out of the person's consciousness. A traumatised psyche is therefore unable to handle the stream of impressions of reality in a balanced way. It permanently resists reality by denying, suppressing, and not wanting to know about the traumatising experiences. Unlike stressful experiences, it is not possible for an individual simply to recover from traumatising experiences, which remain psychologically active until the specific trauma is worked on.

From the basic findings of psychotraumatology, I have, step by step, developed the theory of 'multi-generational psychotraumatology' (Ruppert 2001, 2002, 2008, 2011, 2012, 2014). At the core of this theory lies the 'symbiotic trauma'. We refer to 'symbiotic trauma' when a child, being existentially reliant upon the psychological and physical care of his mother, does not receive enough warmth, contact, nourishment and, most importantly, love, thus rendering him defenceless, powerless and helpless, causing him psychologically to split off his existential fears, his anger, sorrow and pain. The child's psychological development is therefore neither integrated nor stable; he finds it difficult to establish a healthy ego-structure and his autonomic development is blocked. He remains fixated on his mother his whole life as his primary survival strategy of continually trying to get his mother's love and achieve some kind of contact with her. I have named the psychological processes that develop as survival strategies from a symbiotic trauma as 'symbiotic entanglement'. (Ruppert 2012, p. 120ff.)

I am very happy to be able continually to develop and refine this theory due to the many clients that I have accompanied therapeutically in their psychological explorations, and so I have added a further category to the original model which differentiates between four categories of traumatisation (existential trauma, loss trauma, symbiotic trauma and bonding system trauma). This additional categorisation stresses the traumatisation that is caused by lack of love and through violence in our earliest relationships. It makes the presence of perpetrators and victims in early relationships the focal point.

So there are two forms of traumatisation that dominate in most of the people who come to me for therapy:

- the traumatisation of their need for love and their ability to love, and
- the traumatisation of their sexuality.

I include both these forms of traumatisation within the larger context of traumas caused by human violence. On the periphery of this sphere we also have the traumas that have been caused by natural disaster (figure 1).

1.2 Traumatisation through natural disaster

There are many natural disasters that can traumatise people: fire, water, heat, cold, wind, landslides, earthquakes, lightning and viral or bacterial agents. Often with such events there are many other people, whole villages or towns that are affected by the natural disaster. Those who are actually traumatised by such events are usually those who have no way of taking any action to protect their health and their life. As a rule, natural disasters

Traumatisation by Natural forces

Traumatisation by Violence

Traumatisation of Sexuality

Traumatisation of Love

Early Psychotrauma

Figure 1: Traumatisation with the key aspects of violence
and lack of love.

trigger help and support, and lead to solidarity between those people who have been affected most and those who still have the resources to go on living. As a rule, natural disasters also set in motion the attempt to achieve better protection from such dangers in the future, to take preventative measures and develop effective rescue and support plans, even if there are frequent obstacles in the form of conflicting political and financial interests. We cannot suppose that 'nature' intends to cause violence against us; we can only deal with the forces of nature objectively, use them to our advantage and protect ourselves against them as much as possible.

1.3 Traumatisation through human violence

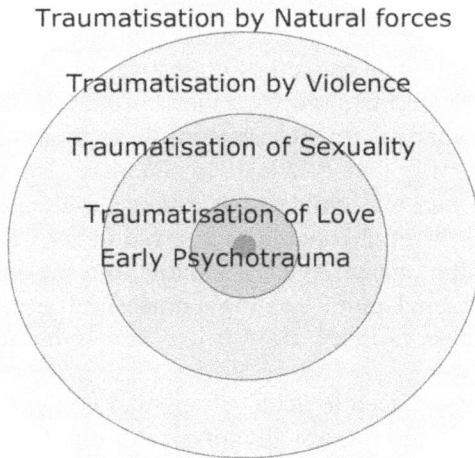

People use violence against one another in many different ways: through physical strength or superior weaponry, through insults and verbal abuse and by the withdrawal of existential resources, both material and emotional. Not giving another person the help they need can also be seen as being a perpetrator, for example if someone purposefully withholds water from a person who is dying of thirst. In this way perpetrators turn other people into victims.

There are individual as well as collective forms of violence. If, for example, a man hits a woman, that can be a traumatic experience for the woman; if the government of a country declares war on another country, that can lead to the mass traumatisation of many men, women and children. If whole swathes of a countryside are rendered uninhabitable, the environment and crops are destroyed, populations enslaved or exploited in the name of capital growth and personal gain, causing immeasurable pain for many people, this is also violence, even if it is hidden behind 'economic considerations'.

Violence can be used to achieve personal goals, for example if an individual wants to possess the physical body, the money or the property of another person, or if a person wants to impose his will on others without consideration of their needs and interests. Achieving lasting power over others and controlling them can be violence in itself.

Violence can also be a legitimate means of protecting oneself against violence from another or others. So it depends on the reason for using violence, but the danger of using violence is that it can always lead to traumatisation of the perpetrator as well as the victim, thereby setting off a spiral of continuing and increasing violence.

Victimhood and Victim Attitudes

Victims of violence are traumatised when they are rendered powerless and helpless, and the activation of their stress programmes actually increases their powerlessness, because the perpetrator reacts to the victim's stress reactions with the use of even more violence or by denying them help. A child's crying, for example, can provoke a mother to hit her child, or leave him on his own, denying him any good connection with her.

A victim survives such a situation by suppressing his stress reactions and his longing for help, which he can only achieve by the process of psychological splitting or fragmentation: the stress reactions and helplessness do not cease, but they are forced out of the person's consciousness and are not transformed into action. This means that an internal hyper-excitation is present that is no longer visible externally. Should the threatening situation continue for a long period of time, the victim has to learn to control his inner agitation in order to endure such a situation. In the end this leads to the victim no longer having any conscious access to his fear, his pain, his feelings of shame or anger caused by the ongoing violent situation.

In order to survive a trauma of violence therefore, the victims have to blank out the fact that they are a victim and ignore it. Instead they retreat into survival strategies that allow them to believe they are not victims of violence and that they do not need help, attitudes such as "Things that don't destroy me can only make me stronger!", "I'm not that easy to knock down!", "I can take a lot – much more than others!", or "I can manage it on my own!".

A victim of violence also sees the perpetrator in a particular way: she is unable to see the perpetrator as a perpetrator. She is therefore likely to idealise him; she may see him as vulnerable and in need of help himself; she will defend his aggressive outbursts, and concerns herself more with his needs than with her own, so that she may have some advanced warning of how he might behave. Victims of violence usually show a psychological fixation on the perpetrator. This kind of trauma survival strategy, which I have termed 'a victim attitude', will cause the victims to suffer from many symptoms (depression, migraine, insomnia etc ...), but the person does not connect these symptoms with the violence they suffered, and may continue to suffer, at the hands of a perpetrator. Their symptoms of suffering become puzzling 'illnesses', which they try to deal with but without success.

This 'victim attitude', which over the years becomes ingrained as 'psychological illness', is in fact encouraged by social structures and services, which tend to blank out the existence of violent relationships, and more often than not side with and defend the perpetrator. As a result it is very easy for people as 'patients' to then become victims of those who treat their 'illnesses' (doctors, psychiatrists, psychotherapists, nurses, social workers et cetera ...), who avoid investigating the real cause of the 'illness' symptoms. Violence that is primarily aimed at the psychological destruction of another person is the most traumatic form of violence. It gives the victims the most pronounced feelings of powerlessness and triggers the deepest feelings of hatred towards the perpetrators. This can then cause endless spirals of violence: victims become perpetrators who create new victims, and the use of violence itself becomes a trauma survival strategy that causes further traumatisation. Because the victims' hatred cannot usually be acted on with the actual perpetrators it is suppressed, and as a result explodes at the next opportunity onto others not connected with the original perpetration, but who offer the opportunity for the outpouring of hatred because they are weaker and unable to defend themselves.

Violence can also be embedded in the laws, rules and cultural norms of society. The application of these laws, rules and standards causes some people in society to experience violence, without the keepers of these laws, rules and standards seeing themselves as perpetrators. One example of this is the unfair distribution of land, which gives wealth and prosperity to a few and allows many others to starve. Economic systems that are based on the exploitation of human labour are perpetrator-victim systems. An individual born into such a system will either become a perpetrator himself given the opportunity, or he will remain a victim. On a familial level, for example, there are children who are forced by extreme violence to become perpetrators them-selves, being made to steal or perpetrate physical violence on others.

Violence can be used consciously, but it can also be used unconsciously and people can be traumatised without any particu-lar plan or malicious intention being behind it. This is frequently the case in parent-child relationships, for example if a traumatised mother simply does not notice how much she is traumatising her child with her inability to love and to be emotionally present. What society regards as victimhood and perpetration depends on its perception and degree of sensitivity. The more people in a society are struggling to survive, the less willing they are to recognise victims as victims, or see perpetrators for what they are. An investigation into the history of childhood during the last 4,000 years put forward by the American psycho-historian Lloyd deMause shows clearly how insensitively children have been treated and traumatised in many ways by their parents and other adults all the way through from ancient times until today. (deMause 1980)

Perpetration and perpetrator attitudes

The fact that perpetrators also traumatise themselves by their perpetration is a further characteristic of the traumatisation of humans by other humans. In a psychologically healthy person, the reality of having severely harmed another human being so much as to traumatise them will cause feelings of guilt and shame, and fears of exclusion from society. Perpetrators have to split off these difficult feelings and block them out of their consciousness. Nevertheless, these feelings of guilt and shame, and the fear of being held to account for their actions, still exist within the psyche.

So perpetrators develop what I have called a 'perpetrator attitude' in order to cope with the internal psychological impact of their perpetration. The most common perpetrator attitudes are: denial, playing down the violence and aggression, placating the public, demonstrating social responsibility, hiding behind social structures ("I was only carrying out orders!", "I'm just doing my job!"), or using economic or financial constraints as an argument. Perpetrators often ridicule their victims, stigmatise them as sick or crazy, and portray themselves as the actual victim. Perpetrators have to rationalise their deeds, and so they have a massive need for theoretical constructs that justify their antisocial interests and actions. The disguise of perpetrator-victim relationships is the crux of every ideology, whether it has a patriarchal, nationalistic, racist, sexist, religious or even scientific bias. Such ideologies give perpetrators a clear conscience to carry on with their violence and demand respect for their actions. On this basis they can even experience pleasure and satisfaction when they carry out their destructive actions.

1.4 Traumatisation of love

From a psychological perspective 'love' is a feeling that is either present in a personal relationship or is not. Two people can be fond of one another in a loving way, or it might be that only one of them loves the other, with the other not reciprocating the feeling. Love develops and evolves in specific personal relationships. To love means that one has the ability to love; it also means that one has a need to be loved. And because the lover wants to be loved himself, he also needs to discover what his loved one loves. Someone whose love is not reciprocated is unable to learn what real love is. If someone is not loved he is left alone with his need for love unfulfilled. If someone receives a false response to his love he learns false things about love.

Love as an internal attitude can be transferred to other things, for example to the work a person does (job, hobby), to other living organisms (animals, plants) or to inanimate objects (mountains, the sea, cars, houses . . .).

Loving oneself is of paramount importance. Self-love means having goodwill towards and sympathy for oneself, even if, and particularly when, one has made mistakes in life. It means looking after oneself, and not causing harm to oneself.

Love, the fact of loving and being loved, has its evolutionary origins in the mother/child bonding relationship. Without the feeling and attitude of love, the mother/child relationship would simply be a battlefield for existential resources, characterised chiefly by fear, aggression and stress.

A child, developed from the union of egg and sperm within the mother's body, doubtless has characteristics that cause the mother great stress. He lodges himself in her womb, feeds himself from the maternal organism, and alters her metabolic processes to suit his needs. He forces himself onto the mother from within. If a mother does not want the child growing inside her, and is not prepared to love him, she will see herself as his victim and regard the child as a perpetrator. It is only the mother's love for her child, and the associated affection and compassion she feels for the new life inside her, that allow a woman to tolerate and accept this child, give him the protection he needs for his development and welcome him as a new person. Only then will she have the strength and endurance necessary to:

- feed, change diapers and look after the child,
- remain patiently with him while he plays and makes new discoveries,
- be always on the alert so that nothing happens to him,
- give up her own freedom so that she is there for the child when he needs encouragement or when he is ill.

How can a mother bear all that for so many years if she does not love her child? A mother's love for her child is not only of paramount importance for his development, but the ability to love her child protects the mother from becoming frustrated and over-whelmed. Bringing up a child she does not love is one of the most excruciating ordeals for a mother; it is a permanent stress for her and fosters unbearable feelings of futility. It is just as essential for the child not to have to experience himself as a parasite to his mother, sucking her dry and perhaps even causing her death. The child needs his mother for his very survival; without her he is lost. His greatest fear is of not being loved by his mother, of being abandoned by her, and so already the unborn child will show consideration for his mother so that he can thrive. He is actively concerned about the preservation of her life and of her wellbeing. He loves his mother because she is his foundation, enabling him to develop his life energy. In the beginning the child's love is directed to his mother, and then towards other people he is dependent on. He can only begin to love himself if the love he directs towards others is fully reciprocated, if his mother and father and others reflect back to him how lovable he is.

In this respect we are all, male and female, included in the evolutionary process of the development of love as a fundamental issue for life, because each of us began life as a child in our mother's womb. Since men do not experience a child growing in their body, the subject of love is less challenging to them in later life than to women who have become mothers. For a man, competition with other men is often an experience that makes more of a conscious impression on their psyche than love. Unconsciously, though, a man's initial love of his mother and the sort of love his mother gave him still continues to affect him.

Healthy Love

Love that is experienced as right, appropriate and 'healthy' means

- appreciating the loved one, with all his or her particular characteristics and uniqueness,
- having empathy with him/her,
- understanding his/her point of view, attitude, and way of thinking,
- behaving constructively with him or her,
- without losing contact with oneself and one's own needs.

Loving in a 'healthy' way means accepting another person as she is, being well-disposed towards her, serving her well and encouraging her in her development, satisfying her need for support, security, belonging, being welcomed, as well as for food, warmth, and being seen, touched and understood in an appropriate manner, and respecting her autonomous needs for her own way of perceiving, feeling, thinking, wanting and acting. Healthy love is based on trust; it is true and real. Love and lies, love and deception, love and betrayal, are all mutually exclusive.

Healthy loving is very different to the state of being in love which, looked at from a biological viewpoint, is a more instinctive and hormonal reaction to the intensification in readiness to couple and commit as a partner. Being in love is a psychological state in which an individual's own symbiotic needs are projected onto another person whom the individual hardly knows, does not actually really trust and does not really open up to. He tries instead to make himself as positive and as attractive as possible towards his loved one. Men and women in love create their own ideal picture of the other person; they see the world through 'rose-tinted glasses'. They hope that this person will fulfil all their expectations and bring them the love they dream of (Precht 2009). The state of being in love is a state of stress that leads to 'butter-flies in the tummy', racing heart, weak knees, and causes the individual to lose touch with reality in regard to their perception of the other person.

Healthy love on the other hand is real, lived love; it is an integral part of a solid relationship. It is based on openness, trust, acceptance of responsibility and loyalty. It is still open to debate whether the state of being in love does evolve into a permanent and constructive love between partners or, even into real parental love.

Love between partners has its roots in the love each of the partners received from their parents. This is because all children are dependent on their mother's love for their healthy psychologi-cal development. If they also receive real love from their father, this will constitute a solid foundation for their healthy psychologi-cal development. If children are able to show their need for love in an appropriate way, they will develop their ability to love in a way that helps them create constructive relationships. The rela-tionship between the need to be loved and the ability to love remains balanced. There is no contradiction between the love shown toward others and self-love. Children who have been loved and able to love in this way become adults who are able to behave lovingly towards their partners and their own children; they can react appropriately to their symbiotic needs as well as their striving for autonomy. Psychologically healthy adults can clearly differentiate between love, fear, anger, sorrow, pain and sexuality and can behave in an emotionally straightforward way with their own children. What they do in their private as well as their profes-sional life they can do with unequivocal loving and friendly feelings.

To love means connecting emotionally with another person, thereby uniting two lives, for better or for worse. So not only can love make an individual happy, it can also mean a shared life of suffering. Both the ability to love and the need to be loved have to pass through a developmental and maturing process. Love is not static; it can only remain alive if it evolves. Thus it is quite possible for love to end at some point.

Love that causes Illness

Parent/child and couple relationships are intrinsically relationships of love. If love is missing in such a relationship, then the most essential part of the relationship is lacking. Such relationships then become purely functional. Conflicts in functional relationships cannot be solved with goodwill but only with cold objectivity, intellectual debates, and ultimately with aggression and violence.

Under trauma conditions, 'loving' also becomes a survival strategy. This can assume different forms:

- The lack of love frequently goes unnoticed.
- The fact that love no longer exists is denied.
- Love is dismissed as "romantic nonsense that one cannot afford" or as "psychological rubbish".
- Money and property are used as compensation for authentic love.
- The addictive search for the state of being in love is intended to take the place of real love.
- The longing for an all-embracing, perpetual and everlasting love is lived out in the imagination and in religious, spiritual or esoteric worlds.
- By 'sweet-talking' someone and telling them what they want to hear, the semblance of love is created, but this actually conceals rejection and indifference.
- Narcissistic self-reflection is disguised as love.
- In the worst case even violence is presented as love.

If parents are traumatised, their attachment ability suffers and with that their ability to love. This is noticeable first of all as a negative effect in the person's relationship to their partner, followed by their relationship to their children. The fact that mothers and fathers may be incapable of love is expressed in different ways towards children:

- by rejection with or without physical violence,
- by unpredictable oscillation between focussing on them and ignoring them,
- by offloading their feelings of trauma onto the children,
- by being needy and clingy towards their children,
- as hope that the pure and innocent love of children will compensate for everything else.

It can mean various different things to a child if he is not loved by his own parents to the extent that he requires for his healthy development: I am not noticed! I am not important and neither are my needs! I am being physically and emotionally abused! I shouldn't really be alive! I shouldn't be here! I should be someone else entirely! These are unbearable experiences for the psyche of a child. If the child's basic human need for his parents' love is frustrated it can build until the feelings of fear, anger, shame and pain are intolerable for the child and he has to split psychologically in order to be able to endure and remain in the attachment relationship to his mother and father. A child who is unloved by his parents, or overloaded with illusions of love and offers of entangling love, has to suppress his uncontrollable feelings and split off his need for love (which is always directed towards his parents) from his real experiences.

Depending on other individual circumstances, their personal nature, their position in relation to their siblings, or their gender, children react differently to this traumatising relationship with their parents:

- Some become ill and express their distress through physical symptoms.
- Others rebel, cry out their fears and act out their anger.
- Yet others withdraw into themselves, creating distance internally from their parents without being able to detach themselves emotionally from them.

Unloved children develop different survival strategies of love:

- They struggle constantly to get contact with their parents and have their attention, either by being extremely good and well-behaved, or by rebellious, destructive behaviour with outbursts of anger or provocation.
- They deny their own needs and copy their parents' survival strategies. They suppress their feelings and don't accept the obvious reality.
- They try harder to love their mother and father despite everything – to the point of complete self-abandonment.
- They put themselves completely at the service of their parents in order to ensure their psychological stability.
- Their parents' wellbeing and their relationship, sometimes even the whole family, becomes the entire focus of their attention, which often means accepting constraints on their own life urges. They identify more with their parents' or relations' problems and needs than with their own. To them love actually means being prepared to remain a victim.
- They will even absorb their parents' trauma feelings as if they were their own and as if they could lift the burden from their parents' shoulders. Their mother's fears and their father's sorrow become more important than their own concerns and needs.
- Even if a child's parents use violence towards him, he does not see it. Instead, he blames himself if his parents are 'cross' with him. The more brutal and cruel traumatised parents are towards their children, the more affectionate and loving the children may become.
- Responsibility gets turned on its head. It is no longer the parents who are responsible for the child's survival and wellbeing, but the child who feels responsible for his parents and their wellbeing. He feels guilty if he sees his parents suffering. He feels he is a burden to his parents.

As a rule, children of traumatised parents are trapped in a trauma of love, in an extreme process of self-denial, self-abandonment, and the reversal of perpetrator – victim roles. The normal relationship of responsibility between parent and child is also reversed. These children cannot find their way out of this trauma of love without help from outside.

I use the term 'trauma of love' or 'traumatisation of love' as being synonymous with the term 'symbiotic trauma' in order to highlight the far-reaching effects if a child is not loved by his parents because they are traumatised themselves, and so continuously traumatise their child instead of loving him. As a trauma of love only occurs when the mother of the child is already traumatised, and the mother might already be a victim of her own parents' inability to love, relationships have to be looked at from a multi-generational perspective. A traumatised mother lacks the crucial psychological abilities and resources she needs to be able to give her child the care and love he needs, particularly in the early phase of his development. As a result, the trauma experiences of the previous generation flow into a traumatisation of love, and often the experiences of the generation before that as well.

The essential characteristic of a trauma of love is the lack of self-love. In its place is an excess of self-criticism, self-judgement, and self-denial. One has the feeling of always having to be there for others, not being allowed to indulge oneself at all, never being good enough, always being a bad child, a bad mother or an incapable father. Basically, in a trauma of love those concerned cannot differentiate love from violence and fear, or themselves from others.

It can also be extremely painful for traumatised parents when they become aware of their inability to love their children. Being caught up in their own survival strategies and trapped in their inability to feel is agonising for them. Being unable to cope psychologically with the role of being a parent exacerbates the trauma of love, which traumatised parents as a rule are burdened with from their own childhood. It is only when they realise their own trauma of love from their childhood that traumatised parents become aware of the full extent of their acts of perpetration towards their children, which are mostly not intended consciously.

Once they experience compassion with themselves as victims of a trauma of love, then they can also recognise that self-accusation and self-judgement are of little use to them, as well as to their children. The only thing that helps with respect to their own perpetration is accepting themselves and loving themselves.

1.5 Traumatisation of Sexuality

Love and sexuality are different phenomena; they are controlled by different physical and psychological processes, and different bodily reactions and behaviour patterns come into play, as well as different hormones and psychological needs.

Biology of Sexuality

Looked at from a biological perspective, sexuality is one of several possible forms of reproduction in living organisms. Other forms are cell division, sprouting or asexual reproduction from egg cells without fusion having taken place with a sperm cell. Reproduction using two biological sexes has the advantage of increasing the diversity within a species. The resistance of newly created organisms when competing with others for available resources (bacteria, viruses, other more highly developed organisms) is improved by diversity. One pest is easily able to wipe out a whole population if that species is not genetically diverse, but it is more difficult if there is genetic variation within the species. Sexual reproduction tends to create two extreme variants within a genus:

- One version ('female') is the organism that has 'eggs' – a set of chromosomes enclosed in a covering of nourishment in which a fertilised egg cell can immediately continue growing. In some species the female offers the newly developing organism their whole body in which 'the young' can develop until their birth. The female organism with its primordial egg cells only needs a limited supply of gametes to achieve reproduction. A supply of 300,000 to 400,000 egg cells is created originally in a woman, which is then reduced to about 400 at sexual maturity.

- The other, 'male', version specialises in bringing a set of chromosomes to these egg cells. In order to achieve this, the organism has a special fertilisation organ (the 'penis') and a large amount of self-propelled chromosome packets ('sperm cells') in order to reach an egg ready to be fertilised. For reproduction to be successful, the bearer of the sperm cells has to create a large number of new cells continuously (in humans there are approximately 300 million sperms per ejaculation).

In nature there are countless variations of sexual reproduction, of the way in which gender-specific behaviour is practised and how the offspring are treated following successful reproduction. Human sexuality is one of several possible forms, as is shown by looking at closely related biological variations, the great apes. Chimpanzees, bonobos, gorillas and orangutans show different forms of sexual activity, develop different gender role patterns and have different ways of caring for their offspring.

The main aim of biological evolution is the survival of individuals so that they can reproduce and multiply. Evolutionary biological strategies are constantly adapting and making new conquests; they test the boundaries within which their life is possible. In doing this, individual organisms are sometimes subjected to borderline experiences:

- Because the strategy of sexual reproduction encourages maximum differentiation between the sexes, females and males develop in a quite different way. Women are predetermined to bear the high physical risks and costs of pregnancy and birth on their own, which can sometimes even end in death. They are biologically as well as psychologically and psychosomatically programmed to identify to a large extent with the wellbeing and woes of their children and to put their own interests on the back burner.
- Men, on the other hand, concentrate on asserting themselves against other men in competition for sex with women. They are subject to a sexual drive that at the height of their virility, when they are between 18 and 30 years of age, they are

sometimes scarcely able to control, and they can run high social and health risks for their sexuality that may even end in death for them.

- While their higher ability for compassion gives women an evolutionary advantage, because they are able to empathise better with the needs and afflictions of their children, the same ability is for men perhaps an evolutionary disadvantage, because too much empathy would prevent them from asserting themselves against other men.
- Because the brain has played an increasingly important role in human evolution and the skull has become correspondingly larger, the passage of a child through the female pelvis and birth channel can be an extremely painful experience. Giving birth can even become life-threatening if there is not sufficient cooperation between the unborn child and his mother. On the other hand, a birth can be the ultimate orgasmic experience for a woman and give a high level of emotional reward.
- Since multiple births constitute more of a burden for parents, many multiple fertilisations and twin or triplet pregnancies actually end in the womb. A life-and-death struggle may occur between the organisms competing to be born. Existential traumas can therefore even occur in the womb.

It would be illusory to think that we humans can operate outside the constraints of our biological evolution. We have to accept them as preconditions in order to achieve our full potential psychologically, socially and culturally. The more we accept our unconscious, psychosomatic evolutionary moulding, the better use we can make of the freedoms available to us. 'Nature' does not make rules or lay down the law for us humans concerning the way we ought to live our lives together. It makes offers that we can either accept or ignore. Knowledge of natural processes is an advantage because it removes the credibility of ideological prejudice.

Psycho-social Conditions of Sexuality

Our sexual development begins long before we are born; the sexual organs begin developing from the third month of pregnancy. The child who will become a woman develops ovaries and later the uterus, fallopian tubes and vagina. To become male, the growing organism has to be exposed to testosterone so that the testicles develop as gonads. It is possible at this stage for unfulfilled processes to prevent the sexual body form from being completely developed and for children to be born with atypical sex characteristics, ('intersex'), where both sets of sexual organs are present at birth.

In order to develop healthy sexuality we human beings usually need a further 10–14 years before the whole body is available for the task of reproduction. During this time sexual organs continue to mature, the primary and secondary sexual characteristics develop, and girls and boys are prepared for their roles as women or men, mothers or fathers. Before girls and boys are able to reproduce, their erogenous zones are already sensitive and can produce orgasms and feelings of lust.

The time leading up to sexual maturity is also a socialisation process for a child's sexuality. Until they reach maturity, girls and boys watch the way adults obey the conventions of sexual behaviour. They experience norms for men and women, and the values and taboos of the society in which they are growing up. Thus, for children to develop a healthy sexuality, they need to be in the society of adults who can deal clearly and appropriately with the subject of sexuality. Only in this way can children take responsibility for the basic power of reproduction within them. Children have to learn which forms of sexual activity are appropriate for their physical, psychological and social level of maturity and which are not. Self-determination in relation to their own sexuality is a basic requirement for a child's own healthy development as well as for their ability to establish healthy relationships.

The frequent lack of transparency in social groups and whole societies regarding sexuality is shown by the prevalence of child sexual abuse, prostitution, pornography, sexual exploitation, sexual violence in couple relationships and the frequency of pregnant women being deserted by the father of the child. These events are psychologically and socially devastating. Attempts to remove the impulse to act out blind, animalistic compulsions through the use of rigid sexual norms and moral concepts of human sexuality more commonly fail rather than succeed. Even liberal sexual concepts and practices frequently ignore the psychological distress and conflicts that sexuality in relationships can cause. It remains a significant challenge for every generation to find the appropriate way to deal with the female and male form of sexuality and resulting relationships. We still have to become aware of our own consciousness so that we learn to deal with our sexuality in a responsible way and continue "the process of civilisation" (Elias 1976) in a good way.

From a purely physical viewpoint, the sexual act, i.e. the penetration of the woman's vagina by the man's penis, is actually quite rough if it is not transformed into a joyful union between the sexes by loving feelings and tender touch. It is often easier for a man to reach orgasm quickly as the climax of mutual sexual stimulation; a woman usually needs longer in order to achieve an orgasm in physical contact with a man. Women need to want the sexual act consciously; they need to trust the feelings of their own body and to be emotionally open towards the man they are with. This is the only way they can come out of their head with its inhibitions and relax into their physical reactions and feelings. The fear of unwanted pregnancy and being deserted by the man can considerably reduce a woman's enjoyment of sex, or even eliminate enjoyment completely. For women in patriarchal societies who cannot exchange their sexuality for the promise of marriage, there is a high risk that they will not only have to bear the physical and emotional burden of bringing up a child on their own, but they will also be socially stigmatised, denounced and criminalised as 'dishonourable'. (Metz-Becker 1997)

Sexual Violence

Just as with love, sexual needs and abilities can also be the result of traumatisation. This happens particularly during childhood:

- when sexual feelings are touched upon too early and originate not from the child but from others,
- when sexual arousal occurs in relationships in which the adolescent child should actually be lovingly protected and encouraged by adults,
- when sexual acts are demanded of the child or adolescent against his will by the use of threats, blackmail and violence.

In such cases the child's or the adolescent's physical reactions are in complete confusion, as are his emotional answers, and the way he mentally classifies the relationship. The child does not know whether his physical reactions are appropriate, he can no longer sense his true feelings and he is completely disoriented in his perception of the person abusing him. Is his father, mother, brother, sister, grandfather, grandmother, etc. being good to him or is what he's experiencing through his body and his genitals inappropriate, painful, disgusting and forbidden?

The child has no alternative but to split psychologically, especially if there is no adult he can turn to who could help him out of his confusion. He has to suppress his perceptions and behave as if nothing has happened. He has to stifle his fears and anger, his shame and disgust and sometimes his emerging feelings of pleasure as well. He has to deal with the person who has just sexually abused him and used violence towards him and now behaves as if nothing had happened. He has to go on living with these people and is practically and emotionally dependent on them. This results in many and varied survival strategies used in a trauma of sexuality:

- attempts to suppress their own sexual impulses,
- deadening of feeling in their own body,
- confusion of identity,
- blanking out consciousness of who the perpetrator is,

- different forms of 'eating disorders' ('anorexia', 'bulimia', eating to make oneself fat),
- using drugs to suppress negative feelings and overcome lack of feeling and sensitivity,
- transfer of painful experiences to others (younger children, then later even their own children),
- basic mistrust or even contempt of the opposite sex (men's contempt of women, abused women's hatred of men),
- illusory attempts to control sexual violence, for example by promiscuity, prostitution or sex addiction,
- controlling the sexuality of their own children (for example sexually traumatised mothers often perceive their son as a perpetrator and try to suppress his sexuality with the use of violence or with suffocating love).

The more comprehensive and profound a person's traumatisation of sexuality is, the more varied the symptoms are that result from it. Sexual needs can no longer be brought into line with the person's own sexual abilities. The sexually traumatised person does not know what to do with his sexual needs: Who should I turn to? Who can look after my needs?

Nor does a sexually traumatised person know how he can cope with his sexual potency so that he does not cause harm to others. Just as his own sexuality was destroyed, a sexually traumatised person often ruins that of others. Thus, sexuality does not become a blessing that creates new life, but a further weapon in his own psychological struggle for survival.

Sexual traumatisation can also occur at an adult age. In war particularly, both sexes are often raped without restraint. Soldiers rape other soldiers and they rape women where they can get hold of them. The women of the 'enemy' are often subjected to sexual violence on a massive scale. The sexual trauma is usually a result of a trauma of love. That is usually the case where interfamilial sexual abuse occurs. The child who is not loved by his mother is fair game for other family members to act out their sexual urges on him, or use him for their own trauma survival strategies and attempt to compensate for their own trauma of love through him.

1.6 Sources of Early Traumatisation

While I have so far based the development of my theory on insights into postnatal attachment and trauma research, in recent years I have also focused on the stock of knowledge and experience in pre- and perinatal psychology. Authors, both male and female, who have particularly addressed the psychological aspects of pre-natal experiences and birth, are (amongst others) Chamberlain 2010, De Jong 2004, Emerson 2012, Janov 2012, Janus and Haibach 1997, Krüll 2009, Levend and Janus 2011, Meissner 2011, Schindler 2011, and Renggli 2013.

The findings of pre- and perinatal psychology clearly show that from the beginning the human organism is not just an accumulation of biological cell structures, but a living creature whose psychological qualities are also present and growing right from the start. They develop alongside the physical structure of a child. Perceiving, feeling, thinking, wanting, remembering, being aware of the self, are psychological processes that do not begin after birth. They are nascent in the growing child in the first weeks of pregnancy and grow rapidly in quantity and quality until the moment of birth. We have to take into consideration that 'psyche' is not the same as 'awareness'. The majority of psychological processes take place unconsciously. Only a small percentage of our perception, feeling and thinking is conscious and can later be remembered and expressed in words. This is true for our whole life. We must not confuse 'awareness' with the ability to put something into words. There is a pre-verbal awareness, and an awareness beyond verbal forms of expression.

Thus a child's psyche can react to traumatising influences in his environment before birth. It has to be able to do this so that the child does not die early of psychological over-stimulation in such circumstances. So a psychological split as a reaction to a trauma experience can take place before a child is born (e.g. if abortion is attempted, or there is an intrauterine inadequacy, or the child gets stuck in the birth canal during birth). I have now experienced many constellations where representatives of the pre-natal child at first come into the constellation full of drive and vigour, but then

27

suddenly collapse because they do not receive any response to their vitality. They will then retreat and freeze.

In relation to possible early traumatisation there are some basic questions:

- Was the conception an act of love or violence?
- Was the time in the womb a period of being 'in paradise', when the growing child was looked after and felt safe? Or was this already a kind of 'hell', with existential or loss traumas, or a trauma of love, or a traumatized bonding system offloading its perpetrator-victim dynamics onto the new life?
- Was the birth a gentle transition into life outside the mother's body, or was the person pulled out, pushed out, dragged out, or cut out (caesarean section)? And all this inducing massive feelings of fear, regardless of his resistance or the idea that it is against his will?
- Are the first hours of life an experience of being welcomed and having his needs recognised, or is this the first frustration of his basic needs, the impact of which will possibly continue throughout his life?
- And what about the care of the child after his birth – does he receive enough physical nourishment and emotional contact, or is he already in danger of starving or dying of loneliness?

As their therapies progressed, many of my clients, both male and female, came closer to their traumatising pre-natal and birth experiences. What shows up about their conception, their time in the womb, the circumstances of their birth and their first weeks following their birth, is often quite extreme, as the following examples show:

- Some were conceived by their father raping the mother.
- Mothers were continually raped throughout the pregnancy.
- Whilst still unborn, and throughout the pregnancy they experienced their parents arguing violently, and their mother was beaten by the father. They were harmed when their father kicked their mother in the belly.

- The mother did not want them; she had repeatedly hit her pregnant belly trying to force an abortion.
- The pregnant mother sat in an air-raid shelter to try and protect them from falling bombs.
- Their mother did not eat healthily during pregnancy, drank alcohol, smoked or used hard drugs.
- Their birth had taken many hours and they were forced into the delivery.
- There were problems during the birth process because their mother was unwilling to cooperate because she did not want the child.
- A caesarean section was carried out and the child was pulled out of the womb without their cooperation and against their will.
- They were separated from their mother in the hospital because, according to dates, they were premature even though they were completely healthy.
- When they became ill following the birth as a result of abrupt separation from the mother, they were kept away from the mother for an even longer time and taken to a specialist hospital in isolation.

We humans are evidently real experts at survival. Even before birth we can react by splitting off the psychological processes of trauma. We can arrive in this world already psychologically split. Our healthy parts are then kept in the background, and we try with the help of survival strategies to survive the time up to our birth, and possibly continue in this way for the rest of our lives. But that is not a successful introduction to life! We are able to lose our connection with our physical needs very early on. Growth and regeneration, our need for phases of rest and phases of activity, may be out of sync with each other right from the start; instead we are programmed for stress, adaptation and perseverance.

Wolfgang

Wolfgang came to therapy because of his gallstones. Although he knew that his birth had been life threatening both for him and for his mother, and he had spent the first year of his childhood with his grandparents on his father's side, he thought that his childhood had been harmonious and trouble-free. However, his constellations had shown how traumatising his birth and first year of his life had been for him. He had had to stifle his fears, his despair and anger in order to adapt to the situation of his mother being unable to develop a secure emotional attachment to him, and had pretended to him that his childhood had been happy.

Viola

Viola, who had already worked for a while on her various psychological and physical symptoms in trauma therapy, suspected an unresolved trauma situation because two weeks after her birth she had been taken to an orthopaedic surgeon with developmental dysplasia of the hip and she had been fitted with a plaster cast. In her constellation the dysplasia was shown to be a result of her difficult birth. She had been stuck in the birth canal for hours and, as the representatives in her constellation experienced it, this had been a life or death struggle for her. The representative for her mother, whom Viola had set up in this constellation, was completely negative and did not want to help her child be born. This corresponded with all Viola's other experiences, showing that her mother had not wanted to have her as her fourth child.

My own early trauma experiences

The puzzle of my own physical and psychological symptoms also made sense when I became conscious of my beginnings in my own constellations. I was unplanned and arrived too early for my parents, straight after their wedding. My mother was still in shock following the terrible accidental death of her father. She grew up in a poor farming family and received little love, being the sixth of nine children. Work, diligence, an undemanding nature, and religious solace were her escape from poverty and psychological distress. In her childhood and adolescence she had experienced the hardship of the National Socialist environment and World War II. She was therefore unable to give me healthy love, warmth and tender attention. She stopped breastfeeding me much too early, and instead gave me a milk powder which would have nearly killed me if a doctor had not realised what was happening and saved me from an early death by altering my nutrition.

My mother also gave me to her mother and her sister to look after me very soon after my birth so that she could return to work. No wonder then that I became a 'crying baby', and my father, who couldn't stand my crying any longer, screamed at me in my cot and shook me so hard that I froze in fear of death and had to split at a very early age. I immediately became silent after my father's violent attack and outwardly became a well-adjusted and good child, but internally I was very afraid, shy and reclusive, and often escaped into a world of fantasies.

We have to assume that very sensitive beings, like unborn and newborn children, are at an extremely high risk of being psychologically traumatised at a very early stage of their existence. Their physical body and their psyche, which are just in the process of developing, can easily be seriously and permanently harmed. We can assume that the earlier a psychological traumatisation takes place, the longer it will last and the more difficult it is to treat and to heal. It therefore seems likely that much of what appears in later life as so-called 'anxiety disorders', i.e. panic attacks, social anxieties, fear of sharp objects, fear of flying etc., originated in a pre-, peri- or postnatal trauma. An unborn or new born child cannot regulate its over-excitation. Its limited ability to move and express itself means that it quickly gets into a state of helplessness and powerlessness, and then is flooded with fear and pain. (Harms 2008) The same is true for other basic feelings such as anger and sorrow, which can develop into so-called psychological or attachment disorders if they are not 'co-regulated' by caring parents. (Brisch 2014)

In view of the many risks in our natural and social environments, the probability of early traumatisation is extremely high. We therefore have to prioritise the protection of unborn and newborn children. We have to recognise or, even better, to empathise with this high level of vulnerability. We know it intuitively, but anyone who has suffered an early traumatisation will unconsciously tend, emotionally split and numbed as they are, to expect others to be capable of enduring similar things without complaint.

1.7 Traumatised and traumatising mothers

Sources of early traumatisation may of course be natural disasters, but there are human perpetrators who attack mothers and unborn children. Also the mother herself can be the cause of her child's early traumatisation if she does not want the child she is carrying. The more aware I have become of the manifestation of early traumatisation in my clients, the more I have come to believe that the many complications that can occur during pregnancy, birth, and in the weeks following are caused by the traumatisation of a mother while she is pregnant or during giving birth. This connection is most immediately apparent in the case of a sexually traumatised mother: a woman who has split from her body due to sexual violence, who reacts to physical contact with fear and disgust, who connects sexuality with pain and humiliation, has great difficulty in regarding anything she experiences with her sexual organs as joyful or pleasurable, rather than threatening. She will therefore resort to her well-established splitting mechanisms during her pregnancy and while giving birth, and will be unable to allow full physical and psychological contact with her child. She is also more likely to expose herself to situations that re-enact her trauma in the pre- and peri-natal phase of pregnancy. She will offer medical or birthing 'helpers' little resistance even if their advice is not really helpful or is even violent. As a result the growing child comes up against barriers to emotional contact with his mother right from the start, as well as physical rejection by her.

I therefore think it is advisable and necessary to extend the concept of the trauma of love explicitly to include the time before birth, as this is when interactions take place between the mother's traumas and the growing child's own early trauma experiences. In some cases it is even more difficult to differentiate between them than in the phase following birth. It is often impossible for the unborn child to feel psychologically at home with his traumatised mother, and connect with her in a healthy way. From the viewpoint of the trauma of love, everything that traumatises a mother also traumatises her child. A mother's experiences cannot be separated from those of her child as far as conception, pregnancy and birth are concerned. What is good for the mother is also good for her child. Anything that harms the mother also harms the child:

- A woman who was raped (whether within marriage or not) will not look forward happily to having the resulting child, who will be growing from the start inside the body of a woman who is already rejecting of him.
- If a mother loses a child in an accident or through violence, this will affect her bonding with a subsequent child.
- A woman traumatised during pregnancy becomes a stressful environment for the child growing within her.
- If the mother is traumatised while giving birth, her stress and panic are transferred onto the child.
- The child is psychologically unable to bear being separated from his mother after he is born, and even if he is allowed to return to his mother, he will find her traumatised by the separation and will have extreme difficulty in re-establishing an attachment with her.

The subject becomes even more complex if we take into consideration that a mother can be not only the victim of a trauma herself, but also can become a perpetrator who traumatises her child. For example:

- A woman can try to abort the growing child, or to kill herself and the child.
- She can choose to behave in ways that severely harm her child: smoking, drinking alcohol, using drugs, taking medication, going to discotheques with pounding noise levels, eating unhealthily.

- A mother can also become a perpetrator by not preparing for the birth properly, or by choosing to have a caesarean section.
- A mother is also a perpetrator if she denies her child skin contact following the birth, chooses not to breastfeed her child even though she is able to, if she leaves her child alone for too long or neglects him, beats him, or continually criticises or humiliates him.
- Above all, a mother is a perpetrator if she allows her child to be sexually abused in his early years, closing her eyes to the fact that it is happening.

There are many complex reasons why a mother becomes a perpetrator to her child, thereby traumatising him:

- She may be too young, or uneducated, and so unable to understand the needs of her growing child.
- She may not have had a mother herself, either because hers died giving birth, or she had not been able to develop good maternal feelings towards her child.
- She may have been sexually abused as a child, and so any physical contact with her child may stimulate feelings of shame and disgust.
- She may have become pregnant again too quickly, and each subsequent child might have driven her to the edge of her psychological capabilities.
- She may have such profound psychological problems that she is unable to recognise her child's needs.

A social environment in which mothers are encouraged to see their children as ceaselessly demanding, and advised to avoid spoiling them at all costs, which was a widely held view in Germany after World War II, (Chamberlain 1997, Brisch 2014, p. 70) is the final blow in causing mothers to treat their children without compassion. Being taken into care, as is increasingly happening to very young children, will also force them to split off unendurable painful feelings, and live in a state of permanent stress. (Brisch 2013)

1.8 Fathers and early trauma

There is a German saying: "Becoming a father is easy, but being a father is very difficult". *Having* a wife and children is very different from *being* a partner and father. In patriarchal societies men tend to see women and children as their possessions; their 'family' is an accumulation of their rules, of 'dos and don'ts'. Their own healthy feelings hardly develop beyond jealous control and surveillance of the other members of the family.

Men in modern societies are rarely prepared for their role as fathers. They are usually unprepared for the transition from partner to father. They often do not understand that with the birth of a child their partner is in a completely different psychological place. The man might have been the central focus for the woman before, but now it is the child who is the main focus for the mother. Her partner, and her relationship to him, takes a back seat. Men often feel aggrieved by this, and feel jealous of their own child, and as a result bury themselves in their work or hobbies. This can become a vicious circle with the woman feeling left on her own to look after the child, leading her to criticise her husband, who then withdraws even further. (Garstick 2013) And a woman's diminished interest in sex after the birth of the child can be the last straw in their relationship, which they experience as burdened with stress and conflict. So having children can drive couples apart instead of binding them together, and can be the cause of separation and divorce.

A further problem is that traumatised people are attracted to other traumatised people. Men and women often consciously choose their partner by appearance, but unconsciously their trauma history dictates their choice of a partner. As a result children often have two traumatised parents, particularly when whole generations have been traumatised by war or natural disaster. (Bode 2004, 2009) If a child looks for protection from one traumatised parent, he is easily drawn into the trauma dynamic of the other. This is most obvious in the case of sexual abuse: if a child turns away from his mother because she is emotionally unavailable and incapable of loving, and towards his father, the father may misunderstand the child's need for closeness and touch and may act out his own frustrated sexual needs on the child. This is more likely to happen if the father is himself caught in a painful love trauma from his own childhood; he is almost incapable of distinguishing unconsciously between being a child and being an adult.

In modern societies the traditional role of the man as the breadwinner of the family is becoming tenuous, and the more women are defined by their role as members of the workforce, whilst their role as mother is hardly acknowledged, the more men expect that women will earn their own income. (Allmendinger 2013) However, the disappearance of old role models might also be a chance for fathers to end their psychological tendency towards rationality and sexuality, and discover their potential for emotion. Children can be an excellent training ground for learning to love in a healthy way. Our world will probably become all the more humane the more men see and feel the world from a growing child's perspective.

1.9 The traumatising potential of midwifery and obstetrics

Mothers and fathers are not the only cause of early traumas. The parents may live in an environment that ignores or plays down the risk of a child's early trauma and so contributes in many ways to the psychological traumatisation of unborn and newly born children.

A child's early trauma may be caused by one of the many people with good intentions who accompany the pregnancy and birth processes, and who nonetheless do things that traumatise the child, and often the mother as well, through their lack of knowledge or sensitivity and empathy for mother and child. When looked at more closely, modern obstetrics should not be underestimated as a cause of early traumatisation. In their fixation on early intervention aimed at saving life, many doctors overlook the possibility of traumatisation of the psyche of mothers and unborn and new born children. It is very worrying if, of all people, those working in professions that are supposed to help (for example doctors, psychologists, nurses, midwives and social workers) do not recognise the traumas of their patients and clients. The reason for this lack of recognition is usually that professional helpers are unaware of their own traumatisation. Since many people who take up the helping professions are themselves affected by love traumas and sexual traumas, they do not see the love and sexual trauma in those people who have put their trust in them and need their support. In addition economic and financial interests in health and social care systems can contribute to early traumas being perpetrated and implicitly accepted.

Pregnancy management and obstetrics, which are predominantly oriented towards medical technology and medication, making mother and child the object of treatment, constitute a large risk factor for early traumatisation:

- Examinations during pregnancy are increasingly intensive and invasive, supposedly in order to reduce the risks involved.
- The mother is often swamped with stressful interventions before and during birth.
- The worldwide percentage of caesarean sections for no urgent medical reason is increasing dramatically.
- The sensitive phases of developing contact and bonding between mother and child directly following the birth are severely disrupted by medical procedures.
- The period after the birth can lead to an early traumatisation if the new born child cannot stay with his mother. Long periods of separation from his mother can very quickly overwhelm a baby.

It seems that modern obstetrics have almost completely displaced the ancient art of midwifery, and are turning pregnant women and the birth process into medical emergencies that need operations and monitoring by doctors. (Metz-Becker 1997, Tew 2007) Thus expectant mothers develop their own natural abilities less and less, and submit helplessly and powerlessly to doctors, surgeons and anaesthetists. Modern obstetricians have learnt how to cut a child out of his mother's womb quickly, but far too few doctors are aware of the profound wound this can cause to the psychological health of a child and his mother.

1.10 Assisted reproductive technology

If we look closely at the types of IVF and assisted reproductive technology: are they also a source of early traumatisation? Is the wish of some parents to have a child being bought at a cost of traumatisation for the child? It remains to be seen whether the many forms of assisted reproduction, 'artificial insemination', the increasingly used forms of *in vitro* fertilisation, egg and sperm donation, embryo transfer and surrogate mothering are more than just a footnote of evolution. However, it is certain that in the case of artificial reproduction fundamental developmental processes, primarily the secure mother/child attachment, are lacking, or severely disturbed, in children conceived and born in this way. (De Jong 2004, p. 103ff.) For children not conceived and carried in a natural way, the risk of developing a trauma of love in relation to their parents, who are already extremely stressed by the reproductive technology measures, is not to be denied.

Up until now not many children conceived and carried in this way are in psychotherapy; if they were it would enable us to make more substantiated assertions. With an increasing number of people having started their lives in Petri dishes and surrogate wombs, this sort of early trauma will probably increase and appear more frequently in psychotherapy practices.

1.11 Early experiences of violence

The concept of early trauma includes not only pregnancy and birth but also the first years of infancy. We therefore have to consider all forms of violence affecting new born children and infants up to one or two years of age. There are a large number of possibilities:

- Unnecessary medical operations are frequently carried out on infants: for example, shortening of labia which are 'too long', removal of genitals to make a confused gender clear.
- Infants may have their genitals mutilated for religious or mythological reasons, for example circumcision in males, female genital mutilation in girls (removal of labia and clitoris).
- Painful operations and treatments are carried out on infants allegedly for reasons of hygiene and health (e.g. enlargement of the urethra, administration of enemas).
- Children who are restless and cry a lot are sometimes shaken and hit to quieten them.
- Parents may not give their infants enough to eat and drink, or abandon them in their urine and faeces.
- Infants may suffer oral sexual abuse within their family.
- Infants sometimes suffer physical and sexual abuse in foster families, homes and in hospitals.
- Some infants are tortured in every imaginable way for pornography by perpetrator organisations operating covertly.

In wealthy nations of the world, potentially 1 in every 10 children has experienced extreme violence. (Streeck-Fischer 2011) Psychotherapists have to be prepared for all these forms of violence and neglect. The symptoms shown by an adult who has experienced violence may be inconspicuous (for example nail-biting, too much gastric acid, a nervous tic around the eyes), but behind these symptoms there may be a yawning pit of early experiences of violence.

Such early experiences of violence are particularly devastating when the perpetrators are people the child depends on for care and love, their parents or other carers. My therapeutic work with clients who have suffered these early experiences of violence has led me to conclude that the more violent these perpetrator parents are towards the child, the more persistently the child idealises his parents. Children traumatised by violence develop strong loyalty to their abusers as a survival strategy, and this even extends past the abuser's death.

1.12 The 'Constellation of the Intention' – a trauma therapy option

We could ask ourselves whether it is really necessary to look at our birth experiences or the time during pregnancy. Isn't it all too long ago? Can we even access this time if we can't consciously remember anything? However, early life experiences form the foundation of our psyche, and we should really include this in our therapeutic exploration. There may well be deep insights available for the person working in therapy on his childhood and adolescent problems, his relationships and work conflicts, but his pre-natal and perinatal experiences are often not addressed. Therefore the individual may still only consider the consequences of the symptoms, rather than their source. Particularly when symptoms are persistent physical ones, or degenerative symptoms in an older person, it is advisable to explore for their deep-rooted causes in an early trauma.

So, if conception, pregnancy, birth and early infancy can be a time of fundamental and manifold traumatisation, then this fact must be taken into consideration in psychotrauma therapy.

It will by now have become clear that treating a child without supporting his mother to explore her trauma is going the wrong way, as is, for example, attempting to treat a mother's postnatal depression without understanding what this has to do with the child she has just given birth to, perhaps under traumatising circumstances. If a therapist works with children, he or she must always look at the possible traumatisation of the mother. It has to be made clear to the mother that her child will only be able to lose his psychological symptoms if she is prepared to work on her own traumatisation.

As I tend to work with adults in my practice, I cannot say very much about working directly with traumatised infants, children and adolescents. However, through my work with the 'Constellation of the Intention', the therapy method I have developed over the last few years, I do see a wide spectrum of situations and psychological structures from a person's complete life history. Pre-natal and perinatal experiences can be revealed through the representatives set up in constellations.

Procedural method

The method I use for the 'Constellation of the Intention' is as follows:

- The client who would like to do a constellation describes his current situation. In order to begin he has to formulate an intention, for example "I would like to discover more about and be able to feel what it means for me to have been born by caesarean section."
- If he is in a group, the client can choose a group member to be a 'representative for his intention'. In one-on-one sessions, I offer to be the representative for his intention.
- When the representative for the intention has been chosen and placed, the exchange and dialogue between the representative for the intention and the client begins.
- Depending on the way this encounter between the client and his intention develops, I intervene as therapist. For example, I may suggest adding more people to the constellation (for example, his mother during the birth process).
- If, during a one-to-one session when I am a representative myself, I might suggest laying cushions on the floor to represent other people. However, to avoid confusion for the client, I make sure that I send a clear signal to him or her when I alternate between my role as the intention and my role as therapist.
- I end the constellation as soon as I have the impression that the therapeutic process has led to a good result and the client's intention has been completed.

It is important to note that the intention is a part of the client who is setting up the constellation, but it should always be understood as a category of the method. It is the path leading to an answer to the client's question. It is also important that the therapist does not try to improve the client's stated intention. The intention the client has decided on and formulated at that moment is the best intention he could have now. It is precisely that particular intention that will allow him to progress, because it is his own intention. Experience with the 'Constellation of the Intention' has shown that it can direct the focus towards traumatising experiences from pregnancy, for example if there was an attempted abortion which the client survived. Traumatising birth processes can also be accessed, as the example with Manfred at the beginning of this chapter shows. Such constellations allow an insight into, amongst other things, the situation of clients . . .

- who were separated from their mother immediately after birth,
- who were subjected to painful and invasive medical treatment,
- who were sent to different foster mothers and child minders as infants.

The 'Constellation of the Intention' is a relatively gentle way of exposing the deeper psychological layers that have been built up around an early traumatisation. There are already a number of therapies for dealing with pre-natal and perinatal experiences, for example primal therapy, body therapy, Pesso-Boyden system, holding therapy or holotropic breathwork. The 'Constellation of the Intention' is a new option that enables better access to pre-, peri- and postnatal traumas.

1.13 Why is the 'Constellation of the Intention' reliable?

To what extent can the 'Constellation of the Intention' be a valid tool to enable a client to access his early trauma more easily, and uncover his earliest experiences and feelings that are not consciously available to him? As I see it, no outrageous assumptions are necessary in the 'Constellation of the Intention', because the processes that this method brings to light are astonishing in themselves. They are a challenge to our everyday consciousness:

- How is it that representatives seem to hit the nail precisely on the head when they make statements of their experience about the inner state of the client and members of his family, without having even the slightest knowledge of the person they are representing?
- What sort of psychological exchange of information is it that takes place?
- What means are used to transfer this knowledge?

I think that the different brain structures we have are set in a variety of ways in order to exchange information with other people, and function as transmitters and receivers in the following way:

- The left cerebral cortex communicates via spoken language.
- The right cerebral cortex communicates with the right cerebral cortex of another person via pictures, facial expression and gestures.
- The limbic brain system resonates through emotions such as love, sympathy, joy, fear, anger, sorrow and pain with the limbic brain system of others.
- The brainstem is connected to other brainstems through signs and signals concerning the fundamental processes of life (e.g. breathing, eating, moving, and sleeping).
- The nervous system that runs through a person's whole body reacts on the autonomic level directly to the body of another person with no need for words.

The most important requirement for a representative in a constellation is the willingness to be open to these communication processes, and to be available as a mirror of the client's psyche. Broadly speaking, constellations with representatives can be described as a complex process of mirroring and resonance. Through the encounter with himself the client develops and matures internally. In this way he is able to recognise and understand himself, and he can learn to love himself. Of course some information that emerges may be inaccurate, or may be misinterpreted. My experience has shown that certain things are necessary in order to make the 'Constellation of the Intention' a reliable therapeutic diagnostic and treatment process:

- The client has to take complete responsibility for his constellation. Thus the struggle to formulate his intention, perhaps days and weeks before the constellation, is a good sign that he is genuinely addressing his trauma.
- The therapist must not attempt to correct or improve the client's intention, but must accept it as it is.
- In his therapeutic interventions, the therapist must also stay within the frame of the intention and not try to give more help than the client has asked for in the present moment.
- The therapist must not reinterpret the intention, turning it into something it does not relate to, even if he knows that the client has other issues to address, perhaps more than he is willing to work on at the moment.
- The representatives must remain in their given roles. They may not swap over into the role of a therapist in order to help the client, even if the process has stagnated and the client has lost contact with his intention. They must not allow themselves to be tempted to fulfil the expectations of the constellation facilitator nor those of the other participants, and they must distance themselves from their own assumptions and speculations.
- The participants in a group may not actively intervene in the constellation, even if the client's fragmented trauma energies take hold of them.

In my experience ambiguities may arise if

- the client strays away from his intention,
- the facilitator does not concentrate fully on the constellation and jumps to conclusions about the interaction between client and intention, leading the process in the wrong direction,
- the facilitator's own traumas are triggered and he loses his overview and becomes proactive,

- the representatives use the vacuum produced by ambiguity to introduce their own issues,
- the group as a whole becomes too active in the mistaken belief that they are helping a facilitator who has lost his grip on the constellation process.

With every psychotherapeutic approach there is always the possibility that trauma situations are unconsciously re-enacted. During a 'Constellation of the Intention' the original traumatising situation is, as a rule, consciously created. However, in order to prevent the re-enactment leading to a re-traumatisation, the points mentioned above must be strictly observed.

1.14   Steps to Trauma Integration

According to my basic model (see figure 2), a patient's traumatised psychological structures are split off from his consciousness and suppressed by trauma survival structures. How much he is able to, and would like to, deal with the trauma depends on his intention.

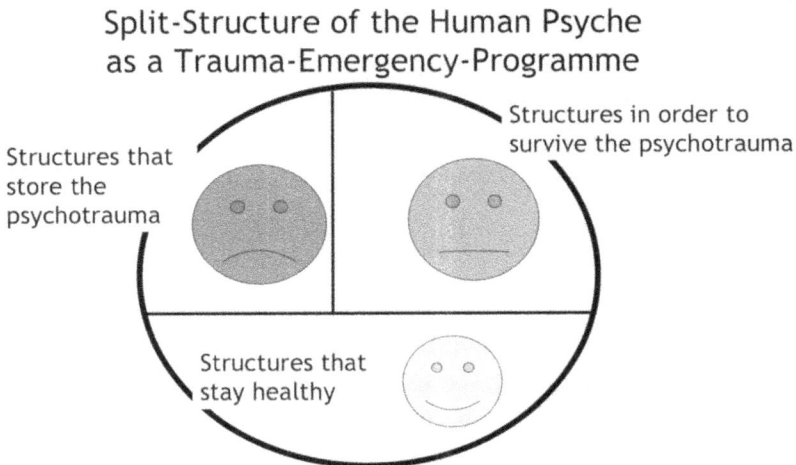

Figure 2: The basic model of the psychological split caused by trauma

The client's current intention could lead to his own trauma survival strategies becoming more obvious, and so more easily changed. Or the client might already have built up sufficient healthy structures that contact with the split-off trauma energies becomes possible. Experience has shown that processing and treating traumatised life experiences usually moves through a four-step cycle (figure 3).

- Strengthening the healthy psychological parts,
- Weakening and disempowering the trauma survival parts,
- Establish contact between healthy and traumatised parts,
- Stabilising what has been achieved and giving a fresh start to a healthy development.

Integration of Split off parts during Trauma therapy

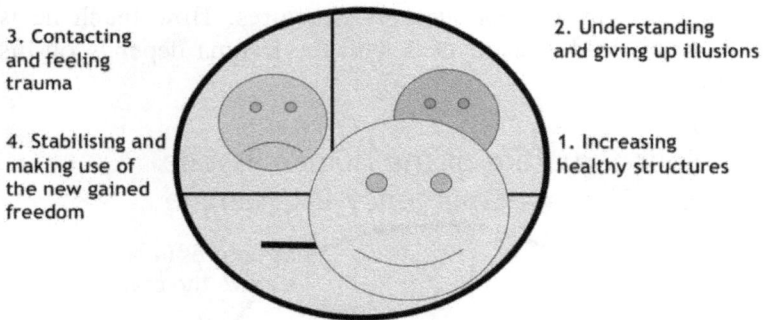

Figure 3: The basic model of the integration of traumatised life experiences

With the 'Constellation of the Intention' it is essential that the client recognises that only he can provide the help he needs. He cannot delegate his healing process to someone else. It is of no use to him if others treat him lovingly if he is unable to accept himself with his traumatised parts. He will resist and oppose well-meaning offers of support with his survival parts, until he is ready and able to encounter his split-off trauma feelings, especially if he is internally still in a perpetrator-victim split.

With early traumatisation we must presume that there are very few, or even no, conscious memories. The experiences, particularly if they were traumatising, usually only become visible through physical reactions and symptoms. A person's trauma is often written on their face, and in and on their body. The representatives see it, for example, in the eyes or the corners of the mouth, or feel it in the client's cold hands, which show that something is acting in the background of which he is not consciously aware. One of the signs that indicates an early trauma is the inability of the client to hold eye contact with the representative of his intention. Other signs are, for example, dropped or raised shoulders, stooped posture, stiff neck, stiff arm and leg movements, strong restlessness or persistent lack of emotional reaction. Chronic physical diseases such as rheumatism or allergies can also be the result of early trauma.

The 'Constellation of the Intention' process deals with each step in turn, which the client takes responsibility for by formulating his next intention. The process does **not** try to release trauma energies or force muscular reaction by physical manipulation, such as pressure on certain painful areas. The 'Constellation of the intention' does **not** re-enact a birth process, or retrospectively 'heal' an attachment process with the mother that never actually took place. Neither does it try to penetrate more 'deeply' into trauma energies than is possible at that moment in the contact between client and his intention by accelerating breathing or movement. In this way the focus is centred on the client's will and autonomy and he or she can decide how much trauma recollection should be allowed. She defines whether, when and how deeply she accesses her trauma within the framework of the constellation.

Thus a further therapeutic opportunity opens up to integrate pre-, peri- and early postnatal trauma. As a rule the following is true:

- All medical and psychological therapies that do not take into consideration the possibility of clients being traumatised and therefore psychologically split, are in danger of re-traumatising the client. They can therefore make the splits deeper, rather than integrating them.

- Therapies can even help a client's survival strategies if they convey illusory experiences of attachment, contact and love from the parents, which in reality did not happen, and which could not happen because the parents are incapable of constructive attachment and love because of their own traumatisation.
- A traumatising birth cannot be forgotten or resolved by simulating a loving and successful re-birth in a seminar room.

It is an essential prerequisite for a 'Constellation of the Intention' to recognise the existence of a distinct pre-natal psyche that is already equipped with the trauma mechanism of splitting. We also have to assume that unborn and new born children have a strong ability to communicate with their surroundings, and can react very precisely to emotional information, as they seek orientation from the adults close to them, primarily from their mother.

1.15 Recognising Trauma Survival Strategies

In my practical therapeutic work with the 'Constellation of the Intention' I make no theoretical assumptions that lead to any speculation about

- a 'transcendent awareness' of existence at the time of conception,
- an awareness of egg and sperm cells,
- a 'higher self',
- an 'incarnation of souls', or even
- a reincarnation from an earlier life.

Working in the psychotherapeutic field we may often have a lack of knowledge, and maybe are unable to find explanations, but in my opinion we should not attempt to fill these gaps with speculative assumptions and unproven theoretical concepts, but should begin by accepting and tolerating our lack of knowledge. In this way our perception, feeling and thinking remain open to other explanations until gradually conclusive and consistent findings come to the fore. In my opinion that is appropriate as a basic scientific approach.

I think it is of great concern if inconsistent and contradictory assumptions of a spiritual or even esoteric nature are made in the field of trauma therapy. Trauma forces our human psyche to blank out reality, deny it, distort it and whitewash it, in order to survive. We know from memory research how much we create our own biography. If we have suffered a catastrophic childhood, it does not necessarily follow that we consciously remember it as such. Our survival strategies have to remove from our consciousness the unbearable reality of being made powerless and helpless so that we neither perish through fear, pain, shame and overstimulation, (leading to the inability to behave correctly in traumatic environments), nor lose contact with the social communities in which we live.

Particularly if his own parents, either as perpetrators or accessories to perpetration, have caused early traumatisation, a child has to split and then believes that he is responsible for what has happened to him. This is the only way he can create in his psyche a picture of his 'dear parents', who have a 'difficult child'.

Irrational ideas, illusions of a better, ideal world are some of the basic repertoire of our trauma-survival strategies. People with early traumatisation in particular, who have experienced their parents as negative and violent, have to create an ideal vision of love, security, family and world harmony in order to hold onto their will to live and retain some measure of self-esteem.

In my opinion such survival strategies also form the basis for the widely-held dualistic way of thinking: separating body from mind and looking at them independently, and treating them therapeutically as separate entities. It is above all the survival strategies in a love trauma that strive to ensure that the parents who are incapable of love remain the focus of the child's love. Children are more likely to blame themselves for their suffering than to admit that their parents are traumatised parents.

It is therefore in the sphere of 'spirituality' that survival strategies find concepts such as 'ancestral mothers' and 'ancestral fathers' and 'cosmic forces' to compensate for what they cannot find in their actual mother and father. The child may try to avoid blaming his actual parents, instead blaming himself by believing himself to have been a perpetrator in a previous lifetime, thinking that he himself has chosen his difficult parents in order to work off the old 'karma' through present suffering.

Another widespread survival strategy is to imagine the removal of the experience of lack of love by internally bonding with those who are deceased, for example, grandparents who died prematurely, or a sibling. A twin sister or brother who might have been in the womb but subsequently died, can be a particularly suitable candidate for the projection of love that is not available from anyone living. Imagination knows no bounds when painting a picture of how wonderful life would have been if a brother or sister had lived, how much they would have loved each other and shared everything in life.

It is also a popular survival strategy to reduce traumatising experiences of violence and perpetrator-victim dynamics to a simple experience of loss, which makes reconciliation possible with relatives who are actually the perpetrators.

It is easy to fall into the trap of parent idealisation, thereby not recognising a perpetrator-victim dynamic between parents and children. Some regard the abstract concept of parenthood as being much more important than actual parenthood, arguing that the person's own life came from his or her parents and they would not have been there at all otherwise. They are thereby drawing from a biological fact – it is true that without their parents these children would not have existed – a psychological conclusion: the parents do earn *per se* respect and appreciation, whatever they did to their children. 'Respecting' parents then becomes a 'law of nature'. "Accept what is!" is a popular formula in which this ideological equation of natural facts with psychological needs is cloaked.

But psychological givens do not result from biological facts. Nature and psyche are different phenomena. The human psyche is not blindly subservient to biological self-preservation and reproduction, or it would be superfluous. It is able to evaluate the particular quality of human relationships emotionally and to understand them mentally. Thus, if parents behave violently towards their children and do not love them, it is a good reason for those children not to focus their love on their parents any longer. Children do not have to protect their parents or excuse them if they have been treated with violence by them. An individual can only succeed in no longer directing his love towards his traumatised parents if he is able to let his psychological child self grow up, to mature and behave lovingly towards himself.

In some cases the parents are so massively traumatised that a child's healthy psyche cannot exist and develop near the traumatised psyche of the parents. The parents' traumatised psyche completely monopolises the child's psyche. Such children can only exist psychologically if they extricate themselves completely from their parents' influence, which they cannot do until they are able to leave home. Only then can they become their own person and develop as an individual. In order to take this giant inner step successfully, there has to be a social and societal environment that does not blindly pay homage to an idealised view of parenthood, but looks closely to see what qualities the parents actually have.

The introduction of arbitrary ideas, beliefs and ideologies into trauma therapeutic procedures does not support the processes of healing and integration. It disrupts and confuses them, offering new suggestions for the trauma survival strategies and keeping the splits alive. It is too easy for the trauma survival parts to distract attention away from the reality of the trauma and flee into the spheres of wishful thinking and fantasies. Traumatisation processes make it essential to confront ourselves with as much clarity and unambiguity as possible.

1.16 Early consciousness?

Consciousness seems to be a more recent 'invention' of evolution, and not a vital component of life and reproduction. Consciousness distinguishes humans from other living creatures, and if we lose our consciousness or have to give it up we are relegated to an animalistic level of development.

I do not want to suggest in any way that we already know everything concerning our consciousness and the depth of psychological processes. There is a good deal we know little about at the moment. There are still many unanswered questions that require scientific research in the field of early trauma and the beginnings of human consciousness. Some reports from people about their pre-natal and peri-natal experiences sound as if the people concerned had consciously experienced everything, and were able to think about it and talk about it. Much that comes to light in therapy concerning pre-natal experiences is confirmed when the parents are asked about detailed circumstances of pregnancy and birth. Child therapists also report astonishing results when they communicate directly with infants about their birth experiences and the infants miraculously lose their symptoms. (Emerson 2012, Eliacheff 2011)

But if we assume that conscious psychological processes require a fully developed neo-cortex, then the questions arise as to when perception and feeling, thought and conscious reflection begin. Nerve cells develop about 15 days after conception, and after eight weeks the growing child possesses a primitive brain that develops rapidly until the moment of birth. (Nilson and Hamberger 2003) There are various explanatory models for the possible existence of pre-natal 'transcendental' consciousness. (McCarty 2013, Renggli 2013) How much thought is there at this point without words? I don't know, and others are also unable to say with certainty.

Conscious memories of early traumas may be through the transfer of the mother's feelings, images and experience of procreation, conception and pregnancy to the child. Is it also possible that the child absorbs the psychological content of his mother's psyche directly? Perhaps we sometimes simply play with our own fantasies, or it plays with us, when we empathise with these early processes during therapy sessions. Free association and translation of rudimentary feelings into imagery are not unusual devices in therapy, and are ones we humans frequently use if we move into areas with few clear points of reference. In summary it seems to me that there are many unexplained questions in this field, and some things that seem miraculous to us at this moment in time may eventually produce a scientific explanation. In my practical work I often trust physical reactions in my clients more than spoken words; the early roots of our psyche are presumably more physical than intellectual.

2
Conception as a source of early trauma

Marta Thorsheim

2.1 Conception where the parents have healthy psychological structures

In ideal circumstances a child is conceived during a sexual act between two psychologically healthy people who love each other and want to start a family, or extend their family. These parents are able to procreate and conceive a child from the healthy structures of their psyche. Following conception these happy and privileged children grow in a loving womb; the child is wrapped in warmth and security and is well nourished. Right from the beginning, both parents take an emotional interest in their child's development. For the child this means that after he is born the care, warmth, love and security he needs are there for him, and his parents will promote and support his individual development to healthy autonomy.

Many people imagine that they are the product of loving parents who could not wait to hold their child and to form a loving bond with him, but unfortunately in reality the situation is often very different.

2.2 Conception if the parents are traumatised and have survival parts

Conception can take place when a man and a woman are in their survival or even in their traumatised parts. Children are sometimes conceived during rape, or in other situations where force is involved, either from within steady couple relationships or outside of them:

- conception can have happened from a moment of thoughtless desire;
- the parents might have tried for a child following the anguish of losing a previous child;
- some children are conceived as status symbols for the parents,
- others as proof that the mother or father was not at fault if a previous relationship of theirs had been childless;
- children may also be conceived in order to ensure the mother's material welfare;
- children may be a form of pressure to prevent the man from leaving the woman,
- or they may be conceived in the hope of saving a troubled relationship.

Every child conceived in one of the above ways has a different kind of start in life. As early as conception and throughout the pregnancy there may be a transfer of negative feelings, emotional states and illusory ideas from the mother to the child. The child may then experience his time in the womb as inhospitable. The conditions for a loving bond between parents and child are absent right from the conception. What the growing child thereby often experiences from the mother is lack of interest, or even icy coldness.

2.3 Past and current sexual relationships between the sexes

Modern western attitudes have changed considerably regarding sexuality:

- Old norms have increasingly disappeared since the 1960s, mainly due to the availability of good contraception so men and women can now enjoy sex without having to worry about pregnancy.
- Liberalised abortion laws along with more effective abortion methods have steered development in the same direction.
- 'Freer' and 'safer' sex has become part of female emancipation and the demand for equal rights between sexes.

- In addition, western standards of education, particularly the education of women, have improved considerably.
- Migration to towns and cities, where sexual morals are less rigid than in the country, has also furthered sexual liberalism.
- Travel has become more common, which has expanded horizons as regards potential sexual partners.
- Methods of communication have become more effective, with the increase of mass media. Television and the internet have shrunk the world and allowed the exchange of information and stimulus in relation to sexual practices to become faster and considerably more comprehensive.
- Religions are increasingly losing their influence on sexual behaviour.
- Attitudes and values relating to couples living together and sexual behaviour generally are becoming noticeably more liberal. Nowadays there are, for example, openly gay presidents and ministers.
- This all means that men and women may have several sexual partners in the course of their lives, and that sex before marriage has become the norm.

These profound developments have by no means been global, and today migration from areas with the old, traditional values and sexual norms mean that western countries are confronted by issues such as genital mutilation in girls and boys, forced marriages, and even women being killed in the name of 'honour' if they resist patriarchal sexual and relationship norms. Men's needs are set far above women's in the very patriarchal cultures of the orient, as was also largely the case in Europe 100 years ago.

Even today, in certain countries and families embedded in the values of a farming culture, a woman has to bear a son in order to guarantee an heir for the family farm, the shipping company, the firm or the royal family. And the culture and politics of some countries still consider girls of less value than boys. In extreme cases, young girls are either murdered straight after birth, sold or given away.

Some of my clients come from countries where it is normal for women to be kept as slaves, or sexually abused in families they have married into. The daughters, and sons, who come to therapy bear the psychological traces of the traumatic way in which their mothers were conceived and brought up. They themselves are traumatised through their mothers and fathers, and have developed massive survival strategies, which are defined by their culture of origin. However, the split-off trauma feelings are generally the same, regardless of the respective culture. The children conceived in the next generation suffer similar disorientation in their process of self-discovery. Seen from a historical perspective, our idea of a partnership being based on love is very recent; marriage was traditionally very much an arrangement to secure an inheritance and property ownership and to establish ties of loyalty between different families, preferably from the same social class. In this worldview, individual romantic feelings were seen as irrational and provocative.

2.4 Traumatised parents – a historical constant

Modern times have seen drastic changes in the social framework for sexuality, as well as conception. There are hardly any social obstacles nowadays if a couple wants to have a child. At the same time we are aware that relationships between men and women, and between the child's potential biological parents, are not always harmonious. Equality in law and real life are very different. Expectation and reality are miles apart both in couple and parental relationships.

Insights gained by psychotherapists show that the traumas carried over from childhood to adulthood are one of the main causes for this. The person's own traumas, as well as those transferred from earlier generations, can lead to psychological splits and symbiotic entanglements. This affects the love between a man and a woman, and the relationship between them as parents. Traumas have an extremely negative effect on the process of the child's attachment to his parents that is so vital for the child.

If a couple have sexual intercourse under the influence of their survival parts, satisfaction is frequently one-sided, i.e. one partner enjoys the sex act and the other endures it. This can happen if a person is forced to have sex, or allows him or herself to be used as a sex object, perhaps in order to hold onto the partner. If sexuality is practised under the influence of survival parts, bonding emotions and sexual arousal are separated from each other. The act of sex thereby becomes mere physical satisfaction that does not bind the participants more closely together, but rather separates them from one another.

This sort of sexuality can give rise to different reactions:

- feelings of fear, and panic attacks
- accusations and anger
- sorrow and resignation
- psychological and physical suffering.

A woman who, while in her survival parts, allows herself to be used as a sex object and becomes pregnant, is in danger of rejecting her growing child from the moment of conception. She is likely to reject the life starting within her, experiencing it as a burden, and to develop an increasing feeling of disgust and abhorrence during the pregnancy as the new life grows. Sometimes this feeling is so strong that she terminates the pregnancy; sometimes it is not quite as strong but still powerful enough for her to ignore the child's needs and live in an unhealthy way, which leads to problems with the child's development. She cannot connect emotionally with the new life.

A man who allows himself to be used as a sex object or provider of sperm for procreation (for example if the woman wants a child or has a stronger sex drive than the man) is in danger of neglecting the woman even more during her pregnancy, and rejecting and feeling disgust towards the growing life.

The bottom line is that everything that is good for a mother who conceives a child is also good for the child, and everything that is bad for the mother is also harmful for the child. It is a blessing for his wife and his children if the man's sexuality is based in his healthy psychological structures. The following case studies show what effect it can have on a person if at the very beginning their procreation and conception have taken place under the influence of trauma.

2.5 Conception as rape

Clients whose conception was from rape frequently describe experiencing irrational fear and anger that is not appropriate for the situation at the time. They tell of emotional numbness, dreams and nightmares about bombings and war, although they were born long after the war was over. They may question whether they have the right to live. Others talk of a vague feeling of being in a container full of sperm and blood.

Monica: No right to live

> Monica has thoughts of suicide and asks herself: "Can it be that I have no right to live?" But she wants to live for the sake of her children. Her intention is "To have the right to live."
>
> The constellation brings to light that the client has a symbiotic entanglement with her traumatised and guilt-stricken grandmother on her father's side, who doubted whether she had the right to live, as she had been jointly responsible for atrocities in World War II. The grandfather on her father's side and this grandmother, as Norwegians, had collaborated with the German Nazis. The grandfather had killed his own countrymen and was imprisoned after the war when the father of my client was two years old. When the grandfather came home he was just skin and bones. My client's father was then ten years old when he came to know his father. The grandmother left the family when her husband was released from prison, but returned later. The grandfather was severely traumatised and brought up his son extremely violently without any intervention from the grandmother.
>
> Monica's father also used violence towards his wife and children including raping his wife. Monica thinks that she was conceived by rape. Her parents' survival strategy was to feign a normal façade to outsiders, to have a respectable job, a nice house and neat children.

Bjarte: The boy not allowed to be a man

Bjarte describes experiencing anger that he cannot always control. He is 40 and used to be a professional soldier. He never experienced fear during dangerous war assignments. His intention is to discover the cause for this anger in a constellation.

In the constellation the representative of the intention looks out of the window. He's a little tense, closes his eyes, sways and takes one step towards the client who moves backwards and says he feels fuzzy-headed. The intention sinks to the floor with his hands over his head, doubles up on the floor and weeps. The client still feels numb, moves back, away from the intention and clenches his fists. As facilitator of the constellation I ask the client if he would like to hear my interpretation of the picture. He agrees. I tell him that I have the impression that an early trauma is depicted here and that the client has split off a part of himself. The client agrees with this suggestion and now comes into contact with memories and intuitions. He describes how, as a small child, he had to sleep between his mother and father, against his will. Then he remembers that his mother had talked about being raped by an unfamiliar man. She told the story as if it had been a dream, stressing the word unfamiliar. He himself had a vague suspicion that he had been interfered with when he had to sleep between his parents. The fog now disappears and he realises that his mother had misused him as a shield against his father. He says: "I always knew it, without realising. And I also know that my mother was always afraid of my masculinity. That is why I had to hide the man in me." For the young Bjarte it was more important to survive this violent relationship between his mother and father than to experience the boy inside him with his own sexual needs. He split his own needs off and ended up in a symbiotic entanglement, charged with his mother's fear of masculine sexuality. This fear, which he was unaware of until that moment, can be spontaneously woken within him and turned into uncontrolled anger. Bjarte now suspects that his mother was not raped by a strange man but that he was conceived in an act of sexual violence by his father.

2.6 Conception as a replacement child

Some clients relate that they have been conceived because their parents had lost a previous child. Some of these children were even given the name of the dead child. These clients often struggle with the feeling of not being good enough. They can be afflicted with melancholy, lack of energy and immeasurable sorrow. They can also feel that they are the wrong gender, or they search their whole lives for a sister or a brother they have never heard of. They tell of a lack of bonding with their mother: "Somehow she was absent". The child then develops an entangled identity. That means that the child does not know his own self, and is unable to realise his own nature fully, which he would have been able to do had his mother not been traumatised by the death of a sibling. This is a serious matter for boys because in this way they have difficulty accessing their masculine identity. It is also a burden for girls because they are not free to live their own femininity because of their mother's trauma.

Anna: The boyish girl

> Anna came to the seminar because she'd had a breakdown following the death of her mother, and was on sick leave diagnosed with 'burn-out'. Her intention is to regain her physical and mental energy and to see what constraints are in the way.
>
> The constellation brings to light the client's entanglement with her mother's suppressed sorrow following the loss of a son who died at birth. We can see this because the representative for the mother devotes her whole attention to the boy who died two months before Anna was conceived. The client's entanglement with the suppressed trauma feelings of her mother and her profound sorrow about the loss of her first child are reflected in the representative for the mother and also in the representative for the 'constraints in the way'. The latter representative shows the mother's infinite love and her sorrow about the loss of her first-born. She is therefore unable to see Anna, the replacement child. In her desperate attempts to bond with her mother, Anna has unconsciously attempted to be the son her mother lost. She mostly played with boys and pretended to her mother and herself to be

something she was not. This led the adult Anna to work until she was exhausted. Anna's breakdown following the death of her mother can be seen as there no longer being any hope of reaching her mother and being accepted by her.

Following the constellation, Anna contacted me and said that she now had more energy than ever and that she can now show her femininity in a new and good way.

2.7 Conception to replace the individual's own parents

Clients' reports of their parents being influenced by the unconscious wish to create a replacement mother or father when conceiving a child are often very moving. These clients describe their disbelief that their parents are their real parents; they talk about their many attempts to connect with their mother, about their struggle to gain access to their mother's heart without ever receiving a positive emotional answer. We hear how these children often develop an over-generous heart and want to do right by everyone, forgetting themselves in the process. From a young age they split off in their helplessness and resignation the fear, anger and pain, the despair and their whole inner misery at not being loved and accepted by their mother. The child hungrily seeks emotional contact with his parents and thus comes into contact with their trauma energies and absorbs these in place of love. The parents' trauma feelings are superimposed on the child's emotions and feel like his own emotions. These children are therefore unable to distinguish between their own feelings and those of their parents, which leads to internal emotional chaos. They often idealise their parents and accept total blame for the bad relationship. They are angry with themselves.

Mariann: The girl with the generous heart

> Mariann remembers being beaten by her mother and that she sobbed through her tears: "You should be consoling me!" To which her mother replied: "That's not true, you're the one who should be consoling me."

In the course of the constellation Mariann's split traumatised parts come to light: she collapses into the position of a little child, slips past the representatives for mother and father without coming into contact with them and gives up. She sits still for a short while and then slips further, behind an empty chair, while the intention sneaks off behind another empty chair. I ask the client whether she can recognise herself in this dynamic. She says that during her early childhood she had the feeling that she was reaching out with her whole heart to her mother, but there was no one to receive it. As a small child she often ran to the neighbours but they always brought her back to her parents. As the constellation progresses the representative for the mother lies on the floor and starts hitting herself on the head saying: "It's not my arm that's hitting me." The client remembers that she was always afraid of her grand-mother. It seems believable to her that her grandmother might have hit her mother. Somehow she senses that her father wanted to have children and her mother didn't want children but only wanted someone who would comfort her. The grandmother on her mother's side lost her own mother very early. During the war she sent her seven-year-old daughter to strangers a long way away to protect her from the atrocities in her hometown. But the acts of war and battles increased in the new location as well. Mariann's mother never talked about what she had seen as a little child and what happened to her there.

2.8 Conceived into a family of victims and perpetrators

According to Ruppert (2014) a bonding system trauma is defined as perpetrator and victim living with one another in the same system and being dependent on one another. All persons involved in such a bonding system remain trapped in their perpetrator and/or victim states and cannot see a healthy way out of their perpetrator-victim relationships. The perpetrators feel pressurised by the presence of the victim and regard themselves as victims. The victims develop the characteristics of perpetrators, but because they cannot defend themselves against the actual perpetra-tor they direct their perpetrator energies towards people who are weaker than them, frequently towards their own children. And the siblings in a perpetrator-victim family abuse younger siblings or possibly animals.

Both male and female clients frequently describe being subjected to destructive mothers during their childhood. This can take the form of threats, beatings and sexual abuse. Incest is always a highly explosive subject, particularly maternal sexual abuse of sons and daughters. A lot of courage is necessary to bring this subject and the painful memories associated with it into the open and to accept and process the facts. Sexual abuse often activates the dynamic of a trauma of love as well as a trauma of existence. Female perpetrators of incest have as a rule experienced sexual abuse themselves as children and received no help. They carry out the same sexual practices on their own children that they had to undergo personally.

Alexandra

> Alexandra is a beautiful woman in her forties; when she sits down beside me she is in tears. She talks about a family where the current generation and earlier generations have experienced incest, sexual abuse, abortion, children being murdered, and war trauma. This applies to both the mother's and the father's family line. And now her own children are also having difficult lives with drug abuse and crime.
>
> Her mother had told her that she was an unwanted child and that all the children she'd had should have been spots on the sheet, and had said that she'd asked for an abortion, but the doctor had refused her application and instead she had been referred to a psychologist. Her mother had talked about the fact that many pregnant women used knitting needles to attempt to get rid of a child. Being born despite being an unwanted child created a feeling of ambivalence in Alexandra that ran as an undercurrent through her life.
>
> Alexandra also says that her father was violent towards her mother during her pregnancy. During the Second World War he had been imprisoned and was severely traumatised by the experience.
>
> Alexandra's life has consisted of drugs and prostitution. Many times she thought about ending her life. But after years of therapy

she has decided not to run away any longer. She now wants to live. Her intention is "to take my life back and unfold".

Alexandra and the representative for her intention are standing holding hands, looking into each other's eyes. Alexandra tells her intention about her life, cries and stamps her feet. Suddenly she starts shivering and cries even more and her intention falls to the floor.

After a while Alexandra pauses, exhales and says: "I think it was my mother who used knitting needles to try and kill us!" Her intention starts to look at her and slowly she stands up and again they hold hands, crying together.

After a while the process stops. After it has ended, Alexandra starts to recount more about what she knows about her life and how difficult it is for her to take in that this is her reality, and how she is still looking for a mother, and that she is not able to realise that she will never receive the love she so desperately wanted in her childhood.

She says that she has lived her whole life with the feeling of ambivalence and an inner struggle between

- wanting to do something and not wanting to,

- liking something and not liking it,

- agreeing with something and disagreeing,

and that this has led her into difficult situations in life, and conflicting relationships, not only within her family but also among friends and colleagues. She also talks about being almost psychotic at times and that she is easily annoyed and has sudden outbursts of anger directed towards "the wrong people", such as her therapists, her children and her colleagues. She says she now knows that her anger should be addressed towards her mother but that talking to her doesn't help. Her mother always pretends to be innocent.

Alexandra often comes for therapy; she wants to be able to realise emotionally, step by step, what her start in life has meant to her. She also knows that to do this, she has to realise that she has been a victim of the perpetrators in her family from the very first moments of her life, and that it does not help for her to go into fighting and perpetration.

3
Maternal ambivalence during pregnancy

Alice Schultze-Kraft

I have been dealing with the pre-natal period, both professionally and personally, for many years. I am very grateful to be able to access this dimension in all its complexity in my therapeutic work even better through the method of the 'Constellation of the Intention', which gives access to these key issues. Integrating the pre-natal era within the therapeutic process allows us to work on the very foundations of the human psyche, having the potential to achieve profound changes that can radiate to all areas of life.

What follows is all about these early experiences that can over-shadow and influence the entire life of the individual. It is the pre-natal experience of maternal ambivalence – that early shock experienced by many people who feel they are unable to open up wholly to life and to their own vital drive. A child needs a loving response, and a secure emotional attachment at the beginning of his life. In his mother's womb he is in a profound physical symbiosis, i.e. he is practically inextricably linked to her body. It is a huge threat to the child if, in this early phase of deepest physical and psychological dependence, his mother is physically and emotionally unable to respond to him and he does not receive the most fundamental acceptance of his physical and psychological existence. The child experiences existential uncertainty that can have an effect on his whole later sense of identity, his contact with other people, his relationships and his attitude towards life itself.

Wished-for or not, wanted or not – it is not always straightfor-ward black or white. What a pregnant woman says and her outward behaviour are not always clear and do not always reflect the whole truth. The internal dynamics of the psyche are much more complex. As well as open rejection, there can also be indirect or concealed rejection of the child.

Ambivalence means the juxtaposition of conflicting feelings, even if parts of them are completely unconscious. A child can be consciously wanted and unconsciously rejected, and in the same way an unconscious split wish for a child can be concealed behind a conscious unwanted pregnancy. "Unwanted does not mean not wished for. The wish can remain concealed. Fulfilling the long-held wish for a child does not necessarily herald the greatest joy. A child's needs can escape his parents' perception if their own visions predominate." (Lüpke 2011, p. 48) I would like to add that the child's needs are less likely to be perceived by his parents if their own untreated traumas predominate. The more a woman is trapped in her own unconscious pre-natal trauma, the more likely it is that she will be ambivalent about her own pregnancy. This ambivalence can be expressed in many ways and is not always as clearly visible as an open rejection with a definite abortion wish.

There are many external circumstances that increase a conflict in pregnancy: an uncertain relationship or one not offering much support, a father's conflict concerning the pregnancy or even his complete rejection of it, rejection of the partner by an individual's own family of origin, desperate financial straits, unfinished job-training or apprenticeship, medical risk factors, etc. But I experience again and again that unfavourable external factors are seldom the sole cause, and that difficulties arise particularly when the woman's inner conflict is of an unconscious nature. A woman who is grounded, connected with her life force and filled with a sense of primal trust will deal with outward stress factors differently from a woman who is subliminally chronically stressed and psychologically split through her own untreated traumas.

3.1 The faces of maternal ambivalence

Many a pregnant woman has wavered backwards and forwards in her uncertainty and desperately tried to make a final decision. Additional circumstances such as manipulation by a partner or a relative often increase the pressure, so that the final decision for or against the child is frequently not a truly free decision that reflects her feelings.

Sometimes a woman who has successfully suppressed her own early trauma, and who seems to wish for a child with all her heart, experiences unexpected conflict from the start of the pregnancy. Because of the split, this conflict may only show on a physical level, for example in the form of extreme morning sickness. Pre-natal depression can also be a sign of this profound conflict and the woman's own unconscious early trauma. It can also show the ambivalence if a woman only realises very late that she is pregnant, or denies and conceals her growing belly. Sometimes a woman will try to achieve this by starving herself. But outwardly everything seems to be fine. The woman 'functions' as a perfect expectant mother, eats properly, reads up on pregnancy and does everything to prepare as well as she can for motherhood. Yet she is unable to establish a good emotional bond with her unborn child. She might not even notice it because she doesn't knows differently, perhaps because the stress and the feelings of confusion and rejection she had been subjected to by her own mother have meant that she had to split off from her vital drive and therefore from her feelings while she herself was still in the womb. Emotional contact with her mother had then been menacing right from the start.

Frequently the desire to have a child is linked to preconditions. For example, there are mothers who, trapped in their own wounded self esteem, idealise their child before he or she is born (or even before conception), and project their own unfulfilled longings and dreams onto the unborn child, who must also compensate for the mother's inner emptiness. This mother does not offer her child any space in the womb to develop his own drive because she is unable to welcome him and his uniqueness. She longs for her child to provide her with those things she did not experience as a child herself: love, attention and approval. "I would finally like to have someone just for myself" is the desperate unconscious wish accompanying a pregnancy like that. When the mother is confronted with the absolute dependency, helplessness and energy-sapping needs of her infant after the birth, the renewed frustration of her own unfulfilled longings may lead to feelings of rejection and aggression towards her child.

We should also mention the child who is conceived in the conscious or unconscious hope of saving the partnership. It is not infrequent for the intrauterine contract to have an effect on the time after the birth and for the child to continue in his role as saviour and mediator as this task has become the reason for his existence.

In all these cases the child in the womb does not receive affirmation of his own existence, and his existence is not an end in itself. "Pre-natal bonding and relationship research has shown how important the affirmative 'Yes' from the mother is from the very beginning for the unborn child. The quality of this affirmation, whether it is an open or a conditional 'Yes', is received by the child and retained." (Reiter 2011, p. 81) The person who has not received a definite 'Yes' at the beginning of his life remains trapped in his mother's original ambivalence that has moulded him psycho-somatically before he is born. However, the extent to which this pre-natal uncertainty is reinforced depends on the way bonding develops.

3.2 The consequences of maternal ambivalence

A pregnancy that is experienced ambivalently by the mother is hugely stressful for her. As a result of traumas she has experienced herself that have been further stimulated by the pregnancy, she can be in a state of chronic overstimulation, which is transferred to the unborn child in the form of stress hormones through the umbilical cord. Maternal stress can have an effect on the circulation of the placenta resulting in an undersupply to the unborn child. It can also lead to premature contractions. (Huizink 2000) If the child is flooded with stress hormones it can have a negative effect on the birth. The child then reacts to the natural stress of birth in the way he 'knows': with the response patterns from his pre-natal time. The child might then experience the contractions during the birth as life-threatening instead of beneficial. (Hochauf 2008)

An ambivalent expectant mother who is already stressed will tend to be uncertain and fearful during the birth process. There is no stable emotional contact, no 'dialogue' between her and the child. The child inevitably feels this stress as well and experiences the birth process as threatening, which makes it more difficult, which in turn increases the mother's fear – a vicious circle. The likelihood of medicinal measures being taken to induce the birth increases, as does the risk of a forceps or vacuum delivery or a caesarean section.

Negative pre-natal maternal emotions not only correlate with complications during pregnancy and birth, they have an effect on the postnatal time as well. Pre-natal stress can lead to postnatal anomalies such as sudden agitation, motor restlessness and increased crying, and also to an increased susceptibility to illness and further down the line to learning difficulties, tics, behaviour disorders or retarded mental development. (Huizink 2000, Janus 2011)

The pre-natal experience of being unwanted or of having an ambivalent mother definitely leaves its mark. The child's early negative experiences can cause biochemical changes and physiological changes in the brain. (Hüther 2012) Certain situations can reactivate the experiences or they can continue throughout the individual's life – with profound primal mistrust and chronic stress. The extent of the effect of the early insecurity depends on the child's further bonding experiences with his mother and above all on whether the child experiences any bonding that gives him stability after the birth, in other words whether the mother is able to build up an authentic emotionally-nurturing and affirmative contact with her child.

This is where I see an important starting point to use the 'Constellation of the Intention' preventatively: the 'Constellation of the Intention' offers an internally conflicted expectant mother the chance to work in depth on her ambivalent psychological situation. This includes accepting the pregnancy and the reality of the foetus, as well as accepting the growing child as a person in his own right in the context of dealing with her own trauma and particularly her own symbiotic trauma. (Ruppert 2012, 2014) Therapy can help the young mother, after she has given birth to her child, to work on her trauma, and thereby come into good contact with her child.

3.3 The mother's own symbiotic trauma

Maternal ambivalence in pregnancy is the result of intra-psychological splits whose deep causes can be found not only in sexual traumas (e.g. sexual abuse in childhood or rape in adolescence or adulthood) but also frequently in symbiotic trauma. A pregnancy stimulates at a profoundly unconscious level the woman's own pre-natal mother-child bonding experience. It virtually opens the gate to the woman's own pre-natal symbiotic trauma, confronting the expectant mother unavoidably with the feelings and traumatisations of her own mother, to which she was subjected before birth. Unconsciously the expectant mother repeats the bonding pattern she experienced when she was in her mother's womb, whereby "early experience is not present as concrete autobiographical memory, but as a flood of feeling and behavioural and perceptual sentience". (Janus and Haibach 1997, p. 41)

The child absorbs the mother's different psychological structures before birth. It is the mother's split feelings that have a sustained disorienting effect on the pre-natal child. The mother's split emotionality impacts on the child and profoundly unsettles him, robbing him of any emotional support. The child does not know where he stands. "Then that which is indistinctly felt spreads like an inexplicable shadow through the person's attitude to life and sense of self, and he is unable to find a way to deal with it". (Levend and Janus 2000, p. 181) The perpetrator parts, as well as the maternal victim parts assumed by the child before birth, stay with him throughout his life as maternal introjects. If the child was insecure before birth he will become "ensnared in a negative pre-natal state" (Janus 2011, p. 139) and a psychological part of the child will remain literally trapped in the pre-natal dilemma. In later life the original experience is frequently unconsciously reproduced; if the woman becomes pregnant, it is more strongly stimulated and is transferred from generation to generation.

Sofia

Sofia [the name has been changed] comes into my practice completely distraught. She has known for a few weeks that she is pregnant. Agitatedly and under intense pressure, she says that she can't cope any more: it's threatening to tear her apart internally. She repeatedly has the feeling that she is possessed by uncontrollable and destructive anger. At such times she experiences the growing child as a demon intent on consuming her from the inside, draining her strength and destroying her life. She is permanently sick and hardly able to eat anything. This terrifying and alarming anger suddenly springs up inside her and she has no idea where it comes from. Then again, she says, she feels mortally afraid and is petrified that she would not survive giving birth. And in the midst of these debilitating feelings there are moments when she feels love for the child, notices him and talks tenderly to him. She has sometimes thought about suicide in the worst moments of despair, but that isn't like her, she has never had feelings like that.

Several constellations reveal how closely Sofia is connected with the feelings and the inner drama of her mother through her early symbiotic trauma. Her mother had not wanted to become pregnant and had had to marry a man she had only known a short while and did not really love. The uncontrollable anger turns out to be her mother's anger, which was directed during her pregnancy towards the father of the child as well as towards Sofia. It is also the anger of the symbiotically traumatised grandmother who had felt unappreciated and unloved by her husband in Nazi Germany and abused by him for the sole purpose of having children. The angry perpetrator part that constituted a threat to Sofia before she was born is now directed towards both her unborn child and herself, so that she slips into her own early trauma feelings of powerlessness and terror that are usually expressed physically. The suicidal thoughts also turn out to originate from her mother. Her mother did not appear to have attempted an abortion, but strong perpetrator and 'abortion energies' appear in the grandmother during constellations. By fantasising about killing herself, Sofia's mother enacted both perpetrator and victim attitudes: she threatened to abort herself. So through her pregnancy Sofia came into contact with her own pre-natal symbiotic trauma. Triggered by her pre-natal distress, she experienced the unborn Sofia as perpetrator and blamed her for her predicament. During the therapeutic process Sofia cautiously comes into contact with her frightened and powerless pre-natal parts. The more she realises and affirms her own embryonic distress and early neediness, the more she is able to accept her child. The image she has of a greedy monster alters. More and more, she sees and feels a gentle little being she wants to care for, love and protect. Sofia's fear that she could die by giving birth can be explained by her severe birth trauma when it was a matter of life and death for both her mother and her.

This example illustrates what a huge effect the mother's unprocessed traumatic experiences have on the early mother-child bonding. If the mother's own pre-natal trauma dominates her early bonding with her child, it masks the child's pre-natal trauma and in a constellation it is not so easy to differentiate between them. If for example, in a pre-natal part, an abortion fear becomes apparent, it does not have to mean that the client has herself been threatened by abortion or experienced the wish to abort her child. This fear can also belong to the mother's or the grandmother's pre-natal trauma.

The unborn child not only participates directly in his mother's experiences and feelings during pregnancy, but is also connected with all his mother's unprocessed psychological damage and through this with the unprocessed terror of earlier generations. The theory of multi-generational psycho traumatology (Ruppert 2012, 2014) deals with such complex connections within the therapeutic process.

3.4 Consequences for therapeutic work

Psychotherapeutic work on pre-natal traumas demands a high degree of sensitivity and awareness. The individuals concerned long, on the one hand, for the loving and affirming symbiotic closeness they never knew, while on the other hand their deep-rooted mistrust causes them to view intra-personal contact with profound uncertainty and fear. They are still trapped in a pre-natal symbiotic trauma. They view the world as a threatening and unsettling place, the same way as they experienced the uterus. They were unable to trust their mother who at the same time became a part of them and continues to have an effect on them, and therefore they are unable to trust themselves. They are physically and psychologically stressed in the same way as they were at the beginning of their lives, even if it doesn't seem that way at first glance because their very early split bonding trauma is hidden behind a façade of survival strategies.

In direct contact they might seem very friendly, anxious to appear cooperative and well-adjusted, or they seem uncertain and evasive. Or perhaps they are 'in their head', controlling, manipulative, draining, demanding or reproachfully aggressive. The survival parts and the internalised victim-perpetrator dynamic show very varied faces to the outside world. But behind them is always an immense split-off inner distress.

There is an unconscious tendency to repeat the original experience, which can become apparent when conflicts and misunderstandings are staged (outside the actual sessions as well, e.g. when making appointments or suchlike). When aversive feelings arise in me in contact with a client, I am aware that these can be important signs of an early rejection or ambivalence experience revealed in the context of counter-transference. To enable a healing process the therapist has to provide an open-minded, authentic attitude in a secure relationship space as well as the willingness to address their own unresolved pre-natal issues. The early negative experiences that accompany individuals throughout their lives can be extremely terrifying if they suddenly threaten to overwhelm them, and cannot be assigned to any specific cause on account of the person's deep splits. If during a constellation they become figuratively-metaphorically, physically and emotionally discernible in the intention, and if they can be initially categorized, this initial assignment is often a tremendous relief. The demon suddenly acquires a face and the inexplicable difficulties in life take on a 'sense'. The original painful experience cannot be undone or 'corrected' in therapy. This experience is reality. But the individuals concerned can become conscious that they are still trapped in the insecurity at the beginning of their life, that they still doubt their right to exist.

The realisation that the original threat is past and life is not hostile, the deep connection with the self, the unconditional affirmation of the individual's own existence, the sense of vitality and rich world of emotions, the recognition and living-out of the person's own unique potential, the wish to be involved with the world and other people – all these are further steps away from the old trauma of destructive maternal symbiosis.

4
Unfulfilled desire to have children

Annemarie Denk

I have two children. The decision to have the first child was made, but I did not get pregnant. I was disappointed; I was certain that ovulation and the preceding mid-cycle pain had meant that it had been 'the right time'.

"But how could I become pregnant now?" I thought after a while, since I hadn't conceived after several years in a relationship and not much thought about contraception. I then decided – in the middle of my professional training – to forget about having a child and once again devoted myself to my studies. Today I am convinced that this was the only way for me to be relaxed enough to have my first pregnancy a little while later.

The deep disappointment I felt at the beginning, and my experience with similarly affected clients gives me an idea of how heavily it weighs on the mind when no pregnancy is in sight, even though everything has been tried, and despite following professional advice for years, the desire to have a child remains a dream. It is painful to see how good friends 'simply' have children, and then to feel left out.

Wanting to have children is a normal and healthy need. *Involuntary* childlessness as a result of infertility and/or sterility was recognised by the WHO in 1967 as a 'disease', if, after two years or more of regular unprotected sexual intercourse, and contrary to explicit will, a pregnancy has not been achieved. Since many women in Europe, particularly in Germany, are older when they try for a child, prompt treatment using *in vitro* fertilisation is often indicated from a medical point of view. The diagnosis of sterility, infertility, even illness, is a terrible piece of news for those wanting children. People who have received this diagnosis speak of a huge impact on their lives, of pain and anger, even of a feeling similar to the loss of a partner or the death of a child – the child who was the reason they did not use contraception and who in their imagination has already been born. The diagnosis can plunge people into a deep existential crisis. Feelings of failure are the result, the value of life recedes, self-esteem suffers, and emptiness and depression can follow. If the loss is not mourned, it can leave couples, if they still want a child, to become traumatised parents.

4.1 Statistics

The number of births in Germany has declined from 830,019 a year in 1991 to 715,000 in 2015. For every woman of childbearing age in Germany there are on average 1.42 births. A frequent explanation for the decline in the birth rate is that women are waiting until they are older to have their first child.

In Germany 15% of couples are involuntarily childless; in 40% of the cases the cause is either the man or the woman but not both; in 20% it is both the man and the woman. Physical causes are usually assumed to be the reason. (De Jong 2002) Psychological causes are only mentioned in a scientific medical context when physical, environmental and health causes, such as being overweight or underweight or smoking, have been excluded. Most treatments with assisted conception involve women between 30 and 39. According to statistics, Europe has the largest number of reported treatment cycles for assisted conception in the world, about 55%[3]. However, there are a large number of unreported cases and Germany is the most affected, owing to the relatively restrictive Embryo Protection Law (ESchG). The Embryo Protection Law prohibits egg donation and surrogacy in Germany, although sperm donation is permitted. Unlike other countries, it is

---

[3] ESHRE European Society of Human Reproduction and Embryology, Results from the European register from the annual conference 2011, ART Fact sheet

against the law in Germany to use pre-implantation diagnostics to eliminate disabilities, although the law is being relaxed.

If an addition to the family is only possible through egg donation or surrogacy, Germans have to seek treatment in another country. The cheaper option of assisted conception abroad also waters down the data in Germany. In addition all data concerning assisted reproduction is voluntary and it is only recorded data that can be evaluated. Austria has a government agency where all cases of assisted reproduction carried out in the country have to be registered. According to statements from specialists in reproductive medicine and the European register ESHRE, there have been approximately 5 million births as a result of assisted reproduction technologies since the world's first, Louise Brown, was born in 1978[4]. The baby take-home rate (BTHR) worldwide is approximately 20 to 25% and is therefore comparable with the rate of 25% of women conceiving naturally. Worldwide 1,563 fertility clinics are registered in 53 countries with 1.5 million treatment cycles and 350,000 births annually following assisted reproduction technologies. The most active countries are the USA and Japan. In Belgium, Denmark, Finland, Iceland, Norway, Slovenia and Sweden more than 3% of births are the result of assisted reproduction.

In 1982 there were only five fertility centres in Germany. Today this has increased to 128 centres offering involuntarily childless couples different forms of assisted reproduction. Each fertility centre records its own statistics with the aim of achieving the highest rate of success, thereby attracting new patients for the lucrative treatments.

The naturalness of conception is increasingly giving way to the improving predictability of 'designer babies'. In a film about the help and support available for involuntary childlessness, for example, an American fertility clinic describes how children with

---

[4]   David Adamson, International Committee for Monitoring Assisted Reproductive Technologies (ICMART) at the 2013 Annual Conference of the European Society of Human Reproduction and Embryology (ESHRE). Focus on Production, September 2013. www.eshre.eu/Press-Room/Press-release/Press-releases-ESHRE-2012/5

eyes and hair of a certain colour, with certain talents, of a certain height, etc. can be 'ordered' with all the options offered by reproductive medicine[5]. In some places an individual's 'own children' are extracted as egg cells, examined and 'repaired' decades before pregnancy and birth. Polar body treatment makes this possible with the exchange of mitochondria. The parents could then be, for example, one father and two mothers, as has already been the case in Great Britain. Other variations are also possible: there are already mothers or same-sex couples who no longer bear their children themselves. Shaping and designing children with a person's own or with external genes is not yet possible in Germany, but already being done in other countries.

4.2 What lies behind the desire to have children?

There used to be different economic reasons for having children (for example someone to inherit the farm or to look after aging parents), but nowadays this is only true for some countries in the developing world. The reasons for having children that are listed today in almost all the more developed countries are:

- the wish to bring a new life into being,
- to have a child that gives meaning to life,
- to have the feeling of being a proper woman and a proper man,
- to feel love,
- the longing for bonding and unconditional love,
- to enrich the person's own life,
- to have more quality of life,
- primal longing and desire for a better world,
- to occupy the maternal role that was shaped by a difficult relationship with the person's own mother in a positive way and to fill it with everything missing from that person's childhood.

---

[5] www.aerzteblatt.de/nachrichten/35612/praeimplantationsdiagnostik_ us-Klinik_offeriert_designer-baby.htm from 2nd March 2009

Occasionally a child is also seen as a way to compensate for humiliation and disappointment in life. Social pressure and our own mortality are also named as reasons, as well as the wish to make up for a loss (for example if a parent or grandmother or sibling has died, or in the case of separation or the loss of a partner). The child can also function as a saviour, a source of care and love for the mother or the father, or the wish for perfection, omnipotence, coalescence and unity, or the realisation of an ideal image. A child can also be seen as a way to put new life into a deadlocked relationship. (von Lüpke 2011)

So in many cases the desire to have a child does not actually relate to the child himself, but is supposed to fulfil a seemingly meaningful purpose for the parents.

4.3 Blocks and disruptions in the desire to have a child

As deep as the wish to have a child might be, it still frequently happens that at an unconscious level the reason for wanting a child is also the cause for failure to conceive, for example if a woman wants to compensate for lack of closeness by having a child, while at the same time being afraid of closeness.

If the woman's own experiences as a child, both pre- and postnatal, were defined by negative experiences such as violence, abuse or emotional coldness, a pregnancy may be unconsciously rejected. Other reasons for not conceiving can be a lack of primal trust, miscarriages, abortions, an attempted abortion by the individual's own mother, and dependency conflicts with the mother resulting in mistrust in having her own child. According to Auhagen-Stephanos (2011), fear of self-endangerment and fear of overextension work 'like a contraceptive pill'. In the same way, fertility can be impeded by

- unconscious rejection of the woman's own femininity,
- intensively living out masculine life principles in the person's job and career without integrating feminine parts, and
- relationship problems between partners.

On the fathers' side, in WHO studies of 'healthy fathers', two-weekly checks over a period of 120 weeks have also shown an extreme fluctuation in the number of sperm capable of fertilisation, which is dependent on the father's state at the time. (Fiegl 2012) Here too, we can see how closely body and psyche are linked and how easy it is to make a false sterility diagnosis, possibly leading to an anonymous sperm donation.

Basically we can say that everything previously experienced by the mother and the father that in the case of a pregnancy can lead to far-reaching disruptions in the growing child, can also have a greater effect if the woman is involuntarily childless, preventing conception and leading to disturbances in the growth of the child. In order to create a sense of security and to surround a child with love, the first step for all couples as responsible parents should be to work on their own traumas as far as they can. Pregnancy and birth can reactivate old unprocessed wounds and conflict situations for the mother as well as the father. Early treatment prevents their own retraumatisation and the early traumatisation of the burgeoning life.

4.4 The beginnings of sense and perception

Prior to the use of ultrasound scans, which were introduced into doctors' surgeries in the early 80s, a child's development in the womb was largely invisible. As a result there was no mention of the growing child having feelings. Today there are many studies which show that long before they are born, babies perceive, hear, sense, feel, swallow, suck their thumbs, react etc. and psychologically bond with the mother in the womb. (Krüll 2009, Levend and Janus 2011, Ruppert 2014, Renggli 2013) In a natural pregnancy, egg and sperm cells are permanently in contact with the body of the mother or the father. The sperm cell enters the egg cell and with fertilisation, the sperm cell is in physical contact with the mother. Throughout its whole development the fertilised egg cell remains without interruption embedded in the protection of the mother's body. Mother and child form a physical and psychological unit. (Ruppert 2008)

Pregnancy as protection from sexuality

> Carmen came with the intention of wanting to know why she felt
> nauseous at the thought of her conception. Her parents were going
> through a difficult time then and she knew that she hadn't been a
> wanted child. It comes to light in the constellation that Carmen's
> mother didn't actually want to have anything to do with Carmen's
> father and could hardly bear him near her. She had only tolerated
> sexual intercourse with him and was then happy that being pregnant
> with Carmen meant she didn't have to have sex again for some
> time.

4.5 Assisted conception as a possible source of the emergence of trauma

Hormonal stimulation of the woman forms a part of every assisted
conception, with the aim of getting as many fertilised egg cells as
possible (sometimes as many as 20). This makes great demands of
the women concerned: hormonal provocation of ovulation,
removal of egg cells under sedation and administration of
painkillers, ultrasound scans to check egg maturation, anxiety,
stress, and feelings which permanently veer between highs and
lows. The fathers are also under extreme pressure. They provide
their sperm in an uncomfortable situation. Love, passion, warmth
and closeness are all lacking. In the case of an external sperm
donor love does not enter into it anyway.

With *in vitro* fertilisation (IVF), a procedure outside the body,
the egg cells are removed and mixed for 18 hours in a Petri dish,
in a liquid similar to the vaginal environment, with intact sperm
cells which have been centrifuged and prepared. They are then
kept in an incubator at 37°C. Here egg and sperm cells can find
each other in what is basically an inhospitable environment, but
one in which they are to a certain extent free and independent.

Intracytoplasmic sperm injection (ICSI) starts off in the same
way as IVF, but here one motile sperm is chosen that is then
injected directly into the egg cell. In this case, unlike natural
conception, the egg cell does not have the chance to start the act of

playing with the sperm cell and allowing it to penetrate it, but is pierced by the needle, taken by surprise and forcibly joined with the sperm cell. In order to avoid damaging the membrane, it is nowadays frequently scored with a laser beforehand. When we see under the microscope that single-cell organisms such as the amoeba move away, contract and show defensive reactions, then the question arises as to whether it is not possible that egg cells, although they are not regarded in medical science as feeling cells, can also show defensive reactions if they are treated with violence in this way. (Heller and Lapierre 2013)

In IVF and ICSI, the fertilised egg cells are transferred to the womb by means of a catheter within 24 to 48 hours. Up to three fertilised egg cells are transferred; the others are deep frozen using liquid nitrogen at a temperature of minus 196°C. In Germany, according to the Embryo Protection Law (ESchG), no more than three embryos may be transferred. In countries without ESchG, more could be transferred, with one possible result certainly being a multiple pregnancy.

For the parents the embryo transfer is a highly sensitive time, since it is the moment the woman experiences as the start of a possible pregnancy. It is the moment they have worked towards for months or even years; the moment their wishes, hopes and expectations are fulfilled or dashed. There are many fears connected with this time, with 'listening to one's inner self', searching for physical reactions that would point to a pregnancy and confirm a successful implantation. Expectations run high and often suppress the fact that success rates in general are low. Of 50,968 treatments carried out in 2012 there were 7,020 births, which is 13.7%, according to a statistical summary of the German IVF Register[6].

Cryopreservation is the process whereby cells are frozen in liquid nitrogen to preserve their viability, whilst converting the biological system into the physical state of a solid. Sperm cells are

---

[6] Deutsches IVF-Register. (German IVF-Register). Annual report 2012. Journal for Reproductive Medicine and Endocrinology, 10th year 2013. Special Edition 2. Gablitz: Verlag für Medizin und Wirtschaft. www.deutsches-ivf-register.de

frozen, as well as 'fertilised' egg cells, which are preferred, as they can be kept for longer. The cells are stored virtually in a state of tension, solidification and shock until they are thawed and used. The longest time an embryo has been kept deep-frozen and then transferred resulting in a successful pregnancy was nine years. Other embryos that have not been transferred or have sometimes simply been forgotten, whose existence has been mentally blocked out by the parents or that have been used for research, are unresolved issues, as protests in Great Britain against the destruction of 3,300 embryos have recently shown.

A couple meeting and falling in love today is able to have egg and sperm cells removed and fertilised and when many years later their professional training is finished and they have pursued their careers, the young fertilised cells can then be transferred into the woman's then-much-older body.

4.6 Sperm donation/egg donation/surrogacy

Sperm donation is the solution for many couples where the man has been found to be infertile. In many cases the actual father is kept secret out of fear and/or cannot always be identified. Children resulting from such pregnancies often only find out as young adults. In the last few years it has become more and more fashionable to have an egg cell implanted abroad or to make use of a surrogate mother. What bond is the surrogate mother likely to develop to the child growing inside her? Her work seems to be done when she makes her body available for a pregnancy with an unfamiliar egg and sperm cell. It is even supposed to be a matter of principle that she does not develop a bond with the child because it will be two other people who will be loving the child and bringing him or her up. But what does this mean for the child when he grows inside a mother who offers him no bonding or love? Who does not offer him any emotional contact but only a physical body reduced to its biological function?

This is basically the classic situation for the start of an early symbiotic trauma. (Ruppert 2012) The thing that is supposed to offer protection – the prevention of a bond between the surrogate mother and the unborn child, so that the child does not develop a trauma by being given away after birth and can develop his first bond with his legal parents – turns out to be a traumatising situation in itself. A further trauma experience is added when the child is separated from his maternal attachment figure after birth. It seems that the different forms of artificial reproduction may be traumatising children from their very beginning.

4.7 Consequences of artificial insemination for the children

Artificial insemination is generally a very stressful time for the parents. The whole process from making the decision to use extra-corporeal fertilisation, through hormonal stimulation, radical examinations of both parents, to monitoring the possible resulting pregnancy and continuing medical examinations, leads to extreme stress and anxiety. This also means that the child is under permanent stress. The child's level of anxiety increases in step with that of his mother. (Janov 2011) Stress and anxiety are transferred to growing children and can interfere with their development. (Brisch 2013)

Artificial insemination leads to more complicated pregnancies and births than natural conception. The artificially-conceived child often appears fractious, has problems sleeping or colics (Renggli 2013). Compared with naturally-conceived pregnancies, there are more premature IVF births and IVF children are often born with caesarean section. If the child has been conceived with donated sperm or egg cells, the parents often experience a feeling of being distanced from their child, which then internally alienates the child and, as with surrogacy, gives rise to bonding conflicts and attachment disorders. (Brisch 2013)

In order to be relatively certain of becoming pregnant, in line with the Embryo Protection Law 'only' up to three embryos may be implanted per treatment cycle in Germany; more are allowed in other countries. The result is twins and multiple pregnancies. However, multiple births are particularly difficult for parents to cope with. Having started with the wish to have one child, the parents are often confronted with several children and this is frequently too demanding for them. This can also pave the way for early trauma.

Parents tend to conceal the fact of IVF treatment from their children. 'Artificial insemination', we don't talk about that! It could mean social exclusion or upset the family idyll, or bring back memories of worry and stress. The more reasons there are to keep it quiet (*in vitro* fertilisation, child of an anonymous sperm donor, etc.), the more difficult it is to tell the children their true origin.

Ariane

> Reports about IVF children in different forms of therapy point to the possibility that such children remember that they were in a Petri dish, in the womb or in the freezer, with several 'siblings'. Ariane came to my colleague, Liesel Krüger, to work on the Clay Field,* and without knowing that she had been conceived by artificial fertilisation, formed lots of little clay balls. She put one ball in the entrance to a cave she had made and called pyramid house, which resembled a womb, and said: "That might be me." In another session she said she was mourning her siblings, although she is an only child, and she felt it was her fault that they had died. In many more sessions she kept making hollow balls, which she flattened with a blow of her fist and called "broken eggs".

IVF children frequently show overly emotional reactions and shock, have difficulty letting go of their mother, and are extremely afraid of needles and injections and of being cut. They feel as if they don't belong in their body, don't cuddle with others, as if they are in a trance, and display identity problems and body image disturbances. (De Jong and Thurman 2008; Terry 2011)

Erika De Jong gives an account of a boy who, as a small child, liked to make contact by pricking her upper arm with a sharp object and who played games that resembled his conception through ICSI such as an enemy attack, violent abduction, death of siblings and involuntary captivity. (De Jong 2008) I know a

---

* See p. 238ff below for an account of Clay Field therapy. (English editor)

curative teacher who has contact with IVF children in her work and who confirms these observations and describes how these children are mistrustful in contact with others, show difficulty in adjusting, and behave as if they are on a different planet. An osteopath who treats newborn babies and infants in my practice has so far looked after 15 IVF children, some of them over quite a long period of time. She describes all these children as lacking the initial impetus that is often referred to in biodynamic osteopathy. This is normally displayed as an easy-flowing movement along the vertebral column. In the tissue of the IVF children this movement is very deliberate, the consistency of the craniosacral flow movement is impaired, more 'viscous' compared with other children who have been conceived naturally.

4.8 Alternatives to artificial reproduction

If there is such a high risk of early traumatisation in children conceived using artificial means of reproduction, what is the alternative? The first thing is to remove every blockage preventing the natural burgeoning of a life. This can begin with the adult opening up to their own emotional blocks and connected traumas, looking at and listening to themselves, which will also prevent the child being burdened with transferred trauma survival strategies. Responsible parenthood starts in this way, with needs being recognised that have nothing to do with having an own child and can be fulfilled in another way. In this freedom and openness a child can come into being or not.

With the mother-embryo dialogue (M-E-D) Auhagen-Stephanos (2013) developed a method of therapy for artificial fertilisation that enables better contact between the fertilised egg cells and the parents and thereby to better acceptance of the egg cells in the maternal womb. I recommend this. But why not let couples that want a child, but do not yet have one, use this method of therapy **before** artificial fertilisation? Because there will be many cases where working on trauma clears the path for conception. If there is a possibility of conceiving naturally, this should be the first choice.

Last chance

One of my clients, Maren, came with the wish "to do anything so that she would finally become pregnant and keep the child". She had been trying for five years to conceive and in the last six months had had seven *in vitro* fertilisations. Two had taken, but in both cases they had ended with bleeding after six weeks. Just while she was talking to me I could see how stressed she was. She only had one more chance. Maren's mother had moved from Algeria to France. In the constellations it emerged that this had been very difficult and had been very frightening for her. Her motto became: "I can't cope with this! I can't do it! It's too much!" Her mother's fears weighed heavily on Maren: she had no confidence, neither in herself nor in the new responsibilities of motherhood, although she wanted it so much. When Maren was able consciously to experience the entanglement with her mother at an emotional level, she became very relaxed and calm and was able to breathe deeply for the first time. I told her that my impression was that she would now be able to conceive naturally, particularly as there was no concrete biological reason for her not being able to. However, as she didn't want to forgo her last chance of having IVF treatment, which had to take place 1½ weeks from then, and she didn't want to risk anything, she had the treatment. The next time I saw her she was over the moon: she was 18 weeks pregnant and had not lost the child.

A study of involuntarily childless women who made intensive use of relaxation techniques has shown that 50% became pregnant by the help of this method alone. It is also interesting to note that women who have had one successful IVF cycle are more likely to conceive with further IVF, and doctors use this as justification for further treatment. I think the real reason might be the inner conviction: "I know it's worked once so it'll work again". Women who are involuntarily childless could find that working with techniques to uncover unconscious obstacles and negative convictions could be successful. Here as well, the method of the 'Constellation of the Intention' can bring far-reaching insights and offer support.

5
Abortions and trauma

Gabriele Hoppe

The termination of a pregnancy (abortion) means the specific and deliberate premature ending of a pregnancy which is either unwanted, or endangers the mother's health or her life. The aim of the procedure is to kill the developing child.

Up to the last century, and occasionally even today, books which were written after the Middle Ages on herbs and midwifery would be consulted in the case of unwanted pregnancies, because they were supposedly also a source of good information on abortion practices. 'Herbal lore' (flowers, leaves, bark, roots, herbs) and knowledge of the effect of particular substances was used to induce cramps and labour, or to destroy tissue. Instruments were also used, the aim being to damage the amniotic sac so that labour is induced or to kill the child directly. Various implements were used such as knitting needles, boiled chicken feathers, spokes of bicycle wheels, wire hangers, urinary catheters or other long, pointed and sharp instruments. (Jütte 1993) As recently as the 20th century, not having the knowledge of how to use the instruments effectively, lacking exact anatomical-physiological knowledge, and misunderstanding the true relationship between cause and effect led to such things as the use of extremely poisonous drugs or improper instruments, causing severe injury, or even death, to the women concerned. At the other extreme, the methods used had no effect at all. The latter caused even greater distress to the women, often leading to late-term abortions.

Women from socially modest and poorer classes who wanted an abortion had to use household remedies or seek illegal assistance: excessive physical activity, carrying heavy loads, jumping off walls, massages, fasting, taking poison either orally or inserting it into the vagina (poisons such as hydrochloric acid, hydrogen cyanide, potassium cyanide), douching with highly concentrated salt solutions or soap solutions, or introducing contaminated objects to cause an infection, were some of the measures recommended for abortion. Women who were better off were able – with their financial means – to gain a psychiatrist's referral to a private clinic for an abortion.

If the standard of hygiene is low when an abortion is attempted, or if the person carrying it out is not sufficiently knowledgeable or careful, it is certain to lead to serious complications (bleeding, infection, embolism, infertility), or injuries to large blood vessels, neighbouring organs or the uterus, possibly leading to the death of the pregnant woman. If all abortion attempts failed, the children were often simply killed after they were born. In the past, the legal framework sometimes allowed up to a year after the birth for this. Friesian law, for example, allowed 'postnatal abortion' up to the beginning of the late Middle Ages. A child of under a year was assumed to be soulless and the father had the right to reject the child and to kill him or her. In India it is still usual today for fathers to kill their newborn daughters.

It was often safer for the mother to give birth in secret and as far away from her usual environment as possible, than to have an abortion. In the first half of the 20th century it was customary in Central Europe to house unwanted or illegitimate children in a 'residential institution'. This developed into a line of business in its own right. The children often suffered an early death at the hands of their carers who continued to take money for the children's board from the mothers.

5.1 Frequency of Abortions

The WHO estimates that about a third of pregnancies worldwide are unplanned and that every fourth pregnancy is terminated[7].

---

[7] www.un.org/en/development/desa/population/publications/pdf/policy/ WorldAbortionPolicies2013/WorldAbortionPolicies2013_WallChart.pdf

This means up to about 46 million abortions globally each year. An estimated 50% of these take place illegally and in unhygienic conditions away from hospital or other medical institutions and without qualified medical staff. About 40% of these cause severe medical complications such as infertility or even lead to the woman's death. About 70,000 women die each year following an abortion, particularly as a result of an infection or bleeding. In general, the more restrictive the abortion laws in a country, the less safe the conditions of the abortion will be[8].

5.2 Legal Regulations

According to a study by the Institute for Family Policies, (Brussels, 3.3.2010) within the European Union 138 abortions are carried out per hour. It is estimated that in the last 40 years in Germany about ten million children have been aborted.

The legal framework for terminating a pregnancy varies from country to country. In some countries there is what amounts to a total ban (Northern Ireland, Hungary, many countries in South America and Africa), in others abortion is permissible on certain grounds (most countries in Europe), while in other countries it is largely legalised. There was one abortion for every two births in Russia in 2012[9]. In the USA an abortion is not punishable if the foetus has not reached 'viability'. In Canada the pregnant woman and her doctor have total freedom to decide. In China the government encourages an abortion after a first child, or in certain cases after a second child. 'Sex-selective' abortions have caused an increase in the number of boys born and a reduction in the number of girls. Since the introduction of family planning policies in China approximately 330 million abortions have been carried out[10].

Different legal frameworks are closely connected with the abortion regulations. The most prevalent are provisions permitting

---

[8] www.guttmacher.org/pubs/fb_IAW.html, Jan.2012

[9] www.un.org/en/development/desa/population/publications/pdf/policy/ WorldAbortionPolicies2013/WorldAbortionPolicies2013_WallChart.pdf

[10] www.worldabortionlaws.com/map

abortion within a certain period, or on certain grounds. The former allows the termination of a pregnancy up to a given date (generally within the first 12 weeks following conception) without giving any reason. The latter does not give a time limit but requires a valid reason for an abortion.

Up to the mid 1970s, abortions could not be carried out legally in Germany. Nowadays, abortion in Germany is basically punishable by imprisonment, with laws allowing the following exceptions, provided the abortion is carried out by a doctor with the pregnant woman's consent:

- Termination of pregnancy in particular by doctors and in principle within 12 weeks of conception and following counselling for the unwanted pregnancy, with at least three days between counselling and the operation (time limitation with counselling),
- Termination of pregnancy – with no time restriction – if danger to the life or the physical or mental health of the pregnant woman can only be averted by termination of the pregnancy (medical grounds),
- Termination of pregnancy within the first twelve weeks if the pregnancy is assumed to be the result of rape or a comparable sexual offence (criminal grounds).

5.3 Abortion Methods

No one in Germany is obliged to play a part in terminating an abortion, not even a doctor. If a child survives a late attempt at abortion, doctors are obliged – after the birth – to start life-sustaining measures immediately.

The number of abortions registered with the German Federal Statistical Office in 20122 was 106,815, which represents a live-birth-to-abortion ratio of 8:1[11]. Methods used legally in Germany within the first three months are chiefly: vacuum aspiration up to

---

[11] Figures according to the Federal Statistical Office (Statistisches Bundesamt), www.destatis.de

the twelfth week (approximately 74,000 cases in 2012), curettage between the seventh and twelfth week (approximately 11,500 cases in 2012), and the abortion pill up to about the seventh week (17,252 cases registered in 2012).

These generally used terms tend to play down the situation. The everyday language is helpful when deciding on abortion. The clinical words seem simply to deal with technical processes: "Cell cluster to be removed", "a minor operation". The impression is not given that living people – a mother and child and their relationship with one another – could be affected. At most it seems to be only the body of the mother that is affected at the moment the procedure is done. The impression is given that 'the matter' is finished with as soon as the abortion has been carried out. Often women are relieved after the abortion and hope to be able to carry on with their lives as they did beforehand. The medical terms 'embryo', 'foetus' and 'uterus' have a distancing effect. However, behind these words lies the medical taking apart and cutting up of a living human body, the crushing of the child's head and disposal of body parts from the belly of a woman, or in the case of the abortion pill the induced death of the growing child, under medical supervision, by painful asphyxiation or starvation.

In the case of late abortions (from the twelfth week to birth) the following methods are used in the West[12]:

- induction of contractions to cause abortion (prostaglandin-hormone-method) throughout the pregnancy;
- infrequently also C-section from the second trimester (23 cases were registered in 2012 with the Federal Statistical Office);
- abortion using saline solution or ethacridine (towards the end of the pregnancy);
- foeticide (464 cases were registered in 2012) by injecting a substance as a 'lethal injection' through the mother's abdominal wall into the child's heart (in 2012 there were 95

---

[12] Figures according to the Federal Statistical Office (Statistisches Bundesamt), www.destatis.de

cases of 'embryonic reduction' following artificial fertilisation to "improve the growth conditions" for a wanted child);
- dilation and evacuation, where the cervix is dilated and forceps and a suction tube are used to remove the foetus and tissue;
- partial birth abortion (mainly USA).

From the 24th week an unborn child could survive the drug Prostaglandin, which is given to induce contractions, thereby leading to abortion. However, the birth process would damage the child since the little body, particularly the head, is not sufficiently mature to withstand it. Children who are born alive despite the use of late abortion methods are sometimes 'not looked after following the birth' which means they are left alone for hours although they move, breathe and cry, until they have died. In order to rule out the 'risk of a live birth' foeticide is sometimes used in late abortions.

5.4 Consequences of an abortion for the pregnant mother

In the last century countless women died or bled to death after receiving the wrong dosage, or from taking lethal substances such as potassium cyanide drops, or following negligent abortions. Even today, 'the procedure' is not without risk for the woman on a physical level: abortions carry all the potential risks of an operation. There can also be immediate or short-term complications such as ruptured cervix, bleeding, shock, perforation, infections and their consequences, or the death of the mother. The pharmaceuticals used can also have considerable side effects.

From a mainly medicinal viewpoint, long-term effects such as sterility, higher risk of aborting future pregnancies or an increased danger of extra-uterine pregnancy (EUG), have not been proven to be the direct consequence of an abortion. However, a slightly higher risk of future premature births is thought likely. According to reports from doctors in the USA and Europe, most women come to terms with 'the procedure' physically and psychologically in a few days or weeks[13]. According to the reports, a woman rarely considers suicide following an abortion. However, some women who have had an abortion can suffer from continued grief, depression, sleep disturbances and feelings of guilt or anxiety. They long for the child who is now dead and worry about whether they made the right decision. Women often underestimate the fact that the world appears different following an abortion.

According to a study by Fergusson, Horwood and Ridder (2006) almost every second woman suffers psychologically following an abortion. The close connection between depression, anxiety, suicidal behaviour, substance-use disorder, and abortion was surprising, even for the authors: a group of 1,265 girls from Christchurch, New Zealand, were observed from birth in 1977 onwards; 41% had become pregnant by the age of 25, with 14.6% having an abortion. Of the 90 women who had had an abortion, 42% developed severe depression within the next four years. There was also a significant rise in drug and alcohol abuse in this group of women. This behaviour and these disorders could not be ascribed to any earlier experiences[14].

The decision to terminate a pregnancy is momentous. An abortion alters the life of all concerned and has lasting effects on them physically, psychologically and in their relationships. These effects can be permanent and become more and more pressing as time goes on. Symptoms can emerge that appear 'everyday' and seemingly have nothing to do with this event. American scientists have proven that the symptoms women can have following an abortion resemble those of war veterans. The women concerned experience depression, and feelings of guilt, sorrow, shame and rage. Further symptoms are flashbacks, denial and substance abuse. (Speckhard and Rue 1992)

Attempted abortions can also not be undone. They have a direct effect on the mother and child, and an indirect effect on the father and siblings born later as well as on the wider family. They

---

[13] www.profamilia.de/fileadmin/publikationen/Fachpublikationen/Medikamentoeser_ Abbruch_2012.pdf

[14] www.schattenblick.org/infopool/medizin/fakten/mz2et683.html

also affect those people who were directly or indirectly involved with the abortion/attempted abortion; they affect perpetrators and victims. They have a multiplying effect on the relationships of millions of families worldwide.

5.5 The role of the father

At first sight fathers appear to be left out when it comes to abortion. Often they are not aware that a child has resulted from being together with this woman. Many women take the decision alone, and have an abortion – against the father's will. It is not infrequent for fathers to be told 'when it's all over'. A father-to-be comes into contact – consciously or unconsciously – with experiences from his early life. If these were insecure or traumatising, becoming a father can be unsettling for him or turn into a time of tension and stress. The inner abandonment of his prenatal time might be reflected in this. The father-to-be might dangerously abuse the pregnant woman or put moral pressure on her, or force her to abort the child herself, or have a professional abortion. If the father knows about the abortion, or if he is part of the decision-making process, he might experience afterwards feelings of shame and guilt, depression and pain about the loss, and his inability to protect the child. Following the abortion, the quality of the relationship alters between father and mother of the aborted child. Many such relationships become (more) unstable or break down. (Dytrych, Schüller and Matejcek 1988, Kubicka, Roth, Dytrich, Matejcek and David 2002) It is believed that 70% of couples separate within one year of an abortion.

5.6 The social situation of the pregnant mother

A woman's life cannot be separated from the social context in which she finds herself. In the course of the last century social values in Germany have been liberalised. Against the background of demographic development (large demand for female labour) women have been courted and controlled both by politics and business according to their needs. In parallel, from about the middle of the last century, women have become more independent and developed their own individual way of life to offer themselves a sense of purpose. They have thereby changed their social function and developed the ability to shape their lives socially, economically or culturally, to satisfy their needs and secure their own existence. It is often said that this is the expression of their conscious perception of their civil liberties; on the other hand, it could be a question of women trying to make a virtue out of necessity.

The World War II generation in the western part of Germany used reconstruction and the economic miracle to compensate outwardly for their traumatising experiences. The children of the war generation often seemed to be orphans, or to be with a mother and father who were not emotionally present. The children were provided for, but were often emotionally on their own; they took on their parents' traumas, and a sense of responsibility very early – frequently feeling responsible for their own parents – also without being emotionally available themselves. They functioned and held their own. Traditional role models still existed but could no longer be lived up to.

Nowadays the descendants of these women make careful plans so that having children fits into their way of life. Against this collective background, more and more men, and increasingly women as well, decide not to take on the permanent responsibility of being a parent. The result is patchwork families or single-parent families. In this context there are probably more children who are unwanted.

Mona

"My boyfriend and I didn't want any children. My boyfriend was a 'mistake' and his mother had dumped him on his grandparents to look after. His father moved abroad. We wanted to leave all that behind us and just enjoy life. When I had an abortion at 19, I didn't for a minute think of it as being a person developing. Soon everything seemed forgotten. It was in my second marriage that the past caught up with me when I was pregnant. I was in tears after seeing a film about the abortion pill because I hadn't given my first child a chance."

Children who are unplanned often arrive 'at the wrong time' and are a shock – particularly for the mother. There are many reasons for it not being the right time for a pregnancy: having just started a degree course; trying to live independently, away from parents; a shaky relationship; developing career; the partner's precarious financial situation; own unemployment or difficult financial situation; unease or anxiety about pregnancy, giving birth and looking after the child; having children already who are not well looked after; the woman being over 35. In all these conflict situations there is often a sense of time pressure – sometimes panic – and there are no understanding people available for the woman to confide in. It is understandable that an abortion is quickly seen as the way to end the conflicts, which are sometimes unbearable if the woman is on her own.

Nora

> "Fifteen years ago, when I had just turned 18, I thought I couldn't bear having this child. I just couldn't imagine ever having maternal or loving feelings for the child either during or after the pregnancy. I didn't want the child. I haven't often thought about the aborted child. Last week I was suddenly overcome with an intense feeling of loss. For the first time I looked at images on the internet. Now I keep asking myself what did the child feel during the abortion? For the first time I doubt whether my decision was the right one."

5.7 Psychological consequences and ways of dealing with them

The subject of abortion is still taboo. For a long time the women who have been through it cannot talk about their experiences and the consequences. During their lives they had probably become insensitive to their own feelings. Denial and/or self-reproach will also have come into play. As long as the experience of abortion remains split off, it cannot be psychologically processed. It is therefore effectively contained, or expressed as a physical symptom and possibly passed on as an experience to children born later or the next generation.

Children born later feel the pain in the mother's psyche about the loss of the aborted child and in their experience the mother is not there for them. It is not possible for a secure attachment to develop between them and their mother. The following example shows how intensely a child born after an abortion can experience this.

Louis

> Following an abortion, a mother had another child who was still wetting himself and soiling himself when he was eight. This boy experienced embarrassing situations at school. He was ridiculed and teased by his fellow students when 'it' happened again. There had already been quite a few unsuccessful medical and psychotherapeutic attempts to help the child. It was also very troubling for the mother. 'Independently' of this, at about this time in the course of a therapeutic session the mother, very touchingly, took responsibility for the earlier abortion. After this session the child's problem was instantly resolved.

Symptoms that follow an abortion can be, for example, menstruation problems, headaches, palpitations, psychosomatic sexual disorders, auto-aggressive behaviour or different forms of addiction. Forms of (usually unsuccessful) coping strategies can be:

- avoiding situations that might be associated with abortions,
- being unable to remember,
- breaking off relationships with the people who were involved in the abortion,
- becoming an ardent abortion activist or opponent of abortions, (Johnson 2012, Lindner 2009)
- avoiding encounters with children, or also
- becoming involved with the plight of children in the world.

Many women's traumatic feelings are triggered a long time after an abortion by meeting another expectant mother or encountering children, or even by other mothers talking to one another about their children. Following an abortion, some women are very moved or confused when the anniversary of the abortion or the calculated birth date comes round. This can be particularly intense if the woman is no longer able to bear a child. Sometimes it is difficult for women to become pregnant following an abortion, or they continually miscarry at an early stage of pregnancy, or children are born prematurely, or mothers have dramatic, even life-threatening births. Being pregnant and causing the death of a child, suppressed feelings of guilt and shame, and anxiety can all be linked and split in the mother's psyche. A new pregnancy can trigger the abortion experience.

Against this background it seems unhelpful to 'let bygones be bygones' or to try and remove the symptoms. However, it is worth finding a way of accessing the cause at the heart of the issue. It is a great relief to a woman to be able to talk about the abortion for the first time in the course of therapy. For mothers, processing the subject of abortion during therapy usually takes place in several stages. In the beginning comes the capacity to reflect upon one's own behaviour, to 'mentalise'. (Allen, Fonagy and Bateman 2011) At this point work has usually been done on different aspects of the perpetrator-victim split. Then it is a case of acknowledging the person's own distress in the situation that led to the abortion. The greater the force and pressure were, the more intense the split feelings of powerlessness and helplessness are. Courage and security are necessary to acknowledge the abortion, and step by step accept a suppressed bad conscience, feelings of guilt, pain, fear of social condemnation, anger, sorrow, and regret about the irretrievable loss and take responsibility for what has happened.

With the method of the 'Constellation of the Intention' as a way of representing psychological realities via representatives, the process of working on the issue can be supported and stabilised. As an example, at this point in the process the woman who has had an abortion can set up a representative for 'herself as mother in the situation of having the abortion' and a representative for 'this aborted child in the situation of the abortion being carried out'. This opens the way for contact with the feelings of guilt and shame and also allows a connection to the embodied feelings. Finally the split-off grief can be broken down and the woman can be enabled to empathise with herself. This process of emotional access to the abortion situation requires time and care. Neither cognitive knowledge alone nor swiftly moving on to the next subject is enough to generate change on a psychological level.

A challenging situation arises for mother and child if the abortion is 'unsuccessful' and the child is born following this attempt to kill him. Both have survived. At this point in time the mother has usually suppressed the fact of being a 'perpetrator'. On the one hand giving birth prompts the woman to take on the role of 'mother' and to look after her child; on the other the child, by his very existence, continually reminds the mother of the unwanted beginnings and of her actions. The child's existence might also trigger troubling experiences in the mother from the time before conception. All this can generate despair, anger and even hatred of the child and herself that seethe under the surface or give rise to symptoms. The mother is rarely able, from this starting point, to be emotionally present for this child, or later siblings, and be a loving, predictable mother who provides support and security. These processes often occur at an unconscious level. At most the mother succeeds in looking after her child. In doing so she usually assumes that she has done the best for her child because she – as opposed to the child – does not notice the processes occurring unconsciously. She assumes that being looked after is the loving attention that a child needs.

There are mothers who unthinkingly come to terms with such situations on a permanent basis. There may be a faint hope of change when they start to wonder about the lack of a deep relationship between themselves and their child, although believing they have done everything possible for the child. Sometimes the key to helping them achieve answers lies in looking at the relationship they have to their own mother. It is extremely painful to realise how much the dynamic that initially developed from the abortion situation has traumatised the child and negatively determined the rest of his life. It is hard for a mother to realise that her child can be triggered by her. It is usually a relief for the child, and the whole family, if the mother works on her 'issues' in therapy. Even if it is hard for the mother to bear, it would be helpful for the child if the mother respects the fact that there can be times when the child – who by then may well be grown up – needs to have some space from her until both of them have worked through their perpetrator-victim processes independently of one another, and are free to develop a loving autonomous relationship.

5.8 Children who have survived an abortion

Following an attempted abortion, there can be no more talk of pregnancy as being the ideal carefree time of joyful expectation or preparing a warm welcome. From the very beginning, after the prenatal threat to his life, the child's fundamental and significant experience of being wanted and protected, of being secure and allowed to exist, and of having his needs lovingly responded to is missing. Mothers who try to take their own lives during pregnancy also give the child growing inside them a traumatising near-death experience with all its consequences.

Nowadays it is undisputed that prenatal traumatic experiences leave lasting traces. (Alberti 2012, Bauer 2002, Birnbaumer 1996, Deneke 1999, Huber 2013, Hochauf 2007, Hüther and Krenz 2013, Janov 2011, Janus 2013, Krüll 2009, Noble 1996, Singer 2002, Sonne 1996) Right from the beginning the child feels fundamentally betrayed which particularly affects his ability to 'thrive', his future need for security and his ability to love and enter into relationships, and his self-esteem. He internalises a threatening image of his mother. At this very early stage the child has experienced his mother's shock at discovering she is pregnant and his own existential fear at an abortion attempt. He also experiences being permanently placed in an inescapable and desperately needed close connection with his mother who rejects him and at the same time ensures his survival. (Brisch 2013)

There are only limited statistics of the number of children who have managed to be born despite abortion attempts. The general public is not aware of the life history of most of the children who have struggled to survive the attack on their life. All these lives began with deeply imbued and ever-present victim experiences that affected the individual unconsciously. The child came into the world and from then on had trouble truly accepting the offer of attachment, even though he was dependent on it. At the same time he longed for a secure attachment. The child's post-natal experiences with his mother might have been very varied: at times he would have been at the mercy of a thoughtless shell of a mother who, because of her own traumatisation, was unable to form an attachment; perhaps she was also a mother who would still have liked to be rid of him, and unconsciously created threatening situations, and whose profound hatred was still deeply tangible. The child knew then that he could not trust her.

One line of thought in the case of an overprotective mother is that her behaviour may be an attempt to compensate for an attempted abortion. On the other hand, children who have survived an attempted abortion might experience a benevolent mother who looks after them well without being actually really seen or accepted. Children such as these would sometimes grow up in what, to all intents and purposes, would be a stable world, yet with confusing double messages. The presence of a mother who has not actually recognised the fact that her child has arrived, would activate both an attachment and an escape system within the child. The child would feel confused and be convinced that he could never do anything right. The child does not understand the mother's anger and rejection and feels he has to apologise to justify his mother's actions. He has had to suppress permanently the part within himself that might have been able to see the perpetrator within his mother. The child would have learnt very early to adjust himself to the point of disappearing, and would have known how to behave in order somehow to belong. Some children would have learnt conciliatory behaviour in a threatening environment, for example if they were subjected to a general lack of nourishment during pregnancy, they would have reduced their energy consumption so that their mother had more and would have had a low birth weight. Later they often take on many different adult responsibilities early, or believe at work that they also have to be responsible for the level above them in the hierarchy. They feel better if they can placate the adults; on one level it secures their survival. The child tries to hang on and blanks out the unbearable.

Janus writes on this: "Existential early experiences can lead to lifelong repetitions of the basic situation [as a 'self-healing attempt'] . . . The early feeling of danger and of being unwanted is strangely obtrusive and obvious, and the conflict progresses right through to a feeling of paranoia. Delusional convictions can definitely be reflections of real dangers having been experienced at an earlier stage: *'Dahinter steckt der Teufel.'* . . .* Prenatal rejection manifests itself as an existential conviction that people see the individual concerned in a negative light, and imposes itself on the reality of social perception". (Janus 2011, p. 84ff.)

This can be internalised so strongly that these people have real difficulty in finding a secure place in life in order to feel a permanent sense of belonging. They seek out – often repeatedly – environments where they are subjected to painful bullying experiences, or they abort themselves, so to speak, by (unconsciously) creating situations in which their own – often soaring – career suddenly comes to a halt or an emerging success is suddenly impeded or destroyed.

In order for a person to be able to accept responsibility in later life for his own psychological integrity, it is essential that from the outset the child continually experience a secure attachment and positive relationships. (Brisch 2013, Janus 2011, Ruppert 2014) Following the abortion attempt, the betrayal of the attachment-seeking child, it can be assumed that this child has lost the basis for achieving a secure attachment to his mother. After that she was no longer emotionally accessible for his needs. The child cannot develop fully because he lacks the opportunity to 'mirror'. (Bauer 2006) Although he felt his mother's violent rejection, he still tried desperately to develop the vital attachment relationship with her (Brisch 2013). In order to be able to bear these traumatising situations the child develops individual 'survival mechanisms'. (Ruppert 2011, 2014)

---

* German proverb meaning 'therein lies the devil'. (English editor)

Hochauf (2007) and Huber (2013) describe introject-forming as quasi-synchronous with the traumatisation process. Based on the very close interconnection between mother and child (perpetrator and victim) it is possible for the introject to affect the child's behaviour as 'whisperer', so to speak, imitating, loyal to or identifying with the perpetrator. According to these descriptions the introject becomes active when the child feels better or has distanced himself from anything the 'original' perpetrator (mother) would still find tolerable; or when the perpetrator-identified introject directly affects the child's behaviour, who then 'takes after his mother', which is sometimes proudly pointed out.

As long as the entangled child seeks an attachment with his mother and wants to belong to her, he is not capable of functioning independently, and as a result will show perpetrator-loyal behaviour for the most part. This restricts the development of his own identity.

5.9 'Constellation of the Intention' with Abortion Survivors

Children who have survived abortion attempts are left with traces caused by trauma. The fact of victimhood is 'usually' suppressed. This can be supported by the mother's tales of a 'normal pregnancy'. On a cognitive level the idea simply does not arise that the mother could be a perpetrator. On the contrary, the child often feels connected and in harmony with his mother, identifying himself with her needs and convinced of the ideal image of his mother's womb. Even so, victimhood remains present in the psyche (Ruppert 2014) and it is for this reason that the subject of abortion can also be enacted in a psychotherapy session. Sonne (1996) writes that: "People who have been through the experience of an abortion develop certain common characteristics: they can have the feeling of not being properly there, not being real, and think that life does not mean much to them. It is also typical to have the feeling that nothing really happens, accompanied by a feeling of timelessness and immobility. Their abortion wishes and fears can be acted out in relationships and also appear in therapy as transference."[*]

Not feeling the emotions of betrayal, fear, pain or growing anger connected with an abortion is only possible at the cost of a general lack of feeling towards oneself. An individual who is insensitive towards himself is also insensitive towards others and to his own and others' boundaries. Thus victims can become perpetrators without seeing themselves as such. People with experience of victimhood attract people with perpetrator energy and vice versa. (Bauer 2011) The resulting perpetrator-victim spiral then shapes everyday relationships. This often results in transgenerational experiences of continued reciprocal aggression whilst at the same time retaining the illusion of experiencing a loving bond. (Ruppert 2014)

To begin with, those concerned cannot imagine that their physical or psychological symptoms can have any connection with life-threatening prenatal experiences and the resulting splits. Simply *knowing* about the event (cognition) can help to discover and sort out the relevant facts, but does not lead to the person being able to take actual 'steps out of trauma'. For that there has to be an emotional connection with the situation experienced at that time. The individual is able to access their experience emotionally if their psychological reality connected to the attempted abortion can be represented with the help of other people. Symptoms, or recurring stressful situations, or a concrete question on the subject, can form the starting point for a 'Constellation of the Intention'. Representatives set up for 'the prenatal child' and 'the mother during pregnancy' can enable the victim situation to show and be seen and emotionally experienced. Usually, however, survival parts emerge during this phase that try to perpetuate the split. However, with a clear goal, courage, confidence and careful external support it is possible to connect with the split off trauma emotions. The survival structures then lose their 'job', they are no longer needed. Perpetrator introjects can only change when the client is able to feel the mortal fear, and the entanglement with their mother (perpetrator) begins to be resolved.

---

[*] English translation of German text. Original is in English. (English editor)

According to Ruppert (2014), within the framework of the constellation intention, where intentions address the context of abortion experiences, inner parts become apparent which:

- want to manage on their own,
- need an excessive amount of time until they can trust someone,
- at the slightest doubt of the trustworthiness of another person immediately go on the defensive, and would ideally like to disappear or at least become invisible,
- are afraid of being seen and at the same time are afraid of not being noticed,
- want to persevere, come what may, because of a fear of being lost,
- are afraid that at any moment something terrible will happen again,
- desperately want to cling onto something because they are drowning in their fears,
- want finally to feel safe,
- are entangled in an exhausting survival struggle,
- are 'besieged' by parts of their mother that hold onto them in order to stay 'above water' themselves,
- tremble in fear and want to scream silently.

The more the client is able clearly to specify the event that threatened his existence and the victimhood connected with it, and to feel and acknowledge it, the more the resulting entanglement with their mother can be resolved.

Prenatal existential experiences require particularly careful treatment in therapy. The split off early memories have to be accessed in a benevolent way without words. The client has to accept responsibility for himself and create space for the bad experiences where the early distress can be expressed, specifically named, demonstrated, felt and taken seriously. A space in which something new can develop. The client has to identify perpetrator introjects within himself, and so can no longer be loyal to the perpetrator out of a longing for his mother's love, so that he can stop being a perpetrator towards himself. Questions such as "Am

I allowed to be, even if I wasn't wanted?" or "Am I really allowed to want myself?" are then no longer taboo. Being able to love oneself makes it possible to feel loved; knowing oneself is a prerequisite for recognising another.

Against the background of the 'mass phenomenon of abortion' the size and extent of the inherent potential for possible change is still barely understood. For those concerned it is astonishing how the quality of life and the quality of relationships can change if these central traumatic entanglements in the context of survived abortions can be resolved. Symptoms change for the better or disappear completely. The person's own needs can be constructively formulated. Self-awareness becomes apparent; enjoyment of one's life, stability and effectiveness in oneself become perceptible. There is more and more evidence of relaxation, lightness and 'supporting energy'. Being more in tune with oneself allows new possibilities for belonging and being pro-active. Perception of the world alters. Creative goals are set outside the perpetrator-victim dynamic.

Hildegard

Hildegard was born in 1959; she is single and has no children. She has had therapy sessions with Franz Ruppert over the last few years which she describes: "It was my 'completely normal' parents' incurable diseases that made me want to go to therapy in the first place. My father died of cancer, my mother as the result of a stroke. My aim is simply to die of old age at some point.

"I've been doing constellations for three years and I no longer doubt their results; so much has been proven to be true and the constellation results fitted well with the facts I knew. And right from the beginning, my health improved after every constellation: my blood pressure returned to normal, allergies disappeared, as did my permanent back problems. My 'healthy way of life' till then had just been a survival strategy!

"To a certain extent the changes are quite subtle:
- I don't injure myself any more since I saw that my mother wanted to have an abortion when she was pregnant with me. I used to nearly always have a plaster on my finger or a sprained ankle...

- My ingrowing toenails have got better since my embryo felt in one constellation that my toenails were curling up through fear! I feel better altogether, I've got more strength and energy and haven't been ill for three years.
- My voice has improved a lot; it's stronger and clearer. I can sing loudly again, high notes too, which I couldn't do for a long time. I'm much more relaxed than I used to be. And I've now got proper boundaries, I don't attract arguments any more; I have the feeling that now I calm people down who are upset, rather than adding fuel to the fire, as I used to do because their agitation upset me.
- I'm very glad that I've now understood my life retrospectively. I always felt at the mercy of my circumstances; it always seemed to me that I didn't have a choice. I always had to pick up the pieces. It is only now that I start to see that I can shape my own life, that the latent danger is over. I feel better than ever before.

"Several constellations were taken up with work on the issue of abortion survival and it was only afterwards that this was revealed as the issue at the heart of all the previous constellations. It started with me wanting to feel the fear that my intention had felt in a previous constellation. Two representatives had said that they couldn't think, couldn't feel who they were and what constellation they were in. It became clear for the first time in this constellation that my mother's abortion attempt when she was three months' pregnant with me was the reason for this fear. Once, when I asked her about my birth and her pregnancy with me, my mother told me that the doctor had said it would be dangerous for her to be pregnant again following the operation she had just had because of an ectopic pregnancy. That is probably the reason for considering and attempting an abortion.

"In a further constellation I took as my intention the sudden hearing loss that I had suffered ten years previously, and again I was in a prenatal situation. The representative said that she was three months old. For about quarter of an hour this embryo lay twitching and trembling in mortal fear in my arms; it was as if we were experiencing the throes of death. I cried and wept for a long time while holding the embryo; then the constellation slowly relaxed; the embryo part was afraid to open her eyes and didn't want to go on living so that she didn't have to go through that situation again.

According to my mother, her pregnancy with me and my birth

went normally. In another constellation I had been afraid of my mother during the birth. I was born at home and if the midwife had arrived any later, I wouldn't have survived the birth. I had waited until the midwife was there – that's what the constellation showed. I was the third child and later had more siblings. In a further constellation it became quite obvious that one of my mother's relations – a Catholic priest – had carried out an exorcism and had abused me as a newborn baby. Even so, to a certain extent my life had been relatively normal. I never married because my parents had set a bad example. When I was 33 years old I had an abortion myself because I simply couldn't imagine then that I would survive a pregnancy. My relationship at that time had just ended. Basically my relationships were about as chaotic as my relationship to my mother at my conception and during pregnancy: I was unable to build up any trust in other people. I always wanted to be free and in control. In one constellation where my intention was about me being overweight, it transpired that I didn't want to have children so that they didn't have to experience the fear I had experienced and survived.

"Now, with hindsight, I can say that I lived my whole life 'provisionally', as if my life wouldn't last much longer. I always thought that my life would end when I was 20, then 30, then 40 . . .

"I was also always threatened; I didn't take it seriously. Now I realise that I re-enacted my mother's rejection, which I had experienced from the very beginning, over and over again, in a futile attempt to rid myself of this trauma. I can now get on very well without my family of origin. I used to keep trying to contact them because I thought that otherwise I'd be lonely and alone. When I heard the sentence: 'If you give up your identity to adapt to your family, you are completely alone', it shook me up.

"Once I took part in another constellation as representative for the disease cancer and I felt that, as cancer, I was only the compressed fear of abortion. In this case a twin had been aborted and the mother only realized later that she was still pregnant and also told her daughter that she had tried to abort her. It is unbelievable how much clarity and awareness has come into my life through the constellations. I am still in the middle of the journey to myself. It is a step-by-step process and I am glad that it is continuing. I feel privileged to experience it, although it is difficult to bear. The relief afterwards is like having a heavy burden removed; one that I wasn't aware of."

6
Traumatic experiences in the womb

Doris Brombach

6.1 The womb as the symbol of femininity

'Experiences in the womb' is a very emotional subject in the practice of psychotherapy. Firstly it is all about the beginning of one's own existence, the origin of one's own body and individuality. Secondly it represents the time in which an individual is practically 'one' with the mother.

The woman's role as giver of life and as mother is closely connected with the womb. Every month the womb goes through the cycle of life and death and is prepared every month anew to provide the space for the growth of new life. No other organ is so closely connected with femininity and motherhood. For nine months the womb is the home of the growing child. If we assume that this child can perceive and sense very early, we also have to ask ourselves what else can take place in the prenatal phase of this fragile being. How does the child experience his first 'home': warm or cold, accepting or rejecting, spacious or constricting? How do internal and external influences affect him?

We now know that the mother's own experiences of stress and fear are transferred to the child. However, the fact that the mother's thoughts and feelings, in other words her trauma feelings, can be transferred to the child is only seldom taken into consideration. Everything the child experiences prior to his birth is stored in his cells and his nervous system, and is jointly responsible for the development of his psychological experience and behavioural patterns in later life. Using the constellation method it is possible to bring old injuries from the prenatal period to light

and into contact with the split off personality parts which originated then.

In the last three years I have been able to learn a lot through
my own experiences in therapy settings. I have been very
distressed myself by a prenatal trauma. For a long time the subject
of life and death was for me a recurring saga although I was
unaware of its importance or complexity. My father committed
suicide when my mother was three months pregnant with me. This
was a shock for her, and for me as an unborn child it was no less
tragic because at some point, very much later and with the help of
constellations, I realised that I had floated in my mother's womb
in a sea of suppressed feelings that in no way belonged to me. I
was now able to remember the time in the womb and to experience again what it was like to be in a cold and dark environment,
lonely, alone and unwanted. For a long time one part of me
refused to believe what I had experienced. I felt powerless, felt
that only part of me was really alive. The questions that followed,
who was I, what was I doing in this world, questions that I had
often asked myself in my life, became ever more present and with
them the memory of my wish from back then, when I wished I
was dead. The method of the trauma constellation enabled me to
come into contact with my pre-birth self. I experienced how
important it was for me and how healing to be able to 'return' to
my mother's womb, to the source, where my mother's feelings
and thoughts were mixed with my own until you couldn't distinguish one from another. My experiences in such sessions were
sometimes so intense that I was unable to tell if the feelings I felt
belonged to my mother or to me.

In the further course of my studies of prenatal psychology I
encountered the books of Arthur Janov (2012), Ludwig Janus
(1997) and Alessandra Piontelli (1996). Piontelli's psychoanalytic
study in the 90s clearly showed that the period in the womb was
connected with later life. In the study she examined 11 unborn
children with the help of ultrasound scans, amongst whom were
four pairs of twins, whose development she followed for four
years following their birth. Piontelli's most significant realisation
was that there was a striking continuity in behaviour before and

after birth. According to her research the newborn child cannot be reduced to a bundle of 'predispositions' just waiting for the 'environment' to interact with them. According to Piontelli, even in the womb predispositions and environment, or 'nature and nurture', have a strong effect on each other so that it is impossible to look at them in isolation. Constellation work has shown that we have to include the mother's psychological makeup in the 'nurture' part because this is transferred to the child. If the mother feels sorrow, pain, fear or anger, the child cannot distinguish where these feelings are coming from, or who they belong to, and so makes them his own.

I specifically began to include the womb as part of the constellations in my therapy work. What was striking was that in almost all constellations the womb took a position some distance from the mother. For me this revealed the mother's deep split from her femininity and motherhood. It frequently became apparent that the womb was not really prepared to accept a child. The womb expressed on a physical level what the woman's conscious part was unable to articulate.

There are many reasons for this inner conflict in women and mothers. One reason, which will not be looked at in depth here, but which ought to be mentioned, is the influence of society on women's self-perception and how they are perceived by others. Societal institutions with their misogynistic views play a great part in disparaging the role of women. Even if this influence is not as strongly felt today, the effects of misogyny can have a bearing on future generations. Our grandparents and great-grandparents were shaped by a paternally-dominated society; in this view of the world, women were seen as seductresses with fiendish passions.

Even today there are many destructive societal mechanisms that influence relationships between men and women. If destructive symbiotic relationships are not recognised and resolved, the individuals concerned will experience their whole lives in dependency. Work with the 'Constellation of the Intention' can help in this connection by bringing to light the client's obsolete patterns of thinking and their resulting pejorative feelings, helping them to disengage from them.

6.2 Constellations with children

In the past few years I have also been working more frequently with children. Work with children is not primarily aimed at helping the mothers. But it can be very helpful if a mother is aware of her feelings during pregnancy and recognises what an immense effect her own experiences, thoughts and feelings, her behaviour and her view of the world, have on her unborn child and how all this affects the relationship between her and the child after birth.

The difference in constellation work with children lies in the fact that a child still needs his parents while the adults have to learn to detach themselves from their parents. But being more aware can help children to disengage themselves early from their mothers' destructive survival strategies. Mothers are now more frequently bringing their children with so-called 'ADHD' to my practice looking for help. Such unsettled children can easily become tyrants to their mothers. At the root of their disturbed behaviour generally lie traumatic experiences that can be traced back to the prenatal period, often as far back as conception. So I invite mothers to work on themselves as well as their child having therapy. It appears that children are more easily able to remember their experiences and feelings in the womb than adults are. These children clearly show me that we humans are conscious perceptive beings, even when we are in the womb – in other words from the very beginning. The patterns of behaviour from prenatal trauma experiences form obstacles in daily life for many children without them knowing where their aggression, their excessive anxiety or their feelings of guilt come from. The true causes for the behaviour of so-called 'difficult children' are usually hidden in the history of earlier generations and their unprocessed trauma feelings.

That means that a 'difficult child' developed that way during the prenatal period through experiencing unprocessed trauma energies that do not belong to him. A mother's trauma experiences make her womb hard, cramped, cold and unwelcoming. If she conceives, the fertilised egg comes up against these unprocessed feelings that are stored in the womb. The unborn child is at the mercy of these unresolved and destructive energies from the mother's trauma experiences, and they can become a huge threat to him. Miscarriages or stillbirths that have not been properly mourned for example are still emotionally present in the womb, and do not make the psychophysical space free for the new child. It is difficult for the child to take his own place in a womb with such a pre-history. In later life, patterns of behaviour can arise from this that are controlled by attitudes and feelings such as: "I shouldn't be!" "I feel left out". "It's my fault". "I'd rather take a back seat and let others go in front of me".

Working with children is a very exciting field and there is still much to be discovered. If one is able to talk to them on their level, children will readily talk about themselves. Even if their essentially visual language (witches, knights, devils, elves, magicians, etc) means that the tales of very young children have to be 'decoded' first, I have not experienced any child's being unable to remember the time before his birth.

Ellen

A mother came to our practice with her 11-year-old daughter. Ellen was a pale, nondescript girl with short hair that made her look more like a boy. Due to a difficult pregnancy and birth – she had been a twin – Ellen survived but her twin brother didn't. Ellen and her brother were born prematurely in the 28th week. It turned out that Ellen could remember that she had not been alone and she felt guilty and responsible for her brother's death. We did a constellation using objects. I suggested to Ellen that she chose one object for life and one for death and set them up. For life she chose a girl with a sunflower and for death, after searching long and hard, she chose a male, dark figure. She then placed the object for her twin brother next to life and the object symbolising herself next to death. When I said that she might take another object for the dwelling where she had lived for nine months with her mother before she was born, she refused and said that her brother was living there and shouldn't be disturbed and we had to be quiet. She looked anxiously at her mother. I asked her whether it would be all right for her if she set me up – the therapist – as representative for this dwelling. Ellen's mother agreed to this and set me up as representative for this dwelling – the womb. I immediately felt that I had to make myself very small. The same sentence kept going through my head: "I mustn't get lost". I didn't get any further than that sentence. For me, the feeling and thought both belonged to the mother, who began to cry during this process, whereupon Ellen immediately went and stood next to her mother with her eyes cast down and asked her mother to stop crying because it was all her fault, as she wanted more room. The mother did not stop crying. It occurred to her that her own mother had always said to her that if she had children she shouldn't have any boys. The grandmother had also had twins and the boy had died shortly after the birth. The grandmother was convinced that boys were more likely to die after birth because they weren't as strong as girls.

When the first scan showed that Ellen's mother was expecting twins and one was a boy, her first thought was why couldn't it be two girls, because they would have had more will to survive from the beginning. She was afraid that her mother's fears might prove in the end to be right. When she became aware of all this she was able to cry for the first time over the loss of her son, and to apologise to Ellen, the child who survived, for not wanting to have her brother. She could say to Ellen that her brother's death was not her fault. Ellen then said that she was feeling better and she wanted to go home.

Later the mother told me that it had been terrible for her to realise that there was a part within her that was happy that the male twin had died. This was not the only problem in this family that made Ellen's life difficult but continuing to work with mother and child on the transferred guilt meant that Ellen's relationship with her mother was significantly improved. Ellen is now 14 years old. She is becoming a little adult who is more and more aware of what belongs to her and what to her mother.

Otto

Otto is a seven-year-old boy who had massive panic attacks when he had to go to bed at night. His mother has been coming to my practice for some time. One day, at Otto's request, his mother brought him to a session. He seemed to be very determined and immediately told me why he had come, his intention. He said that he was very afraid of monsters, although he knew that they didn't exist. I gave him my box with the Play Mobil figures and asked if he would agree to set up his family and his intention. He squatted down on the floor and immediately began to look for mother and father in the box. He stood them a long way from one another. He then stood his younger brother next to the father. The cat had to be part of the constellation as well. After a while I asked him whether anyone was missing. "No, they're all there", he said. I asked where he was standing. "Here I am!" he said and pointed to the intention. I suggested that he could now set up more figures, for example for his fear and for the monster that was making him afraid. "But there are several monsters", was his immediate reply. Finally he took two figures and set them up close to himself. He then looked at me with fear in his eyes, jumped up and hid behind the curtain. There he crouched, huddled up and with his arms crossed, whimpering quietly. From this moment I was unable to reach him.

I fetched his mother and asked her if this reminded her of anything. It occurred to her that her son had been in exactly the same position in the womb and had not wanted to turn. The doctors had suggested performing a C-section. The alternative was to try and turn the child from the outside. When Otto heard this he started to scream that he didn't want that and that it would hurt. Apparently Otto could remember this situation perfectly.

I asked the mother to initiate contact with her child and to re-experience the situation from back then. After the mother was able to admit that it had been she who had made the decision that Otto should be turned, because she had been scared of having a C-section, Otto stopped crying. "You didn't want me", he said firmly to his mother. She admitted it and apologised to Otto. She now admitted to herself and her son that she had been overwhelmed by the pregnancy and by the thought of having a child and had not felt ready, for private and professional reasons, to accept responsibility for a child.

Otto carefully stuck his head out from behind the curtain and looked at this mother for a while. He slowly crawled out of his hiding place and climbed into his mother's lap. He was now completely calm and said that he now knew who the monsters were. He had been afraid that the doctors would appear again and hurt him and force him to do something against his will when all he wanted was to stay lying down. Otto's fear of 'the monsters' has not recurred since.

The primary objective of unborn children is to grow and to be welcome. We, the parents, should give the children the best possible conditions to do exactly that. In order to do that, we need to have sincere and genuine feelings. If, for whatever reason, unborn children experience crises in the womb or during the birth process, these should be made visible, tangible and understandable to them as, according to my practical observations, these experiences only come to a standstill if they have received recognition, insight and, if necessary, regret.

7

Pregnancy and giving birth from the perspective of multi-generational psychotraumatology

Birgit Assel

7.1 Check-ups create anxiety

The first thing a woman who thinks she may be pregnant will probably do is buy a pregnancy test kit. If she has been hoping to become pregnant, she will be overjoyed if the test is positive. If the pregnancy is unwanted, the woman's feelings will be in total confusion. She now has to weigh up whether to keep the child or have a termination. In this chapter I shall be writing about those women who decide to keep the child and are pleased to be pregnant.

For a woman a pregnancy means that her life will alter completely. As early as the first few weeks her body changes, as does her psychological state. As a result of the hormonal shifts, the skin on her breasts tightens, her sense of smell is heightened, she perceives her environment with added sensitivity, tears flow more freely and her emotions run riot. With the first pregnancy, we women are heading for something completely unknown. Top on the list of priorities is whether, and how, we create a healthy relationship between our unborn child and ourselves.

The next step for an expectant mother in Germany is usually to get an appointment with her gynaecologist so that the pregnancy can be confirmed. Only a few women decide to have all the pregnancy check-ups with a midwife. An ultrasound scan will often take place in the gynaecologist's practice. On the screen an amniotic cavity can be seen and the first signs of life are visible. At this point the woman is frequently six to ten weeks pregnant. The due date can be reliably determined by a scan during the first 12 weeks of pregnancy. After that, using a scan to work out the due date is not so reliable.

I can clearly remember such a first appointment because in the summer of 2012 I accompanied my pregnant daughter to her doctor. However, my daughter and I were in a state of 'shock' after this appointment, because instead of one amniotic cavity on the screen, there were two. My daughter was seven weeks pregnant with twins! From then on the original joy at being pregnant was superimposed with the worry of whether a pregnancy with twins would turn out all right. With hindsight, I don't think it is advisable from a psychological point of view to have a scan so early. I can, however, understand that for a woman who is pregnant for the first time, the first scan is an important event. A pregnancy can also be confirmed via a blood test. Happily, my twin grandchildren developed well during the following weeks. But the fear of the next scan only showing one child accompanied us the whole time.

Once the pregnancy has been confirmed by a doctor, the maternity record is prepared. The blood tests that follow and the mother's details determine whether the pregnancy is a 'high-risk pregnancy' or not. It doesn't take much to be declared a 'high-risk pregnancy': the mother's age alone is sufficient. A pregnancy at 35 years or older is one of the risks, as is a multiple birth.

Prenatal care in Germany introduced a 'maternity record' in 1961. In 1966 maternity guidelines were introduced and the cost of preventative medical check-ups was borne by the statutory health insurance. The maternity guidelines were laid down by the Federal Committee of Doctors and Health Insurances and cover the extent and content of medical check-ups. Midwives were not involved in this process and are still not today. Medical monitoring of pregnancies is becoming more and more documented and the maternity guidelines are continually updated. The services provided by prenatal check-ups have increased by 500% in the last

20 years. Since 1973 doctors have been receiving a fee for the check-ups and have been increasingly driving midwives out of this field. (Ensel 2002, p. 17)

7.2 Prenatal diagnostics complicate the mother-child relationship

In 1990, when I was pregnant with my daughter, my second child, I had a midwife who took over some of the prenatal checks. At the same time she was my confidante. She visited me at home and looked after not only my physical needs, but also my psychological wellbeing. During my pregnancy she was the most important person for me and I could ask her for advice at any time. She was always available on the telephone.

I experienced my first pregnancy, in 1983, completely differently. I was 23 years old when I was expecting my son and I wasn't aware that I was entitled to have a midwife looking after me throughout my pregnancy. My gynaecologist did not point this out to me and he carried out all the checks himself. After one scan he told me that my child's head was too large and that could indicate hydrocephalus. I left his practice in a state of shock and waited anxiously for the next scan in the hope that his suspicions would not be confirmed. At the next scan, when I was 28 weeks pregnant, the relationship between my child's head and body had become normal, but on the other hand the CTG registered contractions that I didn't feel at all. He told me there was a danger of my baby being born prematurely and prescribed medication to prevent contractions that I meekly took for weeks on end. Once again I was very anxious when I left the practice.

There is no comparison between the ultrasound device my gynaecologist used in 1983 and the high-resolution equipment available today. CTG devices have also improved considerably. But the crucial question is how responsibly doctors handle the new technologies. I do not deny that there are gynaecologists who treat prenatal diagnostics responsibly, with sensitivity and empathy, with the interests of the child and the mother at heart, and who carefully explain what these diagnostics can do, and what they can't. However, it should be noted that even if the findings are suspect it is rare that treatment is available for unborn children. Prenatal diagnostics are neither a guarantee for a healthy child, nor an indication of an unhealthy child. "On average 70% of abnormalities are overlooked, while 30% of suspected abnormalities picked up by ultrasound scans turn out to be normal. (...) While an increasing number of new deficiencies can be diagnosed in a monitored foetus, doctors are unable to carry out any treatment: A 'patient' is created for whom there is no help available." (Duden 2007, p 89)

Why do we examine unborn children if we are rarely able to treat them? And what effect do these examinations have on the early bonding between a mother and her child? Many women nowadays feel as if they are 'pregnant for a trial period' until prenatal examinations show the statistical probability of them bearing a 'healthy' child. Hardly a child is born today without going through many levels of 'quality control'. The special examinations, which were originally only for small at risk groups, have become routine examinations for all expectant mothers.

There is a silent agreement today between expectant parents and their doctors; neither party wants to think about the possible consequences, and the counselling that is recommended by the German Medical Journal (*Deutsches Ärzteblatt*) hardly ever takes place. What happens when a scan prompts fears that the unborn child might be disabled? What other tests are then called for? Do these tests endanger the life of a child who may have been wrongly diagnosed and is in reality completely healthy?

The maternity guidelines require three routine ultrasound scans as part of the pregnancy check-ups. The first routine scan takes place between the 9th and the 12th week and confirms the pregnancy. By then the length of the body and the diameter of the head can be measured. The heartbeat is detected and the scan shows whether it is a multiple birth. The second scan takes place between weeks 19 and 22 and measurements are taken of the size of the child's head and abdomen. The position of the placenta in the womb is also assessed. An 'extended routine ultrasound scan' is offered that is also covered by the statutory health insurance. In addition, parts of the body are looked at more closely; for example, are the head and cerebral ventricles normally formed? Are the neck and back well developed? Is the heart visible on the left side? Is the heart beating rhythmically? Is the front abdominal wall closed? The third scan takes place between weeks 29 and 32, when head, abdomen and thighbones are measured. The length of the child and his heartbeat are checked.

The nuchal translucency measurement is not part of the maternity check-ups, and the costs for this test have to be borne privately. An ultrasound scan is used to look for signs of possible Down's syndrome (Mutterschafts-Richtlinien 2013 p. 33ff.) [Maternity Guidelines]. Many gynaecologists advise their pregnant patients to have this test, suggesting that it will provide clarification about the health of their child. The German Medical Journal (*Deutsches Ärzteblatt*) writes: "The doctor is obliged under the treatment contract to point out the possibility of diagnosing abnormalities in the foetus. If the doctor does not point this out or carry out a diagnosis on medical grounds that the expectant mother has agreed to, he violates the treatment contract and may be liable for damages." (*Deutsches Ärzteblatt* 95, 1998) The Maternity Guidelines from 19.9.2013 state: "Doctors are obliged to give special information and genetic counselling before carrying out such tests. This not only covers medical questions, but also psychological and social matters that could be significant in connection with the test and its results". (Mutterschafts-Richtlinien 2013, p. 34)

Prenatal diagnostics have created new markets. Prenatal medicine has been a recognisable growth industry for years. There has been a blood test for Down's syndrome since 2012. The new test is supposed to have the potential to revolutionise prenatal diagnostics again, and is correspondingly expensive.

I personally experienced the modern practice of prenatal diagnostics when my daughter was told she was expecting twins. The fact that she was not drawn into the maelstrom of prenatal diagnostics is all down to her very dedicated and caring gynaecologist. She talked to my daughter about the possibilities of prenatal screening but also said that she advised against it because in her experience it causes more insecurity than security. She said that my daughter's whole organism, her psyche and her body were now intent on preparing two little human beings for life. That would cost strength and energy and any external insecurity could severely upset this process.

Monika Hey

Monika Hey documents (2012) her own story of her gynaecologist carrying out a nuchal translucency measurement without asking her. Because of her age, Monika Hey was automatically categorised as a high-risk pregnancy. The consequences were disastrous for her. The measurement findings were abnormal and Monika Hey was drawn into the wheels of prenatal diagnostics and had no chance of extracting herself. Her gynaecologist referred her to a colleague with a high-resolution ultrasound device. Monika Hey was so deeply shocked about the suspected diagnosis of trisomy 21 that she was unable to think clearly. (Hey 2012, p. 49ff.) The ultrasound specialist confirmed the diagnosis, while Monika Hey just stared at the monitor: she saw the little face and the body of her child – he looked just like a newborn baby. Almost within her reach! The doctor urged her to agree to have further tests. The next one was the first invasive test, chorionic villus sampling. When Monika Hey hesitated, her doctor asked her to sign a document for his own protection, confirming that he had explained to her how serious the findings were. (ibid., p. 61ff.) Monika Hey and her husband finally agreed to a further, more precise test in the hope that it was all a terrible mistake and their child was really healthy. But the trisomy 21 finding was further confirmed and the doctor explained to her that her child had very little chance of survival. The pressure on Monika Hey kept increasing. She was told that her child had extremely severe physical and mental disabilities and surely she couldn't want such a child.

However, a genetic test can only make generalised predictions about the child's disability or disease. For example, it cannot usually diagnose the severity of trisomy 21. (Ensel 2002, p. 146) Monika Hey contended that there were people who lived with Down's syndrome and whose mothers loved them, but her arguments were not taken seriously. Based on the oedemas found in the foetus, the survival chances were very low. The more

quickly Monika Hey agreed to an abortion, the easier it would ultimately be for her. If she delayed her decision any longer she would
have to give birth to the child normally. (Hey 2012, p. 77ff.)

Monika Hey was in a state of shock; her husband was unable to
help her because he felt as helpless as she did. Her gynaecologist
arranged a hospital appointment for the abortion. Mrs. Hey's
gynaecologist had not told her that as she was already 16 weeks
pregnant, the birth would have to be induced. After three terrible
days and several failed attempts at induction she gave birth to a tiny
son and she and her husband were given time to say goodbye to
him.

What followed for Monika Hey were years of suppressed
sorrow, feelings of guilt and depression. The therapists she visited
wanted to prescribe antidepressants, which she refused. She was
severely traumatised by this whole experience, from the diagnosis
of expecting a disabled child through to the abortion. "The doctors
subjected me to a storm that numbed my feelings and froze my
ability to take any action. No-one offered me any information that
I could weigh up and that allowed space for such a decision."
(ibid., p. 78)

7.3 Women in victim role

Before I became concerned with the history of midwifery, I often
asked myself why so many pregnant women place themselves in
the hands of medical obstetricians. Why don't they look for a
midwife in the early stages of their pregnancy who can provide
them with assistance and advice? Even if midwives are only rarely
able to accompany the woman to the actual birth because
maternity hospitals employ their own midwives, there are self-
employed midwives who could carry out the prenatal check-ups.
In addition, the midwife comes to the woman's home and is
always available on the end of a phone.

Through the theory of multi-generational psychotraumatology
developed by Franz Ruppert I have realised more clearly why
many women do not trust their bodies, and are afraid and unsure
about what is their very own métier: carrying and giving birth to
children. For generations many women have been traumatised by

male-defined obstetrics and have acquired a broad spectrum of victim attitudes. They pass on their own unprocessed victimhood to the next generation, their daughters, who again unquestioningly place themselves in the hands of medical obstetricians. They do not develop any confidence in their own perceptions, their own feelings and in their own knowledge, needs and ability to be a mother.

Sandra

A mother and her almost-20-year-old daughter came to an individual therapy session of mine. The daughter, Sandra, loves sport and is very successful. She would like to become a professional athlete. She came with the intention of discovering why she always gets injured coming up to an important competition, so that she is unable to take part.

She set me up as the representative for her intention, and I crouched on the floor, pulled my legs up to my body and made some movements to try and extricate myself from this hopeless situation, but unsuccessfully. I was really suffering and the one thought that came into my head was: I have to get out of here, I can't stand it any more! The young woman looked at me speechlessly and had no idea how to deal with this situation. Suddenly the mother started to talk about her experience when she was pregnant with her daughter: it was her second pregnancy; her son was then just a year old. The pregnancy hadn't been planned and she felt completely overwhelmed at the thought of having a second child. She didn't take care of herself during the pregnancy. In the 8th month she had contractions which were stopped with medication. When I heard that, I was able to make sense of my situation as representative. I wanted to get out but I couldn't. As hard as I tried, I couldn't get out. Something was stopping me but I didn't know what.

The mother went on: When the due date arrived she had stopped taking the medication, but she didn't develop any natural contractions. The birth was then induced using a drip. Progress was very slow and difficult and in the end her daughter had to be delivered using a ventouse suction cup. Until this moment Sandra had had no idea how her mother had experienced the pregnancy with her and that she had been born with the assistance of a ventouse. For me as representative of her intention, it was evident that I had given up trying to escape from the unbearable situation. For Sandra it became clear that a very early child part of her always gave up because there was no point in trying. That is exactly how she sees her present situation: she trains incessantly, does her best, but ultimately it's no use, she feels hopeless, powerless and helpless. For Sandra's mother too the birth of her daughter was traumatic and this was the first time she had talked about her experience. From previous constellations of the mother's I knew that she herself had suffered in her childhood and had been treated violently by her parents. She had never protested against the invasive interventions of the doctors because she had never developed a good feeling about herself.

7.4 Medical obstetrics

On the subject of birth, my focus is on women's emotions. Having a child is hard work. Women who give birth consciously can reach the limits of their endurance if their body gets into an exceptional situation with increasingly severe labour, and contractions that are beyond their control. Sheila Kitzinger writes in her book about 'childbirth' and asks what support can usefully be given. (Kitzinger 1998, p. 277)

I am working on the assumption that a woman who has not experienced any traumatisation in her past will not subject herself to any technocratic obstetrics. This woman has a good feeling of self, is psychologically healthy and able to give birth to her child without any help from outside, or at least amongst women who also know that giving birth is 'women's work'. Birth is an event for which the expectant mother and her child have prepared for 40 weeks. It is the first bonding process between mother and child, and any intervention from outside interferes with this process. A mother's unprocessed traumas prevent her from forming a natural bond with her child during her pregnancy, as to a great extent her traumas cause her psyche and her body to exist separately from one another.

Today, an expectant mother is usually accompanied during her pregnancy by doctors and medical technology. Her psychological state is not of very much interest to the obstetrician during her pregnancy check-ups and is not given much consideration during the birth process either. And if an expectant mother has been relying completely on the medical side of prenatal care, she will also rely more on the midwife and the doctors while giving birth, rather than on her own body awareness.

7.5 The development of medical obstetrics in a historical context

The history of the 'female body' (Ensel 2002, p. 6) reflects the development of power structures in the history of obstetrics. On the one hand there are the midwives, and on the other the medical profession, which has taken over the female body in the course of obstetrics. About 250 years ago a woman was only deemed pregnant when she felt the baby move. The fact that her periods had stopped was not considered a valid criterion. At this time doctors were not particularly interested in the birth process and pregnancy; they left all this to the midwives. In fact doctors saw themselves as healers of disease; obstetrics as such did not exist.

Up until the18th century all perinatal care was carried out by midwives. Their knowledge was based on experience gained during their practical work. There were no apprenticeships: the older midwives handed on their knowledge to the younger ones. They possessed perfect techniques to assist with even difficult births, so that neither the mother nor the child came to any harm. They were able to carry out perineum protection, could deal with anomalies of presentation so that the birth process could continue without danger, they used stitches to repair perineal tears, and were even able to cope with a prolapsed umbilical cord or a placental abruption. They were familiar with birth forceps but these were only used to deliver a stillborn child. (Hakemeyer and Keding 1986, pp. 63–88, Metz-Becker 1997, pp. 25, 31)

With the Age of Enlightenment and the emergence of Dualism, a theory that regarded mind and matter as separate, medical interest in pregnancy and birth grew. The shame involved in treating a pregnant woman receded into the background and she became an object of research. Perinatal care, which until then had been scorned as a 'bloodstained craft', was elevated to a science. For the first time, physicians using appropriate instruments penetrated inside a living pregnant woman. (Rockenschaub 2005, p. 26, Metz-Becker 1997, p. 59) The first maternity establishments were set up in Germany in 1751 under the direction of Johann Georg Roederer (1726–1763). Roederer no longer talked of the pregnant woman but the pregnant uterus. (Kuhn and Teichmann 1986, p. 365, Metz-Becker 1997, p. 60) Social conditions in the whole of Europe in the 19th century for single pregnant women were catastrophic. In order to avoid giving birth in the fields or gutters, women went to the new maternity establishments. Single mothers were the lowest level of society, and if an unmarried working woman became pregnant she was dismissed from service, and often banished from the town. With nowhere to stay and no father for her child, she was ostracised and seen as a 'slut'.

These women were given food and a bed in the maternity establishments, and in return they made themselves available as research objects for doctors and students. (Metz-Becker 1997, p. 63ff.) The focus of their research was not the natural birth process but the many means of intervention: forceps, manipulation of the pelvis, and perforation of the skull using a drill, dismemberment and extraction of a dead child. Caesareans were carried out without anaesthetics. The aim was to carry out as many operations as possible so that students could gain experience. The birth process was regarded as highly susceptible to mishaps, and even when not pregnant, the female body was seen as helpless, weak and ill. Doctors regarded menstruation, birth, and the postnatal and breastfeeding period as physiological diseases. (ibid., p. 59) This included an image of women as portrayed by the director of the Marburg maternity establishment, Eduard Caspar Jakob von Siebold in 1829: "If by virtue of his calling the man belongs to the world, the woman belongs to the man. The woman's sphere of activity is small. All her wishes are fulfilled as soon as she is pregnant (...) since the formation of the body is easier for nature than the formation of the mind in such a way as to suffice the male sex (. . .) It is now the doctor's task to direct women in completing their most important duty (. . .) Obstetrics practised by men (must) be given preference". (ibid., p. 55)

With medical intervention began the nightmare of childbed fever in maternity establishments. The reason for this was the lack of hygiene. Doctors and students moved directly from dissecting bodies to the delivery room. It is thanks to Ignaz Phillip Semmelweiß (1818–1865) that the incidence of childbed fever became less frequent, because he recognised the connection between bacterial infection and lack of hygiene. He demanded immediate and prophylactic antiseptic measures. However, his insights were not recognised by the majority of leading obstetricians. (Zander 1986, p. 30ff.)

Midwives were forced further out of obstetrics. Many of them could neither read nor write. Women were excluded from education; an academic course of study was unthinkable. As opposed to men, they were unable to extend their knowledge by studying anatomy, physiology and pathology. Male obstetricians were well versed in the theory but lacking in practice, while midwives were lacking in theoretical knowledge but had considerable experience. However, that did not help them to protest publicly; they would have had to do that in written form, which was impossible for most midwives. (Metz-Becker 1997, pp. 36–42)

Thus the art of 'female' obstetrics and midwifery became 'male' gynaecology. In 1885 the German Society of Gynaecology and Obstetrics was founded. The members were all male. The first scientific convention took place in Munich in 1886. (Beck 1986, p. 8) At the first German Medical Assembly in 1898 it was said amidst great applause that having female doctors would be of no help to patients, would do more harm than good for the women themselves, would be of no use to German universities and science, and would lessen the reputation of German doctors.

With the increase in hospital births in the second half of the 18th century, the institutionalisation of obstetrics and the exclusion of women from science, 'female' obstetrics became more and more restricted. Midwives were forced out of their field of work or degraded to 'assistants' of male dominated obstetrics. Doctors took over training midwives and checked what they were doing. (Ensel 2002, p. 6) In addition, the medicalisation of pregnancy and birth had begun.

A further dark chapter concerning pregnancy and birth is the time of National Socialism in Germany. It was also a 'dark' time in the history of midwifery. The midwives helped to remove 'unwanted inferior genetic material from the German people'. Forced abortions were carried out on women with so-called hereditary diseases, on Jewish women, on prostitutes and on Soviet and Polish forced labourers. Foreign workers had to go to the maternity establishments. Children were taken away from their mothers and if they looked Aryan, they were placed in Lebensborn homes. (ibid.)

It took until October 2000 for the first woman to be appointed as professor of gynaecology at the Technical University in Munich. Until then, men had occupied all chairs of gynaecology at German universities. Research, and teaching in the field of gynaecology is still mainly male-dominated. (Schumann 2001, p. 2) The power structures between the sexes continue to exist.

With reference to the findings of multi-generational psychotraumatology concerning conception, pregnancy and birth, which form the focus of this book, I put forward the hypothesis that the effects of the history of obstetrics in Germany and the associated crimes committed against women in Nazi Germany are still felt today. My writings show the perpetrator-victim dynamic in the history of obstetrics. In the last few centuries it was particularly unmarried expectant mothers who served as research material for gynaecologists; in the Third Reich it was pregnant forced labourers who were used for teaching purposes.

The 'maternity record' introduced in 1961, was thought up by two men who had been senior consultants in gynaecology during the Nazi period. In other words, doctors who were perpetrators of serious crimes against women during World War II continued their research in gynaecology and obstetrics after the War without being fully called to account.

7.6 Birth and sexual violence

The birth process can cause flashbacks in women who have experienced sexual violence. The loss of control, the feeling of powerlessness and helplessness while giving birth can lead to a panic reaction in the mother. Many obstetricians cannot react appropriately because they are unaware of the woman's history. In a lecture, the gynaecologist Kornelia Schönfeld called for prenatal check-ups to take place in a protected space. Routine vaginal checks that are similar to a trauma situation could trigger retraumatisation. Thus gynaecologists need guidelines that should be learnt in psychosomatic primary care. Victims of sexual violence have experienced terrible boundary violations in relationships. Doctors therefore have to learn to respect boundaries and to give patients detailed information about any medical checks that are necessary. For expectant mothers who have experienced sexual violence it is important that the obstetricians know how to avoid retraumatisation. (Schönfeld 2001)

The experience of birth following sexual abuse

A woman who had been sexually abused by her brother and who had been raped twice under threat of death, described the birth of her son to me: "When the contractions became stronger and I lost control over my body I started to panic. The doctors tried to give me an epidural but I fought them off. Nobody knew what was wrong with me. I was hyperventilating. To calm me down an oxygen mask was pressed onto my face. At that point the flashback was all encompassing. One guy who raped me pressed his hand onto my mouth and nose – and I was back in this 'film'. I lashed out at everyone within reach and from then on I can't remember anything. When I woke up again I was told that I had had a healthy son. They had done an emergency C-section. I was totally beside myself. When they showed me my son it seemed as if he was a being from another planet. I didn't have any feelings for him. It took a long time for me to be able to accept my child."

7.7 Violence experienced by women during the birth process

What particularly concerns me is the fact that even today many women experience violence during the birth process. This violence is often a continuation of the violence they have previously experienced in their lives. Just a routine, and often completely superfluous, vaginal examination can trigger past trauma. (Rakos 2012, p. 10)

It was in the 1950s in Germany that women began to give birth more frequently in hospitals. The delivery room would be brightly lit, the beds were only separated by a curtain so that a woman could clearly hear the screams and groans of the woman next to her.

That was the case when I gave birth to my son in 1983. To the right and left of me were two women who were also about to give birth. One woman was originally from Turkey and she gave free rein to her feelings, which prompted my midwife to complain that the Turkish woman was too loud and hadn't learned to control herself. I hardly dared to make a sound for fear that she would berate me. It was also usual then for a woman to give birth lying on her back – the position that is most convenient for the doctors. I now know that I experienced violence during the birth process. To begin with I was given an infusion with no explanation. When I asked what it was for I was told it was a drip to increase the contractions and speed up the birth. I tried to resist but I was asked if I would rather lie there for hours without any productive contractions. So I gave in. The contractions started straightaway and very violently and during these huge contractions I was given the usual enema. I thought I was going to explode inwardly. I have no idea how I made it back from the toilet to the bed. At any rate I was lying on my back again, my legs in the gynaecological stirrups. When the second stage of labour started, my posture made it difficult for me to find the strength to push hard enough and the doctor used the Kristeller manoeuvre. This is a method used to speed up the birth of the child by pushing the top of the uterus simultaneously with the contractions. The manoeuvre should only be used in the last few contractions when the top of the child's head is already visible. Without any warning the doctor threw himself onto my belly, which was extremely painful. I then gathered that they were going to do an episiotomy, although the midwife had promised me beforehand that she would do everything she could to prevent one. I tried to protest again and was told: "It's not up to you to decide what has to be done, it's our decision!" When my son was finally born he was not put straight onto my belly even though I had been promised that beforehand; he was immediately examined. Luckily he was healthy and had withstood the stress and strain, physically at least. At last he was given to me and we had skin-to-skin contact and an indescribable feeling of happiness flowed through me. He immediately looked for my nipple and drank his first breast milk, the precious colostrum.

I was able to prevent my son being pricked in the foot and being given the silver nitrate eye drops that were usual in those days and that supposedly stung badly. The happiness of being able finally to hold my son in my arms only lasted a little while. The delivery room became increasingly hectic because another expectant mother needed the bed. The stitches I was given to repair the perineum were extremely painful. The local anaesthetic had not worked and I felt every stitch. The entry in my maternal record stated: Natural birth, normal, no complications. In other words it was a typical hospital birth in the 1980s.

I have described my experience of the birth process in such detail because since then I have heard from so many women who had a similar experience of giving birth to their children in hospital, but who, like me, did not realise that they and their children were being treated with violence. For a long time I refused to believe that my son's birth was traumatic for him and for me. Franke's words fitted exactly: "No longer being able to make decisions about one's own body, not being able to escape, not being able to defend oneself effectively (...) For a woman who is in labour and is subjected, against her will and with no explanation, to the interventions of medical obstetrics, who undergoes an episiotomy or whose belly is, without warning, subjected to Kristeller's manoeuvre with a knee or an elbow, it is the equivalent of rape". (Franke 2007, p. 4)

Even though I was not aware in those days of the effect this birth had had psychologically on my son and me, I knew that if I were ever to become pregnant again, I would not expose my child or myself to such treatment. My daughter was born in 1990 at home. I did not do a pregnancy test, but relied instead on my body's feeling. Very early on I looked for a midwife who was prepared to go along with my 'project' of a home birth. She gave me the name of a doctor with whom she worked closely and who would support me in my plan. The birth experience with my daughter was absolutely wonderful. It was fantastic, euphoric, impossible to describe in words. Even today I go into raptures when I think about it.

7.8 Birth and the women's liberation movement of the 1980s

At the start of the 80s there were more and more protests from the women's liberation movement against the increase in technology in the delivery room. There was an increasing number of discussions about the unease regarding gynaecological apparatus: paediatricians, gynaecologists, feminists, the Green Party, psychologists and psychotherapists asked whether the much talked of 'alienation' had its beginnings in the gynaecologist's practice. Eva Reich, an American paediatrician, said that we should start with the newborn baby. The surgeon, Michel Odent, advocate and practitioner of the 'gentle birth' believed strongly that 'life changing' meant to change how one is born. (Schreiber 1981, p. 7ff.) Feminists wanted obstetrics to become the domain of women once more. During this period there were almost more books about birth and pregnancy in women's bookshops than literature with the slogan 'My body belongs to me' on the topic of the law forbidding abortion. The author Eva-Maria Stark's call to women was: "We have to reject the institution of the hospital." (ibid.)

Never before had there been so much speculation, from a psychological and philosophical viewpoint, about the meaning of birth. Arthur Janov believed he had found the key to his patients' later anxieties and neuroses in their birth experiences. For the first time people were thinking that the separation of mother and child immediately after the birth, which was the practice in hospitals, was extremely damaging to the mother-child relationship. Even the rather conservative German Medical Journal (*Deutsches Ärzteblatt*) accepted that during a technically perfect "completely normal delivery, fundamental needs of mother and child were disregarded". (ibid.) The trend towards autonomous birth caught on in the women's liberation movement. It was particularly women with successful careers who emancipated themselves. For the first time a generation of self-assured women seemed to be questioning male obstetrics. (Der Spiegel, 28.7.1980, p. 133)

7.9 Births in the 21st century

What happens in a delivery room today, almost 30 years later? What changes have taken place? In the mid 1980s midwives founded the first 'birth-houses', places to have a baby where there were no doctors.

In the last few years many such birth-houses have had to close because of the high insurance premiums for midwives. In addition, more and more women are classed as 'at-risk' pregnancies and prefer to give birth in a hospital where they believe they will be safer. As an alternative to a birth-house some hospitals have delivery rooms under the direction of midwives. For example this is an advertisement for the Niederberg Clinic: "Midwives are in charge in the delivery room where they are responsible for monitoring and directing natural births. We support your trust in the healthy, natural birth process and encourage you in your own power so that you can manage the work of giving birth according to your ability. We will ensure that you can bring your child into the world in a peaceful atmosphere away from any hospital routine."[15] So far there are 15 delivery rooms in Germany that are managed by midwives.

---

[15] http://www.klinikum-niederberg.de

I doubt whether this is an alternative to a birth-house. An expectant mother who is supposedly 'at risk' cannot give birth in a delivery room run by midwives. And as soon as a birth varies slightly from the norm the mother is transferred to a delivery room where doctors are in charge. "Early dialogue, communication, the relationship and connection are the foundation for a healthy birth". (Hildebrandt 2008) This is the theory put forward by Sven Hildebrandt at an international congress for prenatal and perinatal psychology and medicine in Heidelberg. At the same time he observes that the understanding of modern childbirth is far removed from this. Concern for the risks involved is at the centre of medical obstetrics and unfortunately also dominates the way many midwives think. Midwives who would like to emancipate themselves from the system of medical obstetrics receive little support from the Federation of German Midwives (BDH).

Dr. med. Christian Albring, President of the Professional Association of Gynaecologists, is convinced that giving birth is the most dangerous time in a person's life. Even if the pregnancy has been completely normal, there is a risk that a situation will arise where only an emergency Caesarean can prevent severe damage to the child. No mother or midwife is able to rule it out with complete certainty before the birth. It should therefore be every woman's priority to give birth in hospital through concern for her child. Having a scheduled Caesarean can prevent risks for the child[16].

The birth of my twin grandchildren 2013

When my daughter was pregnant with twins, we looked at several hospitals together because my daughter wanted to have her children naturally. Giving birth at home was not really possible with twins because no midwife would attend. Giving birth naturally to twins requires experienced midwives who understand their craft. Unfortunately there are not many such midwives around any longer. Many women expecting twins are advised to have a Caesarean. There are hospitals in which twins are always delivered

---

[16] www.frauenaerzte-im-netz.de

by Caesarean whatever the history of the mother and the presentation of the children.

First we looked at a hospital close to where we lived. After 30 years I saw a delivery room again, and I couldn't believe my eyes. No tiled walls, no neon light, medical apparatus was nowhere to be seen. In the middle of the room, nicely cushioned and in warm colours, was a huge comfortable bed that could be adjusted into any position. Colourful ropes hung from the ceiling and the lighting was dimmed and intimate. The adjoining room was also painted in warm colours and contained a very large bath. Looking round, I was delighted. I hadn't imagined anything as nice. We were greeted warmly and the midwives were keen to show us everything and encourage us to decide on their hospital. Because she was expecting twins, my daughter was already pretty big, the size she'd have been just prior to the birth if she'd only been expecting one child and the midwives assumed that the birth was imminent. When they discovered she was expecting twins they said: "Oh, then it'll be a Caesarean. We do that in the 38th week here, to be on the safe side." Thirty-five percent of births at that hospital are Caesareans. Here is an extract from an article in our local newspaper: "Are too many children being born by Caesarean although there is no medical reason for it? A midwife who used to work in this hospital believes the main reason for the high number of Caesareans lies in the doctors' concern that they could be sued if there were complications in a vaginal birth. She mentions a further problem: the increasing number of Caesareans means that the obstetricians no longer have sufficient experience to deal with difficult vaginal births." (HAZ, 30.8.2013)

We looked at four other hospitals until we found one that promised my daughter she could have her children naturally, even if they were breech presentations. With the help of a very experienced midwife, my twin grandchildren were born in the 40th week in February 2013. My daughter needed neither pain relief nor an epidural. Both children were completely developed and each weighed as much as if they had been single births. My daughter was able to leave the hospital with both children the day after giving birth. She was very lucky, because it could have been very different. The most important thing was that the right midwife was on duty at the right time, and a female gynaecologist who had also had twins, also born naturally, accompanied her.

7.10 Routine measures and stress during a 'normal' birth

The nicely furnished delivery room, with comfortable bed and large birth pool, implies an intimacy that does not exist. The high-tech medicine is well hidden and not visible at first glance: the blood pressure monitors are automatic machines on wheels; oxygen masks and tubes are hidden in the walls so that oxygen or gas can be given; a movable drip stands next to the delivery bed; clamps and brackets can be fixed to special grooves on each side of the bed so that the woman's legs can be raised and she can be examined more thoroughly; forceps and ventouse suction cup are stored under the bed and ready for immediate use.

It is routine for a CTG to be hooked up during the birth even though there may be no reason for it, which means that the expectant mother is attached to cables as soon as she comes into the delivery room that considerably restrict her movement. Cardiac telemetry is new: here the heartbeat is monitored wirelessly so that cables are no longer necessary. A cannula will also be inserted into a vein in your lower arm so that infusions or medication can be administered. The cervix is examined vaginally at regular intervals to check the progress of the birth. Giving an enema and shaving pubic hair are recommended, which most mothers go along with. An epidural is offered as standard, and also recommended. Hospitals claim that with the options available today a birth need no longer be painful.

During my research for this chapter I looked at the websites of many maternity hospitals that advertise their services. They all claim to meet the highest safety standards. They promise that the mother can have a part in making decisions, but only if she and her child are doing well according to standards of safety. Episiotomies are no longer carried out as a matter of course, but a final decision can only be made shortly before the head appears. If the tissue looks as if it will tear and if the head does not come out quickly enough, a cut will be made[17]. A tear heals much more

---

[17] http://www.babyburg.de/baby-ratgeber/geburt/krenkenhausaufnahme-geburt/ entbindungsstation-entbindungsraum

quickly than a cut. The tissue usually tears at the thinnest place between vagina and anus, (a sort of predetermined breaking point), which is why there is much less muscle tissue involved than if it is cut. However, a tear is more difficult to stitch together than a cut because each layer of skin has to be joined.

In order to have her baby a woman needs safety, a feeling of security and a relaxed atmosphere. In a hospital there are frequently time constraints. The midwives work in shifts and have to look after several women at once. The regular vaginal examinations are carried out by different people and are painful, embarrassing and unpleasant. The permanent beeping of the CTG, and being unable to move freely can lead to stress during the birth. When the body is under stress it doesn't produce painkilling endorphins or oxytocin, but mainly adrenaline. Adrenaline ensures that the arm and leg muscles are better supplied with blood to enable fight or flight, and as a result, the supply of blood to the uterus is decreased and the contractions, combined with the lack of endorphins, lead to very severe pain – one reason so many women ask for an epidural.

This external stress can cause the contractions to decrease or even cease altogether. Added to that the child receives less oxygen, which can cause the heartbeat to become weaker. The birth is then frequently induced if the contractions have not started properly so that the birth process is speeded up. Medication is given to increase contractions, possibly followed by medication to slow the contractions down if an overdose of the first medication was given. Interventions are common in such a hospital situation with the justification being that the safety of the child is no longer guaranteed. Thus the birth ends more and more frequently nowadays with the use of forceps, a ventouse or with a Caesarean. The German Federal Statistics Office recorded 653,215 hospital births in 2012. Of these, 6% were with forceps (3,037 births) or with a ventouse (36,959). Thirty-two percent of the births were Caesareans.

We are therefore left with the suspicion that it is the medical birth system itself that creates most of the problems it was supposed to resolve.

7.11 Giving birth at home

Women who plan to give birth at home because they do not want the routine measures meted out by hospitals are said to be risk seeking and irresponsible, as medical intervention could become necessary. For years the number of home births in Germany has remained at only somewhere between10,000 and 12,500 children[18]. In 2012 according to the German Federal Statistics Office 673,544 children were born, 653,215 of those were born in hospital. Outside hospital, therefore, 20,329 children were born. Assuming that about half of those born outside hospital were born in a birth-house, we can say that only 1.5% of all children were born at home.

7.12 Caesarean births

The percentage of Caesarean births has risen steadily in the last few years. In countries such as Brazil or China it is already 50% and more. What prompts medical obstetricians to carry out so many Caesareans? No one is questioning the fact that a Caesarean can be a necessary medical indication and can save lives. But is it really true that every third woman or every third child is in such danger during the birth process that there is no alternative but a Caesarean?

The suggestion is frequently made in the media that more and more women want a Caesarean because it is, after all, the modern way of giving birth adopted by prominent mothers. (Oblasser, Ebner and Wesp 2008, p. 24) A survey on behalf of the Bertelsmann Foundation on whether the fact that women wish to have a Caesarean has influenced the high percentage of Caesareans actually carried out, has shown that only 1.6% of the women asked had consciously decided that they wanted a Caesarean delivery. Therefore the 'too posh to push' attitude that many women are accused of does not explain the high rate of Caesareans. The real explanation, according to this study, is that many obstetricians are unable to deal with breech presentation,

---

[18] www.spiegel.de 20.03.2013 15:34

which accounts for about 5% of all births in Germany. These children are almost all born by C-section. The same applies to multiple births. In other words there are already too few obstetricians who have the experience necessary to deal with vaginal multiple births and breech presentations. (Kolip 2012, Otto 2013) It is worst for the woman giving birth if she has to have an emergency C-section because she has no opportunity to prepare herself. Such birth experiences are often traumatic, as shown by a study by Jurgelucks. (2004)

Emergency Caesareans

One mother described it thus: "Suddenly everything had to happen immediately. I didn't know what was going on, nobody said anything to me. I just heard them saying section and I was taken into theatre. I panicked and was desperately worried about my child. They had already given me an epidural so I didn't have a general anaesthetic. My husband wasn't allowed to come with me; it was absolutely terrible. Then I felt pulling and tugging. I didn't know whether my child was alive; they didn't show her to me. I was sure she was dead. I was paralysed by fear, didn't feel anything anymore. Finally my husband came and told me our daughter was fine; he'd already been with her. After what seemed like an eternity I was able to see for myself that my child was alive – my husband put her into my arms. But I couldn't believe that she was really my child; I just didn't believe it. That feeling stayed for a long time, although I knew she must be my daughter. But I couldn't feel it." To this day this mother does not know what happened. She has now asked for the hospital's birth report in order to find out. For a long time she was unable to talk about this experience; she felt guilty because she had not been able to give birth to her child normally.

Another 'Caesarean mother' told me that she had been having contractions for some time but the cervix had not opened and she had given her consent for medication to be given to her to speed up the birth. She was told that this was the modern way of doing things, better than a drip or rupturing the amniotic sac. She was given an overdose of the medication and she had a mass of contractions without them having any effect on the cervix. She was then given medication to reduce the contractions. All these unnecessary interventions upset the whole birth process, and her daughter was finally delivered by C-section.

7.13 Planned Caesareans

A Caesarean is planned if the baby's position is abnormal. There are not many cases when a woman can give birth normally to a baby in the breech position.

Equally, a Caesarean is often planned if a woman is expecting twins. In many hospitals a C-section is planned in the 38th week of pregnancy with the justification that the burden on the placenta could otherwise be too great and because the uterus has reached its limits.

The increase in IVF and hormone treatment means that multiple births are more common. In the last 20 years the proportion of multiple births in Germany has risen sharply: according to the German Federal Statistics Office there were 13,270 multiple births in 2015. Every 29th child is now one of a multiple birth. In 1991 it was every 42nd child. Most multiple births are delivered by Caesarean.

Some women decide to have a Caesarean if they have experienced a traumatic vaginal birth or a previous birth had to be finished with an emergency Caesarean. They opt for a Caesarean from the beginning to avoid a repeat of the previous situation.

A further reason is that a Caesarean is often recommended if the previous birth was by C-section. In other words once a Caesarean, always a Caesarean. (Taschner and Scheck 2012, p. 21) There is a slight risk that the scar left on the uterus by the previous C-section might tear. Doctors' fear of being sued has also led to the increase in the number of Caesareans. A Caesarean is wrongly supposed to cover all possible risk scenarios. (Otto and Wagner 2013, p. 10) Studies have shown that the percentage of uterus tears in women giving birth naturally following a previous Caesarean is 0.9% to 0.8%[19]. In their book *Meine Wunschgeburt* [My Ideal Birth] by

---

[19] www.babycenter.de/a8826/vaginalgeburt-nach-einem-kaiserschnitt-vbac

Ute Taschner and Kathrin Scheck, women talk about their experience of giving birth naturally following a previous Caesarean. (Taschner and Scheck 2012) At the 59th Congress of the German Society of Gynaecology and Obstetrics (DGGG) in Munich Professor Dr. med. Louwen stressed that a Caesarean was much more of a risk for mother and child than a natural birth. The danger not only of thrombosis, embolism and bleeding but also of hysterectomy is much higher with a Caesarean than with a natural birth. However, the complications arising from the operation itself have decreased in number in the last few decades. (Louwen 2012) A Caesarean is a serious abdominal operation. Many women underestimate the risks to themselves and their child or receive insufficient information from the doctors. It is not only the mother who is at a higher risk, but the child as well. Louwen points out that infant mortality is much higher following a Caesarean. There may be difficulties in adapting, which could mean that the child needs intensive medical care. The danger is highest if the Caesarean is carried out before the 40th week of pregnancy. (Louwen 2012)

This discussion tends to ignore the effect a Caesarean has on the psyche of the mother and the child. Far fewer birth-assisting and bonding hormones are released: endorphins that boost the feeling of euphoria following the birth, oxytocin that encourages the bonding process between mother and child. During a natural birth these hormones are released by the mother's body and reach her child via the bloodstream. With a Caesarean there is no work done in concert by the mother and her child. A natural birth is a finely tuned interaction. It is not only the mother who accomplishes an amazing task, but also her child. Each natural contraction, painful though it is, brings mother and child closer together. The pain of labour is unlike any other.

With a planned Caesarean, at least the mother is able to prepare herself; her child however is completely unprepared. In effect the child is 'torn' out of the mother's body.

I advise mothers planning a Caesarean at least to talk to their unborn child about it and to tell them what they have planned. A C-section often prevents the mother having initial contact with the child. In most hospitals the child is thoroughly examined before being given to the mother. Unlike a vaginal birth, with a Caesarean the initial skin-on-skin contact is often not possible, even if the child is healthy. Even after four days the endorphins are significantly higher with a natural birth than with a Caesarean. The lack of endorphins released during a Caesarean causes more stress for the baby, and makes the birth harder to deal with. It is therefore harder for the child to come into contact with his mother, which in turn has an effect on the mother's release of prolactin, making breastfeeding more difficult. (Ehlers 2010, p. 22)

Many mothers planning a Caesarean choose to have an epidural. The advantage of this is that the mother consciously experiences the delivery and can see her child straightaway. To avoid making the bonding process even more difficult after a Caesarean, midwives and doctors should aim to ensure that mother and child are not immediately separated from the delivery. If the child is healthy, the paediatric tests can be carried out later.

A gynaecologist working as an obstetrician at a Berlin hospital gave a talk at a conference on 'Mother-Child Attachment'. He said that in his hospital he had worked to ensure that the child was put naked onto the mother's breast immediately after a Caesarean. He had noticed that it was then easier for mothers and children to form an attachment following a Caesarean. (Lebensgarten Steyerberg 2009) It is not done that way in most hospitals; often it is the father who takes on this role. Fathers have told me that they laid their baby onto their naked chest and they had the first snuggling moments with their child.

In Brigitte Renate Meissner's book mothers who have had a Caesarean describe sometimes experiencing their children as 'clingy' and not being able to connect properly with them, or the children being easily startled and much closer to the father. (Meissner 2010, p. 125) If the babies, or older children, demonstrate psychological abnormalities, sleep, eating or development disorders, or suffer from other physical symptoms, this might have been caused by the method of delivery. Further diagnostics and integrative therapy are then called for[20].

---

[20] www.kaiserschnitt-netzwerk.de/folgenfurdaskind.html

The increasing number of Caesareans could also be a sign of the bonding disorders of the expectant mothers, and also of the men and women working in obstetrics. In my view, midwives and doctors in obstetrics who are not prepared to work on their own psychological structures are not able to cope sympathetically and empathetically with a birth.

Birth complications are frequently the result of the mother's earlier traumatisation. They provide evidence of the central thesis of multi-generational psychotraumatology, that the effect of a trauma is continued through many generations and the trauma is repeated in future generations. Traumatisations increase the chance of further traumatisations occurring.

One trauma brings on another

A woman who had been coming to my therapy practice for some time knew that her mother had tried several times to terminate her pregnancy with her. In the constellations it came to light that her conception was very probably a violent experience for the mother. The abortion attempts were unsuccessful and following her birth my client almost died of hunger because she was unable to accept her mother's milk. It also emerged that she had been sexually abused by her father as a child, which also fitted with her own body sensation. Her pregnancy with her son was, according to her, uncomplicated. In the first three months she did suffer with severe morning sickness and vomited frequently. But she was still looking forward immensely to her first child. During the birth process her son's heartbeat became weaker and an emergency Caesarean had to be carried out. For a short time he suffered from lack of oxygen and his life was in severe danger. Her son was full-term, yet when he was born he was undernourished. He was much too small and had to stay in intensive care for six weeks. During that time my client was only able to look at him through a dividing pane of glass. That was the usual procedure in the 1970s. For the son's whole life, his mother and he have not managed to develop a healthy relationship with one another. She had unconscious emotional expectations of her son that he was unable to fulfil. He tried to compensate intellectually for what he could not express emotionally. Several years previously he had broken off all contact with his mother. He rejected every attempt to contact him. He even threatened to take legal action if she did not leave him in peace. She only knows through her daughter, who is still in contact with her brother, that she has two grandchildren.

My client is now able to recognise the deeper interrelationships; that she was unable to nourish her son properly during the pregnancy because of her own traumatisations, and that she did not even notice because she was too caught up in her survival strategies. Even though she had looked forward so much to her first child, her own mother's feelings of not wanting her, as she had not been wanted, had continued to affect her unconsciously. Although she is very sad that she is not allowed to have any contact with her son or her grandchildren, she can understand the situation better and accept it as it is at the moment.

8
Premature birth as the result and cause of traumatisations

Manuela Specht

8.1 Premature births from a medical viewpoint

A pregnancy normally lasts 40 weeks, i.e. 280 days from the first day of the woman's last period. Births before completion of the 37th week are known as premature births. Every year 15 million children globally are born before the 37th week and are by definition premature. Of these children, 1.1 million do not survive. Premature birth and associated complications are the number two cause of child mortality. (Howson, Kinney and Lawn 2012)

The number of extremely premature births, when the child is born before 28 completed weeks of gestation, is steadily increasing. In Germany completing the 24th week is regarded as the prerequisite for intensive care measures. Progress in neonatology and paediatric intensive care have considerably improved the survival chances for 'premmies' in the last few years, so that there is a chance of survival before the end of the 24th week. The mortality rate has decreased by about a third in the last 30 years. (Schleußner 2013)

There are different explanations for the increase in the number of preterm births, particularly those that are extremely premature. Causes can be: multiple births (for example following *in vitro* fertilisation), an infectious disease in the mother (especially urogenital infections), high blood pressure caused by the pregnancy, thyroid dysfunction, dysfunction of the placenta, placental insufficiency, placenta praevia. Diabetes, nicotine and alcohol addiction and other forms of addiction, including heroin consumption, all commonly lead to premature births. Other causes can also be obesity or malnutrition in the mother. Possible risks are also the mother's age if she is younger than 18 or older than 30, and whether she has previously given birth prematurely. Psychosocial triggers for a premature birth can be, for example, chronic stress from juggling multiple factors such as family, household and work; psychological and physical stress such as a sudden death, moving house, losing a job, relationship conflicts and accidents. The child himself can be the trigger for a premature birth, for example through a genetic defect and resulting somatic abnormality. Often there is nothing definite to explain the waters breaking early or early contractions leading to the birth. To medical research, the threat of a premature birth is a multi-factor process that can only be treated symptomatically. There has been progress in the prevention of imminent premature births that has led to improvements in neonatal development but not to a reduction in the premature birth rate. Although many studies have been completed, there is only slight evidence supporting the majority of the diagnostic and therapeutic measures used. (Schleußner 2013)

8.2 Use of 'kangaroo care' to assist survival

The situation of premature babies has improved noticeably since the introduction and development of the 'kangaroo care' method. Marina Marcovich, a paediatrician from Vienna, spoke for the first time in 1992 about the need for gentle care of premature babies and introduced the 'kangaroo' method at the hospital where she was working. 'Kangaroo care' means that the child, naked except for a nappy, lies on the naked breast of the mother or father. (Marcovich and de Jong 2008)

Several randomised controlled studies in Israel, Canada and the USA have been carried out in the last few years. It was found that the children who had experienced skin-on-skin contact very early were less susceptible to respiratory diseases. They were also more resistant to hospital germs. Improvements were also seen in the regulation of the children's body temperature, their heartbeat and breathing frequency. The premature child experiences care and warmth through the skin-on-skin contact. The mother's voice, the smell of her body and the sound of her heartbeat have a very soothing effect on her child. The child needs less oxygen and is able to breathe independently earlier than he would otherwise be able to, and the positive sensory stimulation furthers the development of his brain. Bonding is also helped by the close contact between mother and child. The parents gain more self-confidence in looking after their premature child. Their child is no longer just the child of the doctors and nurses; on the contrary, this method encourages the parents to be part of the process from the start. Mothers who put their trust in this method usually breastfeed their children longer. At the very least, the use of this method prevents long-term neurological problems such as delayed development, or behavioural disturbances such as ADD or ADHD, autism or dyslexia, which premature children often suffer from. (Stening 2007)

8.3 Stress and early births

Research studies from prenatal psychology increasingly show that we should look more closely at this prenatal period. We now know that strong impressions are left on the deep emotionality of the unborn child in the womb. In *Nabelschnur der Seele* [The umbilical cord of the soul] (2006) the Hungarian psychoanalyst Jenö Raffei writes about the intuitive communication between a mother and her unborn child which he calls 'prenatal bonding space'. If the mother is happy about expecting her child, she is relaxed and well adjusted, which is good for her unborn child. The mother's good mood strengthens his feeling of wellbeing. If the mother is stressed and anxious because, for example, the child's father has left her, she might want to abort the child. Or if she is subjected to physical violence in the relationship, this can cause a great deal of stress for the growing child and ultimately lead to his premature birth.

Arthur Janov (2012, pp. 39–40) also talks of a prenatal consciousness, i.e. the experiences a child has before birth are encoded and stored at the deepest biological level of the child.

These experiences define his individual response patterns in later life. He reacts to the environment he finds in the uterus by adapting his life functions, his hormones and neurotransmitters to this reality. The nervous system of the growing child is so well developed that he is physically able, for example, to perceive his mother's conscious or unconscious abortion wishes. It can happen that if the expectant mother is under stress, there is a rapid rise in the level of the stress hormone cortisol in her, which speeds up the child's development. This again can cause a premature birth.

As with every birth, prenatal experience also precedes a premature birth. It is therefore very important to take into account not only the external stress factors, but also to bear in mind the processes taking place, to some extent unconsciously, within expectant mothers which can cause severe damage to the unborn child. Tension, anxiety and stress in a pregnant woman are not always visible to the outside world. However, the mother's increased cortisol levels can have a serious effect on the child's development.

My experience from working with the constellation method has shown that there are new preventative ways of using the 'Constellation of the Intention' to avoid a premature birth.

8.4 Trauma and premature birth

My work with mothers who have given birth prematurely has revealed their own recurring unprocessed traumatic experiences. Sometimes the mothers were conscious of these experiences, but more often they were unaware of them. They were more aware of events after their own birth, either from hearing their parents or grandparents talk about them or from previous therapies. They were totally unaware of their own prenatal experiences.

Dagmar

Dagmar has been coming to my practice for some time. She comes from a family system with severe attachment traumas, and as a child she was hospitalised and also in therapy. With the help of the constellation method, she was able to look at and process many of her issues. In one session she wanted to create a conscious connection to herself and the traumatic birth of her second child, Peter. Dagmar was first pregnant when she was 16 and had to come to terms with her situation on her own. Neither the father of the child nor her own parents wanted anything to do with the situation; they were of no help to her at all. She also felt that Social Services were checking up on her and not giving her any actual support. When she was 17 she had a healthy daughter by C-section. In the same year she became pregnant again by a different man. She was now at her wits' end. She lived with her daughter and a female friend in supported accommodation. The child's father hardly bothered about Dagmar. Her daily life was total stress. She had contractions in the 32nd week and had to stay in bed. Her daughter was already being temporarily looked after in a foster family. In the 35th week she was given medication to inhibit contractions. However, ultimately, a preterm birth could not be prevented. Before undergoing surgery, Dagmar had arranged to marry a young man from a family she was friendly with so that Social Services couldn't later take her child away from her. The child's actual father was in prison at this point. Her son Peter was born by C-section and immediately taken to the nearest paediatric hospital. Dagmar was only able to visit her son on the third day after the operation. The whole situation completely overwhelmed her. Dagmar had no feeling for herself and was unable to establish a relationship with her son. The hospital staff could have brought her any child and she wouldn't have noticed whether it was her child or not. Dagmar was unable to take any action to alleviate the traumatic birth experience. She no longer had any will of her own. She felt completely helpless and powerless in the situation. She just functioned in the way expected of her by the doctors and her family. Ultimately, this traumatic event reflected her own birth experience, to which she had had no conscious access prior to this session. Dagmar herself had experienced a perinatal trauma with her own mother, which she had split off in order to survive. It was only now that she was able to approach her own experiences step by step, and establish conscious contact to herself and her split-off parts. She had given her two children away for adoption because she had been unable to cope with the situation for fear of harming herself or them. Both children are now adults. To this day Dagmar has not seen her children again. Two weeks after the constellation, an initial contact occurred with her children via the internet.

Peter

It was not only for Dagmar that the premature birth of her son brought a fresh trauma and a retraumatisation of personal birth experiences. For the premature child, Peter, the sudden physical separation from his mother was also a trauma: a new, severe event after all the traumatising prenatal experiences he had had to cope with. In the following case example, I describe how Peter may have experienced the separation from his mother and the world of the incubator. In this session Dagmar wanted to know how her son had felt after being separated from her.

As the representative of Peter, the role I (as therapist) had undertaken, I felt completely disoriented, physically twisted, like a coil that wants to move upwards. I wanted to eject myself from the womb silently. I didn't want to live. I just wanted to get out and away. I didn't want to endure any more pain; my whole body was in pain. I had to cough; couldn't breathe. But I noticed that I couldn't escape upwards; the top was shut; no opening; something prevented me from getting through. I was enclosed in a covering with no way out. Breathing was extremely difficult; I kept struggling with it. I kept thinking about ways of getting out and away. Then I noticed that I didn't have to struggle to breathe myself any more. The covering was gone. Suddenly I could breathe freely. I sensed that ultimately I had had to give up; I didn't have any control any more, something outside was even looking after my breathing. I allowed all this to happen and just wanted to sleep. I knew 'something outside' was now looking after me. I didn't think about the 'outside something', I didn't have any questions; the only important thing for me was my condition. I didn't feel any anxiety when I was separated from my mother. Did I ever feel anything except pain? The whole time the word 'mother' never occurred to me once. I was happy to be at peace; it was a bit cold, but the main thing was that it was peaceful. I felt cold but those 'outside' would have to work that out for themselves. I was neither able to, nor wanted to communicate with them. I was very hampered in my movements. My final thought in the role was that they now had to look after my life; they wanted me to live.

8.5 Premature birth and symbiotic trauma

The personal histories of premature children often demonstrate prenatal disruption or even a prenatal breach in the relationship to their parents. Significant events in the mother's life and experiences have consequences for the child. As in the case of Dagmar and her son Peter, there were situations before the birth that were unbearable for Dagmar, and so stressful for Peter that he only wanted to get 'out and away', even out of this life. In the meantime Dagmar was in written contact with her son and confirmed in a further conversation with me that her son still thinks that today: The others have to look after me. Dagmar had not yet met up with her children. There is a great deal of fear on both sides of being overburdened again by being in contact. Fear that feelings could overwhelm them. Dagmar definitely wants to continue working on herself in order to find inner peace.

Birgit

> I had a conversation with a mother who had also given birth prematurely and I would like to summarise her story: Birgit had a terrible childhood. After her sister was born she was just a nuisance to her mother, who constantly criticised her. Both her parents beat Birgit frequently. When she was 15 she suffered from anorexia and bulimia. At 17 she was so badly beaten by both her parents that she ended up in hospital. She started smoking a lot. At 18 her GP could no longer look after her as an outpatient and she was admitted to a clinic. There she regained her strength and began an apprenticeship. When she was 19 she became pregnant by her then boyfriend, but it was some time before she realised she was pregnant. It was only in the 4th month, when she was again admitted to a clinic because of her eating disorders, that it was discovered. She was not doing well. Her family now ostracised her even more. There was only one cousin who looked after her lovingly and brought her food when she was home. The child's father didn't pay much attention to her. He also had other girlfriends. When he did visit Birgit, he hit her. Her parents blamed her for everything; said she deserved no better. As far as the doctors were concerned, Birgit's was an 'at risk' pregnancy and they said she could end the pregnancy at any time. However, Birgit didn't want to have an abortion. In the 33rd

week she was taken to hospital with premature contractions. Everything happened very quickly; even the medication to stop the contractions couldn't stop the birth. Her daughter, Martina, was born naturally in the 33rd week with severe jaundice. She was immediately moved to an incubator.

Birgit was pleased to have a flat stomach again. She was also relieved to be without a child for the time being, so that she could prepare herself in peace and quiet for the new situation of being a mother. She regularly expressed her milk and was able to visit her child on the fifth day. But her daughter was a stranger to her; she wasn't able to love and accept her. It was only after six weeks that she was able to take her daughter home. During her stay in hospital, Martina also had a hernia operation. After such a long time without her child, Birgit felt better. She even tried to breast-feed her but found it very unpleasant and a lot of bother. She became very worried about Martina; she worried about her dying in a cot death. She kept watch over her day and night. She thought she was now a proper mother. After four months she married the father of the child, although she hated him. However, she wanted to make sure that she and her daughter were provided for financially. Birgit soon started working and Martina went to nursery when she was a year old. In the long term Birgit couldn't bear her daughter's need for closeness, love, warmth and security. She often hit her daughter and her daughter regularly fainted from the beating. When I asked Birgit why she thought her daughter had been born too early she answered in a very cool and distant manner that her daughter had not been able to stand being with her as mother: "I wasn't able to develop a relationship with her as a mother. I wasn't in a good place myself; there was no room for her. I could never love her. I could look after her, but that was all. I transferred my parents' rejection onto my child." Mother and daughter still have a difficult relationship today.

The daughter Martina came to my practice once and wanted to look at her problematic relationship with men. In the constellation it quickly became clear that she felt torn apart internally. Her parents' relationship dynamic had made excessive demands of her from the beginning. She not only suffered from the traumatic circumstances of her early birth, but also remained trapped in a symbiotic trauma with her mother.

8.6 Personal experiences with the constellation method

I was present at some of the constellations of a forty-year-old man facilitated by Franz Ruppert, which showed that continuous trauma therapy with the 'Constellation of the Intention' can lead to the individual being able to overcome the trauma he experienced in an incubator and the symbiotic trauma with his mother. He was ultimately able to access the painful and distressed feelings of the child in the incubator from whom he had originally had to split in order to survive.

I am grateful and delighted to have discovered work with constellations for myself as well. Thinking, worrying, and trying to understand rationally had not helped me with my own problems. Today I have a clear picture of what is taking place within me psychologically, both personally and as a therapist. I have found a path that helps me to live my life independently, confidently and free. Today, as an adult woman, I am no longer helpless and powerless like I used to be as a child. Even before I was born, my life was more a case of survival. My first very traumatising relationship experiences with my parents have been a recurring theme throughout my life and have had a huge influence on my physical and psychological health. After many constellations of my own I have arrived at being myself and can live my life autonomously. This is an experience I wish for everyone: to be able to live happily and at ease with oneself.

9

The process of separation and re-bonding: the final birth phase

Dagmar Strauss

Before a mother can hold her child in her arms, both she and her child have to overcome the three birth phases together. The birth begins with the dilation phase. Regular contractions of the uterus cause the cervix, which until then has been tightly shut, to open gradually. In phase two, the expulsion, the child moves down into the mother's pelvis and the urge to push down will help the child move down the birth canal into the outside. The final phase is the delivery of the placenta, when the placenta separates from the uterine wall and is pushed out by further contractions. Recently this phase is also said to include the cutting of the umbilical cord and the newborn child's re-bonding with the mother.

9.1 The first time mother and child meet outside the womb

During the months in his mother's womb the umbilical cord has been the unborn child's lifeline. Throughout the pregnancy this thick, sinuous, elastic blood vessel supplies the child reliably and securely with food and oxygen. The mother gives the child everything he needs to grow and flourish via the placenta. The child in turn sends all the used blood back along the same path. According to Sven Hildebrandt (2008) the placenta is one of the child's vital organs and the placental birth phase is as important as the two preceding phases. He recommends only cutting the umbilical cord once the placenta has separated from the uterine wall and has been delivered. This prevents retention of the placenta, i.e. the after-birth not being pushed out. Once the child has been born, his body receives oxygen via his lungs and nourishment via his mouth. This all happens naturally and harmoniously as long as mother and child are given enough time and a peaceful environment. The powerful contractions of the uterus during the expulsion phase flood the mother and child with large amounts of the hormone oxytocin. Thus, both mother and child are prepared in the best way possible for their first sensate experience, skin-on-skin and face-to-face. Biologically, mother and child are inherently prepared to bond completely with each other as soon as the child has left the security of the womb.

The physical act of childbirth is a profound moment for both mother and child. The child has to re-orient himself towards his mother in the vastness of a strange world. After the newborn child has given up his previous source of nourishment, the placenta, he seeks and finds a new bond at his mother's breast. When he arrives in the world he has only one want and need: his mother. She is his only safe haven because, as a foetus, he has developed an intense emotional and sensory connection with her. As the child is unable to look after himself, his survival depends on him developing a strong bond with his mother. Thus, the newborn child is not only ready to bond, but is actually born with a powerful bonding expectation. The bond with the mother is biologically and psychologically the strongest, most important and intense bond that we humans enter into in our lives. (Ruppert 2012) Strictly speaking, the child's survival depends on a successful bond with his mother because he is unable to fend for himself. In his mother's womb the child has come to know the familiar voice of his mother, her smell, the way she moves, her heartbeat and the rhythm of her breathing and unfailingly recognises her. This tiny being can only focus all his senses on her because his instincts tell him that with his mother is where he should be, and where he can bond. But in order for that to happen there must be no disturbance to the first meeting between mother and child. It takes time – at least two hours – a relaxed atmosphere, a quiet, warm room with subdued lighting and understanding, sensitive people around. The whole birth process can be gently and happily completed in a safe place such as this. Together, mother and child form a new emotional and physically-sensual entity that replaces the prenatal bond and allows another bond to form between them. It is extremely important that this highly sensitive phase is not interrupted in any way so as to ensure a successful transition from the prenatal to the postnatal mother-child bond. The birth process is only complete when the child has found his place at his mother's breast of his own accord and has begun to suckle.

It is essential for the child's wellbeing and his healthy physical, emotional and mental development that he successfully re-bonds with his mother. Unfortunately, however, in many places even today people are still unaware of the immense importance of this postnatal mother-child bonding or of its consequences, with the result that the process is regularly and painfully interrupted.

Knowledge of the natural process of postnatal re-bonding has increased enormously in the last few years. Christine Lang (2009) recommends not putting the newborn baby directly onto the mother's belly but giving the mother time and space to gather her child herself. Initially, the midwife should place the baby carefully onto a warm towel between the mother's legs. During the final birth phase the mother is sunk into deep inward concentration and needs time before she can think about anything external following her exhausting labour during the expulsion phase. Studies have shown (Kirkilionis 2008, Odent 2006) that mothers usually touch their children gently with the tips of their fingers first, then stroke them with the palms of their hands and only then place the newborn child on their belly. This way the mother has time for the first eye contact with her child, time for her first physical contact and time to gather the newborn to herself in the first close skin-on-skin contact. This way of making contact with her child seems to be innate maternal behaviour. The father behaves in a similar way if he is the first to touch his child because the mother is still under anaesthetic following a Caesarean.

With premature babies it is noticeable that the parents only really accept their child after they have stroked him with their hands. (Kirikilionis 2008) Marshall and Phyllis Klaus (2000) write that every baby is born with the innate ability to make his own way to his mother's breast, to take hold of the nipple in his mouth on his own and to suckle. After the exhausting birth the newborn normally rests to begin with and after about 30 to 40 minutes begins to make spontaneous sucking movements and to use his arms and legs to make his way to the breast. He will find the breast on his own with no assistance. It appears to be his sense of smell that shows him the way to the nipple because the amniotic fluid contains a substance similar to a certain breast secretion. The newborn baby knows at birth what his mother smells and tastes like. Unfortunately it is rare in modern birth practice for the newborn baby to be given the chance to connect with his mother's breast himself.

Ray Castellino (2013) is of the opinion that every baby knows how to be born and how to re-bond. Mother and child together start the birth process and carry it out.

Suckling at the breast stimulates the production of colostrum (the pre-milk). This is the nourishment the newborn child needs until the milk comes in a few days later. Michel Odent writes (2006) that colostrum is high in unsaturated fatty acids, vitamins and minerals. It also contains a large amount of antibodies, immune cells and other immuno-active substances that protect the newborn child from disease and help to develop healthy intestinal microflora.

The skin of many newborns is covered with a whitish layer, vernix. This is secreted by the sebaceous glands that are formed from about the 17th week of pregnancy and protect the baby's skin from drying out in the amniotic fluid in the womb. It also has a function after birth, which is to protect the baby from bacterial skin infections in the first few days and also to help keep the baby warm. It should therefore not be cleaned off after the birth. It will gradually be absorbed by the baby's skin.

9.2 The father's role in the birth and bonding process

During the first birth phases the father's presence can be an important support for the expectant mother. Often the fathers go to the antenatal classes as well and are involved early on in the birth process. They can then give the mother good support while she is giving birth, and offer her reassurance and emotional assistance. The level of oxytocin in the father's blood has also been found to increase if he is present at the birth, which makes him particularly sensitive and helps him to enter into a loving bond with his child.

A new father who had a good bonding relationship with his mother himself instinctively knows that his newborn child's relationship to his mother is more important than his wife's relationship to him. He will therefore remain in the background during the sensitive phase of re-bonding. His quiet, affectionate and loving presence provides a safe, protective space for the mother to concentrate on re-bonding with her newborn child in peace and quiet. Only when the child has arrived at the mother's breast and has melted into his mother's gaze can he begin, from this place of safety, to react with curiosity to having contact with his father. If the mother receives support in this way from her partner, her contact with the child will be more sensitive, and the mother-child bond will be closer. (Castellino 2013) If a baby is unable to fulfil his primary need to bond with his mother (if, for example, the mother were to die at birth or not be present emotionally) the child will experience a symbiotic trauma, even if the father is there and ready to bond with him. The child will always endeavour to bond primarily with the mother because he was totally geared to this bonding during pregnancy. The father is the secondary bonding partner and always takes second place to the mother as far as bonding is concerned. (Ruppert 2014) The bond between father and child is different and has a quality of its own, but can never replace the bond with the mother. In order for the father to give the child security and be a loving bonding partner, it is important for him to be involved during the pregnancy, the birth and post birth care of the baby.

9.3 A successful separation and re-bonding

I would now like to invite you to imagine the experience of a newborn baby from the moment his small body emerges from the birth canal to the moment he arrives contentedly at his mother's breast. Let us assume that we are talking about a baby endowed with all his amazing senses and abilities, who senses and feels everything that happens to him during this time. So at this moment we experience how we have worked our way out of our mother's womb. Careful hands receive us gently and lay us down onto a warm blanket between our mother's legs. A warm cloth is laid over us so that we are not cold. It is pleasantly quiet in these unfamiliar surroundings. A warm, diffuse light surrounds us and we can slowly open our eyes and accustom ourselves to the light of the world. The first thing we see is the eyes of our mother as she leans down to greet us. Her look of love pierces through to the depths of our being and we sink into these eyes that we have never seen before, but which are so familiar to us. We feel welcomed and accepted. To our delight she begins to touch us very gently with the tips of her fingers. Completely trusting, we open our senses to see what happens next. She lays her warm, soft hands on our body and strokes our skin. Finally she takes us gently and safely in both hands and lays us on her belly. She is showing us that she has decided to hold us very close to her. We snuggle into her body, listen to the beating of her heart, feel the softness of her body, and smell the scent of her skin. It is all so familiar. We want and need nothing other than this comforting warmth and security, the protection and safety of our mother. We can relax completely and rest after the exhausting effort of our birth. There is nothing anywhere that scares us or frightens us. We feel secure and protected here in our home. Our mother is relaxed and we enjoy the wonderful feeling of our skin on hers. We almost melt into her. Her heartbeat and the gentle raising and lowering movement of her body to the rhythm of her breathing soothe us, and all the commotion of the last few hours can gradually disperse. We are awake and calm; nothing escapes our notice. Our eyes are wide open; we look and listen. Everything is new. Our mother's skin temperature rises by one or two degrees so that we are not cold. Our mother whispers loving words to us. She expresses her joy over and over again that we are there, telling us how beautiful we are and how much she has longed to hold her sweet baby in her arms. We are ready to open ourselves completely and give all our love to our mother. While we lie together quietly, she holds us with her hands and strokes us gently. The room is filled with her quiet presence and everyone present is moved by this first meeting.

We are still attached to the placenta by the umbilical cord. Our lungs have not yet unfolded and we can't breathe on our own yet. After a while we feel how our breast slowly begins to rise and fall. Our lungs start to unfold and air streams through the air sacs. Soon we are breathing regularly and our body is supplied with oxygen. At the same time our blood circulation changes all by itself. The umbilical cord only stops gently pulsating and finally collapses when our breathing and circulation are stable. We are then no longer dependent on it and can bid farewell to our old supply organ, the placenta. It comes away and is also born with a strong contraction. That is then the right moment to cut the umbilical cord.

We know instinctively that we have to find our future source of nourishment; now we have to make our own way to our mother's breast. From the nipples we can smell the familiar scent of the amniotic fluid. Although we have only just been born, we are already able to raise our head slightly in a searching movement and to support ourselves a little bit with our arms, followed by a push from our legs. We search, following the scent, until we can encircle the nipple with our mouth. Then we begin to suckle strongly. We are not the only ones happy and contented with our achievement; our mother is also proud to see how we bond with her of our own accord. The whole stress of birth is left behind when we suckle at her breast. We let go and sleep contentedly. After we have rested, we are curious about our father. Now we really want to get to know him as well. We have fulfilled our longing and our need to arrive safely with our mother; now we want to find ourselves in our father's eyes. He has always been there, quietly, in the background. Our mother was able to lean on him for support and security so that she could concentrate completely on us and our bonding process. Now our father takes us lovingly into his arms. He is very emotional and we gaze into each other's eyes for a long time. Now we are examined and dressed and our father brings us back and places us in our mother's arms. Now both look at us deeply and lovingly.

Every time we suckle at our mother's breast she produces the hormone prolactin (a hormone that enables milk production) so that after just a few days her milk comes in. That ensures our nourishment.

By finding and attaching to the breast ourselves we have completed the bonding process and the birth has reached a good conclusion. Now we have finally arrived with our mother and the initial bond of love is forged. Until the normal milk is available we are completely satisfied by the yellowish, extremely nourishing colostrum that makes us strong and resilient.

In our first days of life we enjoy round-the-clock close physical contact with our mother. Our favourite position is on her belly or tucked between her arm and her breast. We are nourished by her scent and her loving gaze; we listen to her tender voice and feel completely safe. She lives completely for us. We can feel how she kisses our face and hands with joy, sniffs our scent, talks to us when she changes our nappy, caresses us and strokes our soft skin.

Because we are always together, we get to know each other quickly. Mummy soon knows exactly what we need to be happy. The smallest signals tell her when we're hungry. That's when we start to move our head from side to side, our mouth opens and our little tongue licks our lips as we make sucking movements. Our sucking shows our mother that we need her milk. Before the hunger is too intense and we start to cry, she puts us to her breast and we can suckle to our heart's content. Our mother's milk is ready for us whenever and wherever we want it; it is always the right temperature and contains everything we need for a healthy development. Suckling and sucking at her breast give our mother and us an incomparable feeling of pleasure that runs through our whole body. We feel totally content.

Our mother sensitively registers our every need for nourishment, care, security and contact, and fulfils them all happily and quickly. We are completely safe within her love. Our bond strengthens and deepens in the next weeks and months in just the same way as the successful re-bonding after the birth. We are certain: we belong together. It is this wonderful love that gives our mother the strength to be there for us day and night. She is our safe haven, the embodiment of peace and security. We can experience from the very start that our deeply rooted need for unconditional love and affection is fulfilled all the time and that we are safe with our mother, in our family – and therefore in the world.

9.4 Trauma during the final birth phase

Unfortunately this ideal picture of a successful re-bonding does not correspond with the reality of giving birth in our hospitals. In the '50s we started having fewer home births, and moved all births into clinics, even non-risk births. Breastfeeding was not encouraged. Through the radical separation from the mother, newborn babies were traumatised. Thomas Harms (2013) writes that a baby does not have any adjustment mechanism to allow it to understand why the mother is no longer there. There is no psychophysiological defence strategy against lack of bonding with the mother.

A physiological weakness, in particular a weakness of the immune system, is inherent in this psychological weakness and quite a few children therefore suffer from diverse postnatal infections. It used to be thought that the germs in the postnatal room were responsible for this and as a consequence children were separated yet more rigorously from their mothers.

Increasing rationalisation and use of technology in delivery room, and a disregard for the essential needs of mother and child, have led to millions of babies being traumatised, some of them severely, in the last few decades. The child used to be held by his feet immediately following birth. A smack on the bottom ensured that the child cried, because the assumption was that this made the lungs open more quickly. The umbilical cord used to be cut immediately. The child was examined and taken off to the baby unit without having any contact with the mother. Often the first time mothers saw their child was after 24 hours had passed, and while they remained in the clinic they only saw them after that at set feeding times.

It was only in the late '80s that interest in natural birth grew, with mothers able to follow their natural instincts, technology and medication being used less, and cosy and comfortable surroundings being more available. Some hospitals introduced 'rooming-in', where the child was not taken to a baby unit, but stayed next to the mother day and night, and the mother cared for him. This is now standard procedure, but the importance of re-bonding immediately after birth is still ignored to a great extent through ignorance.

Even today the birth process is considered to be complete once the child has been pushed out of the birth canal. In the hectic activity of a hospital there is no time for mother and child to bond gently. It is true that the child is usually laid on the mother's breast, and some time is allowed to elapse before the umbilical cord is cut, but even so everything is still far too rushed. The placenta is delivered, any injuries to the mother (for example an episiotomy) have to be treated, the child is medically examined and reports are written. It is usual for the child to be routinely separated from the mother when they are born. Weighing, measuring, etc. are paramount and the timetable does not allow for any delay.

Technology used in the delivery room comes mostly with glaring lights. There is a general coming and going of medical staff. Busy, noisy activity creates an unsettled atmosphere. The bonding process between mother and child is extremely sensitive and prone to disruptions and it requires absolute peace and quiet, and a feeling of safety. Loud noises, bright lights, hectic time pressure, sterile surroundings and lack of intimacy greatly unsettle mother and child, who are frequently distracted by the events going on around them. It is therefore not possible for them to abandon themselves to the joy of their first meeting. They do not find one another, and the postnatal re-bonding process is unsuccessful. They lose this unique opportunity, and for the child in particular this causes a huge amount of stress, and at worst a traumatisation.

9.5 A traumatically-interrupted bonding process

After going through the ideal sequence of events leading to the successful re-bonding of mother and child, I should like to take you through a scenario which has been typical of the birth process since the 50s, in order to highlight the traumatisation that mother and child might suffer in the worst case during this phase. We will again follow events from the perspective of the newborn child.

We have passed through the birth canal and have been received into the world by the powerful grip of hands in rubber gloves. Immediately our umbilical cord is cut, shutting off the dependably flowing circulation from the placenta and the connection to our previous source of nourishment. We do not know what is happening to us. We are picked up by the feet and swung up into the air, head downwards. We are given a slap on the bottom as a welcome. The shock frightens us to the core and our whole body immediately tenses up; a wave of panic floods over us. Our stomach tightens and we are in danger of suffocating. Our body instantly activates an acute emergency programme. Our level of adrenalin shoots up. We throw our arms outwards, our lungs inflate and the incoming air burns like fire inside us. With a cry we gasp out our first breath. Our small body curls up with fright and shock to try and fend off this pain. Our cry incorporates our whole tension, fear and anger. All the people there take no notice; on the contrary, they congratulate our mother on having a child with such a strong voice. We have no clue, nothing we can use as orientation. The glaring lights dazzle us, the loud noises, the hustle and bustle and all the strange people round us confuse and frighten us. We are overcome with fear and we are powerless to do anything. We look into masked faces and emotionless eyes. Our gender is determined and after thorough examination we are declared healthy – or not. We cannot exchange a single glance

167

with our mother, nor receive a single touch from her. We are taken away, examined by a stranger, weighed and measured, bathed and dressed. Instead of being looked at lovingly by our mother, our eyelids are pulled up and drops of a burning, stinging and cold liquid are put into our eyes (silver nitrate solution, also known as lunar caustic or lapis infernalis, to prevent bacterial eye infections). The shock courses through us. Our little feet are very cold; we stiffen and our body is under extreme strain. An eternity of disorientation begins; we might even have to spend the whole night alone in strange surroundings. It's no wonder if we give up and collapse, numbed.

At some point this eternity ends and we are taken to our mother. At long last she can hold us in her arms for the first time. She is very unsure and does not really know how to hold us. She tries to make eye contact with us. The eyes looking at us are rather sad, exhausted and scared; that makes us very sad. Now we are given a bottle; if we are very lucky, the breast. But that is not usual. The bottle is preferred by conventional medicine. Since being in the world we have had no peace. Finally, in our mother's arms, we can feel secure and relax a little while we are drinking. It's familiar here and warm; this is where we belong.

But as soon as we've drunk our quota of milk the nurse takes us away from our mother again and carries us into the agonizing loneliness of the baby unit and puts us in a bed that is much too big and empty, under neon lights, in the fumes of disinfectant. We cry but our crying is not heard. We feel lost in the fear and loneliness that fills our whole world. Without our mother we'll die; we know that with every fibre of our being. And our mother never comes.

The futile struggle has to stop before we die of overstimulation. The turmoil inside us then stops immediately because we are not aware of our body any more. We feel no mortal fear, no despair, no overwhelming pain of loneliness; we feel nothing. All the terrible, threatening feelings are severed as if with a sharp knife, and buried deep within our psyche, unreachable. The apathy is merciful. We have surrendered to our fate. No crying, no screaming, only exhaustion and resignation. We wake, we sleep, we are taken to our mother every four hours, given our food and taken away again.

We are not allowed to be in contact with our father yet. A nurse holds us, and he is allowed to see us through a pane of glass. When will we finally be allowed to feel him as well? When will we be allowed to look into his eyes, smell him and hear his voice?

At some point we leave the hospital with our parents, but nothing much changes even though we are at home. Our desolate situation continues. Parenting advice warns against spoiling children. The four-hourly feeding has to be strictly adhered to. If you want to have a child who is easy to look after, you should stick to a routine. As before, we lie alone in our bed, day and night. It's supposed to be a peaceful, secluded room so that the child's sleep isn't disturbed – and most importantly, mother's and father's sleep as well. We have quickly learnt that crying is not only useless but makes everything worse. If we want to be with our Mummy we have to be quiet and good. If you cry, you have to go to bed. We long for her so much, so urgently, we need to be close to her, we need her to care for us, to talk to us. We don't want anything else – just to be with her. So we are good. When we wake up in the night in our secluded room we are afraid and we stare into the dark until we go to sleep again. We sleep a lot and that pleases our mother and the whole family: we're so easy to look after! What a good idea, to stick to the parenting advice!

If we experience our birth in this way with our needs being ignored and profoundly violated – our natural needs for complete loving care, constant physical closeness, stimulating contact, support, safety and secure mother bonding – then we experience a symbiotic trauma.

Whole generations of children have suffered all their lives from the serious consequences of the symbiotic trauma they experienced during the pregnancy, during birth or during the separation and re-bonding phase. The fact that re-bonding with the mother after birth has either not taken place or been interrupted means that their psychological and physical health is also affected. Emotionality, ability to feel sensation and enter into relationships cannot develop normally. Current hospital practice with its lack of regard for sensitive processes is one of the reasons for the wide scale spread of symbiotic trauma. It is a vicious circle. The babies who were the victims become today's perpetrators in obstetrics.

9.6 Help for children with a symbiotic trauma

Most people alive today have been deeply hurt at birth in their crucial need to bond with their one source of security and support, their mother. Influenced by commonly held ideas, mothers also treated their children at home in a way that rejected the child's bonding need. They did not dare to follow their instincts and intuition and, without knowing or planning it, harmed their children. The consequences of the symbiotic trauma were not picked up and attenuated, and so the traumatic splitting continued.

The symbiotic bonding with the mother is unique and there is no way of making up for it in adult life. Even a loving, understanding partner is unable to satisfy this need later. Our primal yearning for our mother's sensitive care, for unconditional acceptance as well as emotional and physical closeness remains, though it may be unconscious. He still exists, hidden deep inside, the child left alone in the nursery and the children's room, he is still crying and mortally afraid. Split off from him, and buried deep within his unconscious, are all the overwhelming traumatic feelings of helplessness, powerlessness, anger and despair. This child is consumed with longing for his mother all his life, and seeks her in every person with whom he tries to bond. In this way unconscious parts of his personality always influence his behaviour and experiences, in particular his relationships with partners and children.

These insights into multi-generational psychotraumatology (Ruppert 2008, 2011, 2012, 2014) are regularly illustrated in the 'Constellation of the Intention'. Representatives of the client's early childhood personality parts in the constellation bear out this experience in an alarming way. They express feelings of infinite loneliness, nameless fear and profound despair, and in addition their unfulfilled longing to give and receive love – from their mother. Their birth long ago and the emotional experiences of their early childhood years are continuously lived through in the present. During constellation work, only a cautious approach enables an individual to open up to his own overwhelming feelings of pain and mortal fear and to experience what he must have felt as a newborn child. But it is only if we access the unresolved feelings that we can integrate these experiences into our consciousness. Continual therapeutic support over a considerable length of time is necessary to provide the secure space that is needed for this healing process that requires a great deal of courage and strength.

Healing the early wound

Let me make use of a client's constellation experience to illustrate how it is possible to identify and heal the early wound. From the very beginning this client had not received any loving care from her mother and had therefore suffered a symbiotic trauma. In her trauma therapy process, which was already quite advanced, the client came to the group and her intention was to encounter the child within her who had experienced intense rejection from her mother. The constellation process was remarkably reminiscent of a successful natural bonding between mother and child at birth.

Immediately the (female) representative of the intention lay down on the floor in the middle of the room and curled up. It was clear that the representative was depicting the traumatised child part. The client sat down in front of her and began to touch the representative's body gently with her fingertips. She closely watched the movements that her touch produced. Then she used the palm of her hand and began to stroke the body gently. Ultimately, she snuggled up against the representative's back. They lay quietly like this for some time, in close physical contact. Everyone felt the importance of what was happening and the atmosphere in the room was deeply touching. A little later, the representative of the intention slowly turned round and faced the client and for the first time looked deeply into her eyes. The client then began to whimper quietly and with profound sorrow, and ultimately both were crying with joy and emotion. They lay like that for a while, still hugging one another tightly, and gazing into each other's eyes as if they were recognising and finding one another again. A re-bonding process has taken place here to a traumatised and split child part through eye contact and physical touch. The client was ready to open herself again to the past pain and to give herself the longed-for closeness, attention, loving tenderness and sensitive care she would have needed so badly from her mother.

Only when we have emotionally and physically lived through and integrated our traumatising experiences in pregnancy, at birth and in the bonding phase with our mother, are we able to regain the life energy bound up in this. Primordial vitality, joie de vivre, emotional resonance ability and the re-found good sense of self give our lives their own individual meaning. And only if we develop real understanding, loving acceptance and patience, sensitivity and tenderness towards ourselves are we really able to enter into relationships with other people in a healthy way, so that our encounters give birth to joy and fulfilment.

10
Miscarriages and stillbirths as trauma

Cordula Schulte

All children who are born dead are 'born silent'. I use this phrase instead of the usual terms 'miscarriage' and 'stillbirth'. Silence about them is also commonplace after their death. My first child died 35 years ago from lack of oxygen one day before the due date. This event changed my life dramatically. A fundamental naivety or innocence had given way to the certainty that there are events over which we humans have no influence, but which change our lives totally. I have experienced the depths of despair, and emerged thanks to a process of intense work. My development has been shaped in the last few years by the 'Constellation of the Intention' method. The fact that I am today working in my own trauma therapy practice can definitely be attributed to my own experiences.

Women who have experienced a miscarriage or stillbirth tend to conceal this trauma, or at least qualify it. "It's such a long time ago", "I came to terms with it ages ago", "I've got lovely healthy children now", "Who knows, perhaps it was for the best", and many other thoughts contribute to the magnitude of this loss trauma not being properly realised. Mothers have words for them like 'star children' or 'butterfly children' and find some comfort in not forgetting the child who has 'disappeared'. An experience such as this, and the pain of the loss involved, is frequently not seen as a psychological trauma.

Kerstin

Kerstin comes to my practice because she feels inadequate in many ways. She is an attractive woman and her manner is very quiet and withdrawn. Her reason for wanting psychotherapy does not become clear during the initial consultation. She mentions in passing that she had a miscarriage years before, but amazingly enough this did not matter to her. She even laughed about it in hospital. Her intention is the wish "to be able to accept herself as important". I allow myself to be set up as representative for her intention and go immediately to a door recess to seek shelter. There I have the feeling that I have to orientate myself by means of external objects and a sense of order. Kerstin remains standing alone in the middle of the room and we do not have any contact with each other. She does not realise that she is completely on her own there. After standing a while in silence Kerstin describes herself as an empty husk. During the constellation it becomes evident that Kerstin has lost all contact with her own feelings, such as her pain and sorrow, but also her joy. Her survival strategy is "I will put my life in order" so that the emptiness is not continuously noticeable, and she can instead direct her attention towards the outside world. In Kerstin's constellation, 'order' refers to external order as well as the ordering of objects. While Kerstin remains in this survival mechanism she is unable to engage with herself or with her feelings concerning the loss of her stillborn child.

10.1 The loss of a child – a loss trauma

A loss trauma occurs with the loss of, or separation from, a person to whom the individual has psychologically bonded. The most profound loss trauma for a child is the death of her mother, and for a mother the death of her child. This includes miscarriages and stillbirths. Continuous sorrow and depression can indicate a loss trauma. "The unbearable loss of a person who is unconditionally loved leads to an insoluble psychological conflict and an inner rift. Accepting the loss as reality and mourning it would mean accepting that this person has gone for good and will not return. Psychological survival mechanisms are initiated, because the pain

and the fear of finality at the moment of loss are unbearable".
(Ruppert 2011, p. 102)

10.2 Figures – Data – Facts

If a woman loses her child before the 22nd pregnancy week or the
baby weighs less than 500g, the term used is 'miscarriage' and
until recently the miscarriage was disposed of with the other
hospital rubbish. Whether the dead foetus was birthed naturally or
had to be removed was irrelevant. Before the 12th week it is
referred to as an early miscarriage and up to the 22nd week it is
called a late miscarriage. After that it is referred to as a premature
birth or a stillbirth. The longer the pregnancy continues, the less
risk there is of a miscarriage; during the first few weeks the risk
is 20%, which decreases to about 1% after week 18. As recently
as the 1980s it was normal for the foetus to be 'disposed of' –
regardless of the pregnancy week or the child's birth weight.
Miscarriages were the property of the hospital and the parents did
not have the right to bury their child.

The risk of a miscarriage, ectopic pregnancy or stillbirth,
taken over the whole length of a pregnancy, is about 13%. The
risk for 20- to 24-year-old women is about 9% but increases
considerably from 35 years onwards and for 42-year-old women
the risk is 54%, rising to 84% for 48-year-old women. According
to the Federal Statistical Office (Statistisches Bundesamt), 673,544
children were born in Germany in 2012. We can assume that the
risk of a stillbirth today is approximately 1% to 2% in Germany;
that is about 1,000 children a year or three stillbirths a day. In the
1950s about 20 in every 1,000 births were stillbirths.

At the end of the 1980s people's attitude changed, thanks to
the commitment of many individuals concerned, including
midwives and psychologists, and the way the dead child was
treated before, during and after the birth was recognised as being
of huge importance for a successful mourning process. The
change in attitude was due in part to the recommendations of the
psychologist and author Hannah Lothrop (1945–2000), who in
1991 published her book *Gute Hoffnung-Jähes Ende* [Happily

expecting – sudden end] based on her own personal experiences, and initiated a transformation in the support offered to parents with miscarriages and stillbirths. (Lothrop 2004) Women began not only to perceive their pain and sorrow, but also allowed themselves to show their feelings in public and talk about them.

Many self-help groups were formed which succeeded in, amongst other things, introducing rooms in hospitals that were set aside for mourning. Nowadays children with a weight in excess of 1000g who are stillborn are buried in cemeteries; in some states this applies in excess of 500g.

From May 2013 the regulations in Germany relating to births, marriages and deaths were changed to allow individuals to apply to the civil registry office for a miscarriage to be officially registered. This was not previously possible.

10.3 Therapeutic practice

Female clients come to my therapeutic practice with the most diverse issues: relationship conflicts such as difficulties in a work context, partnership issues, problems with the children, loss anxiety or non-specific anxiety, depression, drug abuse, psychosomatic symptoms – which appear to have nothing to do with miscarriage or stillbirth, but which point to an unresolved and complicated source of sorrow. In initial consultations or in the work of constellations with the women concerned, a stillbirth or, more frequently, a miscarriage is mentioned 'in passing', as if this were something the women have come to terms with quite quickly. When questioned more closely, it usually takes some time for the client to access this event again and for her actual feelings to be allowed to surface. Once accessed, the extended medical history often shows that in the client's own life or in her family history there have been miscarriages or stillbirths at different stages of pregnancy. These events are often not clearly communicated, but only mentioned by the clients themselves or their mothers or grandmothers when they are asked directly. In such cases a genogram shows clearly whether there is an aborted child, a miscarriage or a stillbirth in the family system.

Carola

Carola comes to my practice with a work-related question. Her employer had offered her a managerial position and she had taken it on. However, although she was happy with her new position, she also feared failure and not being able to do this demanding job properly. When asked about private issues it turned out that Carola had had two miscarriages in the last few years and the second one in particular had caused her great distress. She never mentioned these pregnancies in her work environment. She behaved as if nothing had happened.

When working with the intention "I would like to separate my career issue and me" it became clear that she had not finished processing these traumatic experiences despite a course of talking therapy. Her pain at the loss, and her apparent inability to have children, still have an effect on all areas of her life. Carola wanted to keep this 'failure' away from her professional life. However, that wasn't possible, and seemed to be a huge mountain that could not be climbed by a small child.

In the constellation Carola only gradually comes into contact with her 'inner child' who, according to her, doesn't understand anything, was previously unseen, and above all is not allowed to feel anything. When Carola was two years old her mother had died and she had not been allowed to grieve for her loss out of consideration for her father. After this painful occurrence, the little child's life was simply supposed to continue, and her sorrow had to be hidden for decades. Feelings such as powerlessness, helplessness, bewilderment and sorrow were not allowed. And for the adult Carola nothing had changed.

In further therapy, Carola more and more frequently encountered personality parts that are connected to pain and sorrow, but are not in contact with each other, rather seeming to each other to be 'like an only child'. As well as accepting of her deep sorrow, she is now able to contact her child part that existed before the trauma. She was able to remember positive feelings associated with her mother. In this way the familiar feeling of secure bonding was re-activated.

10.4 Miscarriages and stillbirths in the family

Clinical findings show that analysing a profound loss also re-activates earlier unresolved and unprocessed losses such as early traumatic experiences, the untimely death of parents, siblings or previous miscarriages. (Bowlby 1987) This is one of the principal reasons people fear processing the trauma caused by the death of a child. It is partly an unconscious fear of not knowing what will come to the surface when working on suppressed emotions, and partly how the woman concerned will be able to cope with these insights.

It frequently becomes apparent that expectant mothers are barely in touch with their body awareness, with their own maternal feelings, their awareness of the growing child and his wellbeing and emotional state. This is also reflected in the high rate of Caesareans. Advice is sought in books, doctors' recommendations are followed, and suggestions from people close to them are put into practice, people who themselves also have no contact to their inner self, and who pass on their limited perception as an assumed reality. Thus, the attachment to the child is 'imagined' but not experienced.

Vera

> Vera seeks my advice about her difficulty in making decisions at work and at home. This has led to symptoms of exhaustion. Vera feels massively under internal pressure. After a few sessions she talks about her first pregnancy, which was a good and stress-free time when she experienced her child's development in her body. The child was planned and all the check-ups promised a trouble-free pregnancy. Two days before the due date her gynaecologist's examination showed that the birth process had begun but that there would still be some time to go before the birth of the child, who was probably going to be quite big. The doctor advised her to spend this waiting period in the comfort of home, especially as the delivery room was overrun. The next day irregular contractions started and the expectant mother waited for the 'right' moment to go to the hospital, although she wasn't sure how to recognise that the moment had arrived.

While she was waiting for the birth Vera had a vague 'bad' feeling because the child didn't seem to be moving, however, she couldn't quite put her finger on anything and thought that it was 'probably normal'. Her husband only drove her to hospital when the irregular contractions started. The midwife couldn't find any heartbeat and the doctor couldn't find any sign of life either so they assumed that the child had died in the womb.

A 12-hour wait now began, during which labour was induced and the mother was given painkillers and sedatives. Following a natural birth a girl weighing 4.5Kg was stillborn. Examinations did not reveal any pathological findings. Vera tells me that she was able to see her daughter at birth and that she had the feeling as if her daughter were herself, that it was her own birth. She thought, like all mothers, that her daughter was beautiful and talked about feelings such as pride at her 'achievement', and the thought that giving birth wasn't terrible, just extremely exhausting. She said it was dreadful giving birth to a dead child. After peremptory condolences the doctors advised taking the girl to the pathology unit where the cause of death would be investigated. They advised against a burial so that the mother could come to terms more easily with what had happened. Thus, the child was 'disposed of'. Strong medication prevented Vera from taking part in the decision-making process properly. In a constellation it transpired that, even when Vera was a child, her mother had always referred to Vera's birth as a terrible event when she 'almost died' from lack of oxygen and delays, and had had to be given special treatment. She'd frequently had to listen to this story as a child. This account meant that for Vera giving birth was full of anxiety, not the pregnancy. The fact that she was severely traumatised at birth and in the following three days when she was separated from her mother had never been a focus or an issue for her.

10.5 The process of bonding during pregnancy

Up until the start of the 1980s no psychotherapy or other professional assistance was offered following such a severe loss trauma. Besides the mother not being able to say goodbye to her dead child, she was not able to work through her own trauma, which was caused by this event, in the ensuing years. In this way the birth cast a shadow over her further life and her later pregnancies.

What is the explanation for what used to be regarded as the 'normal approach'? It was thought that the mother would experience less pain and sorrow if she were prevented from forming a bond with her child. For the same reason it was not supposed to be talked about later. The idea was to behave as if nothing had happened. Don't touch it! Get it over and done with as quickly as possible so that life can return to 'normal'. The fact that this attitude is questionable is shown by the many mothers who still, years later, are burdened by not having had the chance to say goodbye to their dead child, and who suffer from not having been able to work through the resulting trauma. This attitude only makes sense if one assumes that the attachment between mother and child begins after the birth, and does not happen during the pregnancy. We now know that bonding patterns are already programmed in the interactions between mother and child in the womb, and play a crucial role in prenatal brain development. Thus the newborn baby's personality and his self-regulation have been shaped before he was born. In his book *Der frühe Verlust eines Kindes* [The early loss of a child] Professor Beutel describes three prenatal phases in the development of readiness to bond, which are summarised below: (Beutel 2002, p. 9)

- From conception to the child's first movements (4 to 4½ months) he describes increased emotional lability in the mother, which is also connected with the physical changes taking place.
- As of the first noticeable movements (from the 4th to 5th month) the readiness to bond is significantly increased. This can trigger fear of separation and loss.
- In the third phase of pregnancy as the expectant mother prepares to give birth to her child, the mother already has a firm picture of her child's personality and temperament, which influences how she experiences her child.

10.6 Replacement children and disruptions to the readiness for bonding

"Various forms of compensation also function as survival strategies, for example another child is conceived to take the place of a child who has died". (Ruppert 2014, p. 87) The term used for children who are born following the mother having had a stillbirth or miscarriage is 'replacement children', and the pregnancy is classified as 'at risk'. If the mother is traumatised by the loss of her child during the previous pregnancy, her ability to bond with the later child will be affected. She is unable to give him sufficient emotional care, which will result in a symbiotic trauma with all its manifestations in the replacement child. (Ruppert 2012, p. 8)

The expectant mother of a replacement child is usually unable to open herself emotionally to her child during the pregnancy. On the one hand she is unconsciously avoiding contact with her own traumatised parts, and on the other she is afraid of a further loss, which she cannot rule out because of what happened previously. She therefore experiences ambivalence, resulting in an insecure attachment that is always linked to stress and helplessness. She is stressed by her previous birth experience if there was no opportunity to grieve. "Will it all go well this time?" "Will I notice if something isn't right?" "Can I allow myself to become involved with the child in my womb?" Many mothers who have lost a child in pregnancy can only relax when they are past the stage at which the previous pregnancy ended. Thus, a mother whose child died after nine months of pregnancy can only bond with her replacement child following that child's birth. Until that point is reached she is not prepared to bond with her child because she cannot feel secure.

Corinna

Corinna has come to my practice because of vague feelings of fear and panic attacks. She tells me that she is always confronted with fear when dealing with her children. Following the loss of an unborn child she chose the same doctor for her 'replacement child' because she hoped he would take particular care of her so that the same thing didn't happen again. She also gave an earlier date for her last period so that her due date was earlier as well. This hope and the extra window of time she had given herself enabled her to carry on from month to month.

Throughout her pregnancy Corinna was afraid that something could happen again, and she was unable to develop a natural and unstressed bond with the child in her womb. Even after the birth of her healthy child, her relationship with her child was still influenced by the previous pregnancy in a way that manifested itself as over-protection and a difficulty in becoming emotionally involved with this 'replacement' child.

This example illustrates the inability of women who have suffered such a loss to respond to their children's needs in a natural and unbiased way. They are too afraid that a close bond will always hold the danger of another loss. As a result, 'replacement' children are looked after well, but often the necessary emotional bond cannot be created or, at best, only years later when they have worked on their own trauma in therapy. This behaviour has far-reaching consequences for the 'replacement' children themselves. An individual whose mother has lost a child in a previous pregnancy experiences their mother's grief directly and relates their mother's behaviour to themselves.

Sabine

Sabine comes to my practice because she has problems with her two-year old son. He won't settle down at night and cries until he goes to sleep from exhaustion. The problems have been going on since he was born. Sabine has read various books on the subject and tried to follow their advice. When her child is still not asleep after 20 minutes, she starts to feel aggression. She has to leave the room. In such situations she regrets ever having become a mother. Sabine herself is the child of a traumatised mother. She has tried in vain to reach her mother emotionally. Sabine tells me that her mother had given birth to a stillborn son before she was born, and she always had the feeling that she was a 'replacement child'.

Following a stillbirth mothers are sometimes completely unable to get involved with another child and his needs. As they develop, these children blame themselves because they cannot replace the sibling who has died, and they direct their mother's grief onto themselves. They feel inadequate, and every further bonding relationship becomes more difficult for them.

Ingrid

> Ingrid takes part in one of my constellation groups. After her first child was stillborn she was really afraid that something could go wrong with her second pregnancy. Her first birth experience had made her unable to give birth naturally to her second child. Even after many hours of labour and contractions the birth process was not progressing at all and she had to have a Caesarean. Ingrid wanted to breastfeed her daughter but every time she offered her the breast her daughter cried and tensed her body. This happened repeatedly and Ingrid gave up wanting to breastfeed because she couldn't bear to hear her daughter crying like that. She followed the advice of the neonatal nurse and stopped breastfeeding after a few days. She still feels guilt about that now and thinks that she gave up too early.

10.7 Babies who cry a lot: so-called 'crying babies'

If a mother has already had a miscarriage or given birth to a stillborn baby, the next child will feel her mother's fears and worries. The mother's continuous tension and restlessness are transferred physically and psychologically to the unborn child. Then it can also be difficult for the child to settle after the birth. He might cry a great deal and defy the mother's attempts to comfort him. With 'crying babies' we can consider this type of infant traumatisation as having been transferred through the mother's trauma, in accordance with the theory of 'symbiotic trauma'. Children do not cry without reason, nor is it because they want to manipulate their parents. Excessive crying, hyperactivity, or continuous sleep disorder are the way they express their anguish. Children have basic needs – nourishment, protection, care and bonding – none of which they can satisfy themselves. For a long time after their birth they are dependent on adults and on their parents or other attachment figures who should be providing them with security, and not subjecting them to further stress.

10.8 Constellations concerning a loss trauma

When working with trauma constellations the focus is on the actual trauma in each case, here the loss trauma. Healing can only take place when the individual's own splits become visible and, through their intention, their wish is expressed to re-integrate these parts, and recognise the loss with all its consequences.

When she is confronted with the news that her child is stillborn, a mother is numbed and incapable of any action. Karin describes her experiences as follows: "After I received the news from the doctors of the death of my child, I just lay there with my eyes open staring at the ceiling. I had the feeling that time was standing still and I was in an unreal world, not myself at all. I realised that something unimaginable was taking place but I had a feeling of unreality and absence. I had no sense of my own body and no feelings at all. I lay like that for hour after hour and I have no idea how I emerged from that state. Sometimes I feel like that now."

With the method of trauma constellations it is possible to come into contact with the split-off feelings. With pain that was never properly allowed, with the inexpressible grief, with the feeling of having failed, of not having helped one's child, perhaps not having listened to one's own intuition. The feeling "I should have realised something wasn't right, I should have prevented it" continues at an unconscious level in many of the women concerned.

In order to come to terms psychologically with a loss trauma such as the death of a child before, during or after the birth, the individual has to be determined to accept the loss as final. (Ruppert 2014, p. 87) In 'multi-generational psychotraumatology' the 'Constellation of the Intention' makes it possible to recognise the loss, the devastating emptiness, as well as the consequences, as real. The effects on the mother's future life, as well as on the replacement children, are made perceptible and can actually be experienced. This recognition and acceptance leads the women concerned to their real feelings in a coming-to-terms process.

10.9 Return to 'gut feeling'

When people have learnt to listen to their intuition again, they are able to have a sense of their own vitality, to have good relationships and to get in touch emotionally. They expand their ability to act and improve their quality of life. When women come to be able to listen to their gut feeling during pregnancy and birth again, they usually know very well if they and their unborn child are well and what they both need. They can gauge if something is not right because their own body and the child send signals that are understood. They are in contact with themselves and their child. Women who have been confronted with the terrible experience of a miscarriage or stillbirth and who have had to deal with it, intrinsically know how much they need to grieve and to say goodbye. The fact that women listen more and more to themselves is shown clearly by the change in procedure in the last few years for the trauma of a stillbirth or miscarriage.

11

'Psychosis' following the birth

Petra Lardschneider

'Postpartum psychosis', if it happens, occurs a few days after giving birth. "While postpartum depression usually begins gradually and can occur anytime during the first year following giving birth, it usually begins suddenly sometime between the birth to 14 days after the birth [. . .] The particular danger lies in the hallucinations or productively psychotic symptoms that usually relate to the child and can lead to suicide or infanticide". (Neises and Weidner 2012, p. 1090)

As opposed to 'postpartum depression', when the mother suffers from inner emptiness and torpor, and from the inability to have any emotional contact with the newborn child, so-called 'pregnancy psychosis' gives rise to obsessive thoughts and a desire to take action, both of which are directed at the newborn child. The causes of both 'depression' and 'psychosis' can be found in the mother's history.

Sabine

Sabine, the mother of two girls, came to see me because she was having obsessive thoughts. She was admitted to a psychiatric ward for six weeks with a diagnosis of 'postpartum psychosis' each time after giving birth. Shortly after each birth her thoughts turned to killing her child, thoughts she could not explain because she wanted both of her children. The thought would suddenly spring into her mind that she was a mass murderer. In the maternity clinic these delusions increased in intensity. The thought "kill, kill, kill" was so dominant that she didn't see any way out except by admitting herself to a psychiatric clinic. Sabine felt immense confusion and distress which she could not understand.

What is sometimes diagnosed as 'madness' or 'psychosis' is, from the viewpoint of multi-generational psychotraumatology, the expression of a perpetrator-victim split, which makes it impossible for the individual either to differentiate between being a victim and a perpetrator, or to differentiate between himself and others with whom he is symbiotically entangled. (Ruppert 2012, 2014) Because the birth process can cause feelings of "fear, panic, anger, despair and shame, all the way to complete terror, fear of annihilation, and a feeling of being torn apart" (Janus 1991, p. 30) a birth can also easily trigger the reoccurrence of split off trauma feelings in the mother and retraumatise her.

> Sabine explained that her own mortal fear was in the forefront of her mind after the birth of her first daughter, Marie. She had thoughts such as "I'm an infant and I'm being killed". This thought appeared six weeks after Marie's birth so that she was unable to sleep for seven days. She got into a state in which she had to keep moving in order to endure the feeling "I can't not breath".
>
> With Charlotte, her second daughter, her main thought was to kill her. "Everything was completely blurred. I couldn't tell the difference between my two girls. Who was now which baby?" She mistook Charlotte for Marie, and Marie for Charlotte. The fact that Sabine wasn't able to recognise her children suggests that she was lapsing into a child state herself because her own mortal fear as a baby had been triggered. Sabine describes her inability to feel the difference between being victim and perpetrator. She didn't see her children as children, but perceived them as perpetrators and felt as if she was their victim. Sabine is the elder of two girls. Her parents were married until her father was killed in an accident, which happened when Sabine was 27 years old. At that time Sabine was a member of a religious sect. Her father, who was traumatised by his experiences in the war, came from the former East Germany and had fled to West Germany before the wall was built. His parents stayed in East Germany. Sabine's mother, who was born in 1942, had fled with her mother from Pomerania during the war, when she was three years old.
>
> **Feelings of guilt.** In her first session, a one-to-one session with cushions as markers, Sabine wants to work with the intention "Where does the feeling of guilt come from?" She chooses me as

her intention and stands opposite me. As the representative of her intention, I say that I can't turn to my right. Sabine says she knows that feeling. She always has trouble turning over onto her right side. During the constellation she adds a cushion to represent 'the Sabine who has feelings of guilt'. When she stands on this cushion herself, this part says it can kill and it sees dead children. Sabine asks the intention whether that could have something to do with her grandma and mother when they were fleeing. I then ask her to choose a cushion for 'the grandma' and one for 'the mother' as well as one for a 'person who has killed a child'. Sabine can only clasp the cushions representing the two women to her stomach. She says she can't put them on the floor. After a while she places 'the grandma' and 'the mother' immediately beside the cushion of 'Sabine who has feelings of guilt'. When she stands opposite her intention again she says: "I don't want to have anything to do with it", and lays down the cushion for 'the person who has killed a child' at quite some distance from herself. In the role of the intention, I feel total chaos and hear shots. When I stand on the 'grandma' cushion, I see an image of a farm. I describe this in detail to Sabine. Suddenly she says: "Exactly! I always see that! I thought I was going mad. I don't know of any such farm." She holds her hand over her mouth and remains still.

In the role of 'the grandma', I hold a child's mouth shut to protect us both and want to hide with him. Around me all is confusion: soldiers, screams. I can't bear it! Sabine has still got her hand over her mouth and after a while she repeats that she doesn't want to have anything to do with it. I ask her to add a cushion for 'the child who was killed'. She doesn't choose a cushion, but a big, dark green blanket and spreads it out over 'the grandma', 'the mother' and 'the part of her who has feelings of guilt'. In the role of the intention, I feel at one with Sabine's mother and grandmother as well as with the dead child and the part of Sabine who has feelings of guilt. Sabine repeats again that she doesn't want to have anything to do with it. I suggest that she also puts 'Sabine with psychosis' and 'soldiers at war' down. The 'psychosis' part feels as if it's in a trance, and stands between Sabine and her intention and says: "I feel very central and important. I can't see the grandmother, the mother or any other people." Because of the presence of the soldiers, the grandmother can only remain motionless and rigid and doesn't feel anything anymore. The part of

'Sabine with the feelings of guilt' wants to help 'grandma' and 'mother' and feels grown-up. This situation displays the classic pattern of a symbiotic trauma. Sabine has been unable to develop her own identity because of the lack of any bonding relationship with her severely-traumatised mother. She is therefore unable to differentiate between her own feelings and those of her mother or grandmother. The intention says she wouldn't have a chance. She would have so much liked to establish contact with Sabine. But if Sabine doesn't want to have anything to do with the situation, then the intention feels as if she is sitting on a bench, kicking her heels, and just has to wait. I swap over into the role of the 'mother' and feel violent abdominal pain. I simply can't imagine that I've got any children. I don't want to have children!

Sabine says that her mother had wanted to enter a convent when she was 17. She and the grandmother were the only ones of their generation in the family to have children. I explain to Sabine that we are dealing with a collection of psychological splits and entanglements. It looks as if the grandmother was raped during the war and it feels as if she killed children to protect them from the soldiers.

In the role of Sabine's part with the feelings of guilt I sense that I am disintegrating. The family history is so terrible for Sabine that the only thing she can do is to disintegrate so that she doesn't have to feel her own severe pain and fear. She then doesn't feel her body any longer.

Sabine says to her intention: "I think I have to deal with this. I don't want you to sit on the bench, waiting." The intention comes closer to Sabine and replies that it feels good and says: "We have to know what happened." At the end of her first constellation, Sabine thinks she can now look at this to find the cause of her feelings of guilt.

My interpretation of this is: because of the killing of children during the war and her dramatic experiences as a war refugee from Pomerania, the grandmother was unable to establish any emotional relationship with Sabine's mother. Sabine's mother in turn was unable to develop a healthy mother-child attachment due to the traumatic events in her own childhood. It was only by splitting and entanglement of her feelings with the grandmother and mother that Sabine was able to survive this symbiotic trauma. Unconsciously, she had taken on huge feelings of guilt from her mother and her grandmother. That same evening I received an email from Sabine. The work had greatly impressed her and she was still feeling the effects. Following the constellation, perpetrator energies and anxieties had again arisen within her. But she was now better able to control them. She wrote: "Very strong feelings of hate have emerged, and also pleasure in hating. Something I completely deplore! I know it doesn't belong to me but it's stuck to me. I'd like to send the energies where they belong and not live in illusions any more. I think my grandmother was herself a perpetrator, in the form of an abortion, and now that overlays everything." A week later I get another email from Sabine. She had enormous upsurges of energy and creativity and it felt as if dams had broken and a blockage had been dissolved. She sometimes felt as though she was in several people. She takes up my suggestion to make a drawing of these feelings and this condition. The picture she then made clearly shows her dissociation and is a good depiction of the way she feels beset by a number of people.

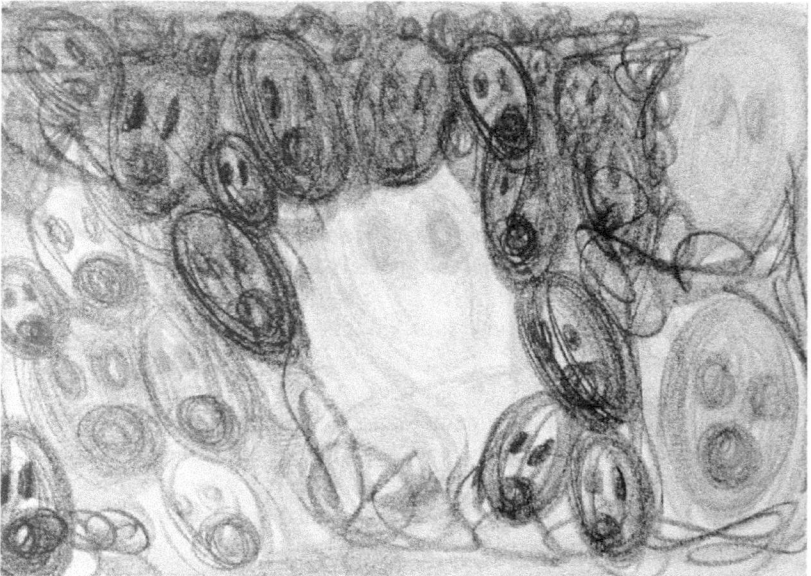

Figure 4: Sabine's depiction of herself in mortal fear, surrounded by people

Sabine draws herself in the centre, in yellow. Surrounding her are many black heads. She says that it all belongs to her; she can't differentiate anything anymore. It feels like a soup. Around her everything is confusion and harassment. There are no boundaries. Every face is shown with an elongated mouth drawn in black. She tells me that the scream doesn't come out of the mouth. The black colour illustrates the mortal fear around her. Sabine went on: "Through my strong feelings of guilt I accepted the blame for everything and wasn't able to differentiate between what belonged to me and what didn't. Now I feel for the first time what self-awareness is or could be. It's almost scary, but it feels wonderful." She said she knew that this was not yet a permanent feeling and that there was still a lot to do.

Sexual abuse. In the course of further one-to-one and group constellations it becomes apparent in Sabine's biography that she was subjected to sexual abuse through a friend of the family when she was eight years old. Sabine's mother was unable to perceive the danger emanating from this family friend because of her own traumatic experiences with her father. She herself had been sexually abused by the latter. Sabine's contact with her father is also disturbed. Her father never really recognised her distress. In one of her constellations it becomes apparent that she was only able to have a relationship with her father in terms of achievement. When she was a little girl, he had taken her on a mountain trek up 3,000m that she had had to get through without stopping.

Fit of rage. In one of the subsequent constellations Sabine wants to look more closely at the fits of rage of her three-year-old daughter, Marie. She can't bear this rage and wants to know where this lies in her. She talks about being pregnant with Marie. Shortly before the birth she was in the bath and had collapsed. The contractions then diminished and Marie slipped back up the birth canal. The doctors gave Sabine an epidural and used a ventouse to deliver Marie. Sabine took no further active part in the birth process. It was a nightmare for Sabine when the doctor pressed so hard on her abdomen to push the birth along. She felt as if she was her own unborn child. It turned out later that it had been a repetition of parts of her own birth, when her mother didn't let her come out during the birth process. After the session, Sabine realised that it was not about Marie's rage, but her own distress as a child, which was directed at both parents. She had been unconsciously trying to transfer her own trauma feelings onto Marie.

Stay centred. The next constellation takes place after Sabine's holiday, which she spent together with her family in an area that in the past was severely affected by war between ethnic groups. Genocide had taken place in this area of the country. She described how she had seen blood in a nearby stream and had been scared by horses. She said she still felt unable to protect her boundaries. She wanted to continue working on this and chose as her intention: "I would like to remain centred." During the constellation it becomes apparent that her survival part talks incessantly so that she doesn't have to feel her anxiety and pain. A few days later she rings me and says she now recognizes the message of the psychosis: "Mothers are dangerous and with the birth of my daughter I became a mother and my own issue was triggered again."

Neediness. At our next meeting she repeats her wish to look at her own neediness. She said the awful conditions of her psychosis had gone. She would like to be able to perceive her child part and come into contact with it. Sabine describes an experience with her mother and her children at the doctor's. When Charlotte cried her mother had started to sing and said: "Now we can't hear it!" Sabine said she remembered that from her own childhood. Even when she had bronchitis, her mother didn't take her seriously and said she was just play-acting. She realised how crazy the situation must have been for her as a child. The needy part of her would like to cry, but there was no one there to hear her. The 'intention' says she has to close her eyes otherwise she wouldn't feel her body. Sabine confirms that she often doesn't feel her body, and now she wants to start experiencing her body. She had tried as a child to access her mother's love by putting on a mask. That was the only way to come into contact with her.

Vitality. This time Sabine chooses her representatives from the group. Her intention is: "I would like to lose the fear of my own vitality and instead enjoy it." The 'intention' talks of a fear. She cannot speak, she feels like she is in a deep sleep – as if on stand-by – and she doesn't know which fear Sabine is talking about. Sabine has the feeling that something happened prenatally. Hearing that, the 'intention' comes alive and says: "Yes, that's right!" During the constellation it becomes clear that Sabine had developed survival strategies so that she didn't feel afraid of her vitality. Again she talks about a mask and about 'doing'; says she knows that feeling well. She says that part of the mask feels like kicking in the womb and the 'doing' is the continuation of it. It is important to the 'intention' to emerge from the illusion, from the 'wish for an ideal family'. She would like to know what really happened. Sabine takes away from this constellation the importance of the mask's protection and of the 'doing'. Both are survival mechanisms that she had not been aware of. At the moment, she says, she can't do any more. Vitality is still too dangerous for Sabine. Sabine's mother's own trauma was triggered and reactivated by her pregnancy with Sabine. "Being alive is dangerous, it means you'll be killed." As Sabine's mother had aborted a child before Sabine was born, the information "I have killed a child" was stored in her mother's womb and her cells. In a phone call a few days later she tells me that she wanted to follow my suggestion of drawing herself as a baby in her mother's womb and that she had felt an inner barrier, similar to the feeling in the constellation.

Mortal fear. In the next session Sabine tells me there is a 'self-denial part' in her that hates itself, that experiences mortal fear and fantasies of violence, and that this is really the 'psychosis part' in her. This part is quick to feel threatened. It is connected to the perpetrator energies, the feelings of guilt and the extreme anxiety of the mother, grandmother and possibly the great-grand-mother, in order to avoid feeling its own mortal fear and pain. It is the mortal fear of the baby who feels threatened by the perpetra-tor energies and cannot differentiate between herself and her mother. It is all there in this part: the mortal fear, guilt and the perpetrator energies. She feels at her strongest and most able to act when in the perpetrator energies. She would like to use her intention to find out which part needs her attention. We set up a

constellation using notes and cushions and during the constellation
Sabine starts to feel as if she is in the amniotic fluid sac. It turns
out later that this is the part of her that feels the mortal fear.
Following my suggestion she puts down a cushion to represent the
mother. I then lead her back into the birth process. I suggest that
she contact the baby in the mother's womb.

Sabine (S): "It's like being in the waters, I'm big here because
it's very cramped and I feel quite big. Oh God, that can't be
true! Now everything's becoming blurred."

Therapist (T): "Pay attention to the feeling, who is becoming
blurred?"

S: "The mother."

T: "Can you see where she is?"

S: "She's sitting on the couch and crying. She is all alone. I feel
heavily pregnant and don't want the child. I feel really pregnant and the poor little one. My belly hurts. I was raped."

T: "Notice these thoughts, at this moment the mother doesn't
want the child. And she feels raped. Feel her body, her
vaginal area, it knows who raped her. Who was it?"

S: "It's not my father, it feels more like the grandfather. I don't
want the child. Oh I can feel so clearly that my mother
doesn't want me."

T: "The mother doubts whether she wants you because of her
experiences. Feel yourself in your mother's womb."

S: "It's cramped and I want to get out!"

T: "Feel yourself as a baby in your mother's womb."

S: "It's so cramped (she holds her own head) – there are
thoughts: 'I don't want to kill you – I don't know what to
do.'"

T: "Yes, there are thoughts, like I don't want to kill you. Who's
thinking that?"

S: "The mother, she's thinking: I've aborted a child and I don't
want to kill you (in other words me), and I can really feel her
sadness. Everything is blurred between me and the other
baby. As if she doesn't really feel me, there's a sort of wall
between us."

T: "Yes, notice, there's an emotional wall between you and your mother... and the thoughts of the mother who had aborted the baby before you, thoughts that are now reactivated at your birth. With a baby in her womb once again, alive this time and wanting to be born. She killed the last baby, it was not alive when it came into the world."

S: "I feel, I want to get out and I can't. It's as if the mother is holding on to me. It's like a thick wall that I have to get through. I know that in everyday life: I want something and I can't."

T: "Yes, you can see a parallel in everyday life and now you can see how it fits together. Feel the situation in the womb, the mother holding on to you."

S: "She's afraid that the baby will be born..."

S: "Now I'm outside. I feel how I am pulled upwards. It's really cold, I'm freezing, I'm sad, no one welcomes me. I can't go to my mother. My eyes dart here and there, I'm really trembling, I feel I'm being washed, held, it's all so unpleasant. I'm totally alone, there's no love anywhere, I'd like to be held in someone's arms, I'd like to snuggle. Why am I so alone?" (She cries while she feels all that.)

S: "I feel the father is watching through a sliding door. I cry but no-one comes. I'm totally alone, it's endless."

While she is taken back into the birth process, Sabine can clearly feel herself as a baby. The 'intention' in the constellation showed that the part with mortal fear needs her attention. In the follow-up discussion Sabine thought this work was a good basis to be able to look at her own pregnancies.

Summary. Sabine has done a great deal of work on her issues in the last few months, and has been able to make progress at the deepest levels of her psyche. The cause of Sabine's postpartum psychosis lies in the biography of her grandmother (World War II, rape, infanticide, flight). Her confusion, anxiety and depression are the direct consequence of her experiences with her severely traumatised mother. Her mother had aborted a child before she had Sabine. When subsequently pregnant with Sabine, the mother was unable to engage with the new baby because she would come into contact with her own unresolved trauma feelings. During the pregnancy she had stopped any emotional contact with her baby. Then there were additional aggravating circumstances for Sabine at the birth of her own daughters. She was given an epidural during the expulsive phase.

In the course of the constellations described here, Sabine was able increasingly to recognise her own victimhood and thereby her own pain and anxiety. She was able to develop more empathy and ability to love herself. With the help of the constellation work Sabine learnt something completely new to her: that she herself is able to notice the changes within her, and this enables her to manage her inner recovery by her own means.

12

Mothers caught between wanting to have a career, having financial difficulties and making time for their children

Christina Freund

When I was three I ran away from home. My mother had shown me the kindergarten I would be going to after the summer holidays. Apparently I couldn't wait: with my ball under my arm I set off without anyone seeing me. When my parents found me, I'd almost reached the kindergarten. They'd asked me where I was going. "To kindergarten. To all the other children. To play!" I had desperately wanted to go to kindergarten. I was lucky and there were places available for a child of only three years old. Like most children in West Germany, I grew up in a 'traditional' family: The mother looked after the children and kept house, while the father earned the money. In contrast, very many children in East Germany grew up in day nurseries because both mothers and fathers had to go to work. (Eichhorst et al. 2007) Since the reunification more and more women have to decide for themselves how they want to live their lives: just be a mother, or have a career, or be a mother and have a career at the same time, or be a mother and have to earn money. (Allmendinger 2013)

Rita

> Rita (30) has suffered for some time from 'burnout'. She inter-
> rupted work on her doctorate only briefly for her son's birth and
> went back to it again straight afterwards. Rita couldn't find a
> suitable nursery for her child, but she didn't want to give up her
> doctorate either. As a result she was only able to work when her
> son was asleep. "I sacrificed myself for my son and for me!" A
> few weeks after handing in her dissertation she collapsed psycho-
> logically and physically.

With the 2007 campaign in Germany to increase the number of
nursery places, the Government created the conditions necessary
to ensure that no woman would have to give up her profession
because she had a child. From 2013 every one-year-old would
have a right to a nursery place. The aim of this paradigm shift in
politics was to allow women in Germany to combine job, career,
earning money and children. In France however, regarded as
exemplary in Germany because of the higher birth rate, there now
seems to be a change in thinking: More and more mothers want to
spend more time with their children; want to be proper mothers
for their children. (Moulin 2013)

12.1 How long can a child spend without their mother?

The new legal regulations concerning early childcare services in
Germany can fundamentally alter the lives of infants and toddlers.
Parents can decide that their children, when they are only a year
old or younger, are to be separated from them and looked after by
strangers in unfamiliar surroundings. These childcare services are
hotly debated in Germany. Supporters of the nursery scheme
claim those against it are over-protective mothers, while
opponents of it see the supporters as bad mothers.

   Very often it is experiences gained in the individual's relationship to their own mother that prevent an objective discussion,
because separation from the mother is one of the primary stress
factors in the life of an infant. The younger and more immature the

child is, the more this applies. It is not the unfamiliar surroundings with strangers that make the child anxious, but the mother's absence. A mother who is present not only gives the child protection and security, but also encourages the child to be curious and explore the world. If the child does not have his mother's presence to reassure him when he is exploring, he will start to become anxious (Brisch 2009, p. 144ff.) Therefore there is a low stress factor for. young children becoming accustomed to nursery, as long as the mother is present. The more secure the attachment to their mothers is, the less stress the children experience. This alters only when the mothers leave the nursery room and the children are supposed to stay there on their own. The children cry and cling to their mothers. They clearly demonstrate bonding behaviour: Mummy must come back quickly! But the mothers go and they leave the children in the nursery. (Ahnert 2011, p. 192ff.)

Lea

Lea (19) is increasingly panic-stricken when her boyfriend has gone out and she is alone at home. She feels abandoned and completely cut off from life. She feels life is taking place somewhere else without her and she is left behind, alone. Her father died in a traffic accident when she was two, and her mother worked a 40-hour week to support the family and Lea was given to a child minder while her mother was at work. She always cried a lot and clung desperately to her mother, screamed loudly and clearly for help, but in vain: her mother left anyway. She pulled herself away and pushed Lea towards the child minder. Lea had to deal with being separated from her mother at the same time as coping with the death of her father. Lea's going to the child minder happened at an incredibly unfortunate juncture in her life and the eight hours a day she spent there was also a long time. The two-year old Lea was completely overwhelmed, physically and emotionally: her father dies suddenly and her mother goes away and leaves her behind. Her panic and fear of being abandoned and excluded from life is a clear sign of an early traumatisation. In this sense, Lea's current panic is a consequence of the disorder resulting from the trauma of her childhood experiences, which she was unable to cope with emotionally. (Ruppert 2014, pp. 65, 66)

This case history shows that the length of time it is all right for a child to be separated from his mother depends on the individual circumstances; there is no one-size-fits-all. It depends on the child and how he is on a particular day. But it was not possible for Lea's mother to take that into consideration: "I had to go to work", was the reason her mother gave, which appears understandable. However, for a two-year-old child this explanation is no help; it serves only to increase her distress further. Lea is supposed to understand that it is necessary for her to be left with the child minder; perhaps she is even supposed to pity her mother. But to do that it is necessary for Lea to split off her pain – the separation anxiety and physical stress. "I became increasingly reserved and quiet." Clients frequently attribute words to themselves such as 'brave', 'good', 'big', and 'sensible'. As Ruppert (2012) emphasises, these are clear signals for trauma survival strategies in the case of a symbiotic trauma, and a sign of a symbiotic entanglement between mother and child.

In the following constellation, Lea's symbiotic trauma, which preceded the separation, becomes visible. Initially Lea's intention ("How will I get rid of my fear?") reflects Lea as a traumatised two-year-old. She clings desperately, crying loudly, to the big Lea. When the representative of the 'mother who always tore herself out of Lea's grasp' comes into the constellation, little Lea becomes silent and hides. The mother, on the other hand, cannot bear her daughter's distress. She becomes a distraught little child herself who needs help – abandoned and alone.

Little children adopt their mothers' evaluation of their environment, which is why the mother's reaction is crucial in situations when the child is being separated from her. (Brisch 2009, p. 144ff.) When the mother left Lea with the child minder she was probably overwhelmed with feelings of anxiety and pain herself. This meant that Lea was even more unsettled at the separation. It was obviously difficult for her mother to leave her child with the child minder. Therefore Lea was unable to feel secure with the child minder. In this way the child's normal anxiety at being separated from her mother was increased by her mother's unresolved trauma feelings. Lea's mother herself grew up with a mother who didn't want to be a mother. She was only there occasionally and if she was actually present, she was forbidding and unapproachable. Because of this, Lea felt the anxiety and distress of her needy mother. She looked after her traumatised part. As a small child Lea didn't want to leave her mother alone, always wanted to be with her so that she could give her the care and security she had lacked.

How long children can be separated from their mothers is defined by the quality of the mother-child relationship. A child can be happily separated from their mother as long as they feel secure and looked after. If they become insecure or ill, they will need contact with their mother. Additionally, a child can only be happily separated from their mother as long as the mother herself is happily separated from her child, in other words feels secure while she is away from her child. (Ahnert 2011, p. 197ff.) The mother needs to be empathetic and feel her own attachment needs as well as those of her child in order for both to cope in a healthy way with their separation.

12.2 Crèches and nurseries in stress studies

How does a stressful separation affect a child's development? Can a child minder replace the mother? Does being in another's care harm children? Or do the children even benefit from it? Such questions are controversial in the light of the continuous increase in the number of nurseries.

A series of studies (Achenbach, Dumenci and Rescorla 2002, Baker, Gruber and Milligan 2008) has looked at the development of children in crèches and with child minders compared with children who remain in the care of their mothers. All the studies show an increase in the number of behavioural disorders of children in third-party care compared with children looked after by their mothers. The children appear more anxious, more depressed, and more aggressive. They are less able to concentrate and more frequently display delinquent behaviour. However, different publications put conflicting interpretations on the relevance of the connection between third-party care and behavioural disorders. (Böhm 2011, p. 318) So, remarkably, both opponents and supporters of crèches feel their viewpoint is validated by the research results.

The most comprehensive of these studies is the NICHD study (NICHD Early Child Care Network 1994). This large-scale study started in the USA in 1991 and investigated the cognitive and emotional development of children and their behaviour. In all, 1,364 children and their families were examined from birth to the end of Year 6 at school, and re-visited when the children were 15 years old. The data collected was analysed from various perspectives and the results published in more than 300 scientific articles. In the process the link was again confirmed between third-party care and behavioural disorders.

The researchers were able to make even more precise assertions: there is an association between the start of childcare in nurseries and its duration and the observed behavioural disorders in children up to 15 years of age, regardless of the quality of the childcare. That means that the younger children are when they go to childcare and the longer they are there, the more negative characteristics they display. (Böhm 2011, p. 317)

A further outcome of this study surprised the researchers: parents' influence on their children was much greater than expected. Even if the children spent the whole day in childcare outside the family, the quality of the parent-child relationship influenced the child's development more strongly than the third-party care. (Böhm 2013b, p. 28) Children who were securely attached to their mothers remained securely attached, despite being in childcare, and in the same way, children who were insecurely attached to their mothers remained insecurely attached. Evidently the quality of childcare cannot improve the mother-child attachment. However, the insecurely attached children became even more insecurely attached if their relationship with their insensitive mother was continued with poor-quality childcare. (Ahnert 2011, p. 170)

Third-party care in a crèche is very stressful for young children. For that reason children between one and two years old are particularly susceptible to infectious illnesses, as the NICHD study has shown. (Ahnert 2011, p. 164ff.) Further studies have therefore looked at the effects of stress on young children. In the *Wiener Krippenstudie* [Vienna Childcare Study] (2007–2012), for example, measurements were taken of the cortisol level of 65 crèche children aged between 10 and 35 months (Dattler, Funder, Hover-Reisner, Fürstaler and Ereky-Stevens 2012). The concentration of this hormone in the blood alters during the day: it is highest in the morning just after getting up and drops continuously to its lowest level at midnight. The values measured in the morning and during the day are indicators of a person's stress level and the way they deal with it. After the children in the Vienna Childcare Study had been in the crèche for two months, researchers took saliva samples from them to measure their cortisol levels. It was evident that the younger the children were, the more sensitively they reacted to stress. After just ten weeks in a crèche, children under two had a much lower level of cortisol in the morning, and the level rose again in the afternoon. So the longer the children were in the crèche, the more the level flattened out over the course of the day. That means these children were no longer able to cope with their stress and had descended into a state of permanent stress. (Ahnert, Kappler and Eckstein-Madry 2012, p. 87)

These results are worrying. The paediatrician Rainer Böhm observes that the cortisol levels of children in crèches is comparable with that of children who have experienced emotional, physical and sexual violence (Böhm 2013a, p. 122ff.). This unresolved stress from the first years of life apparently leaves lasting traces. In the NICHD study the early morning cortisol level of the 15 year-olds was measured. The earlier the teenagers went to childcare and the longer they were there, the lower the cortisol values were, even more than ten years later. The levels were similar to those in the group of 15-year-olds who had grown up in hostile or abusive families (ibid.). In addition, the Vienna Childcare Study has established that the quality of the attachment to the child minders influences the ability to cope with this stress: thus, the cortisol value of the securely-attached children also fell, but only four months after first going to the crèche. That means that the quality of the care can delay the stress to children under two years old, but not normalise it. In other words, it is not sufficient protection for toddlers. Since the children's sensitivity to this stress decreases the older they become, this will probably only be successful when they reach kindergarten age.

In my view, the children's behavioural disorders observed in the studies are also symptoms of the enormous stress, or the symbiotic trauma, they experienced in early childhood. Their hyperactive, aggressive, impulsive, thoughtless, but also their quiet or reserved behaviour, are all attempts to cope with early and lengthy separation from their mothers. In this sense the non-availability of the mother is traumatising for infants or toddlers.

12.3 Are traumatised mothers more likely to place their children in crèches and childcare?

There is not yet a research project that investigates a possible link between a mother's traumas and her child's third-party care. I am therefore going back to my own therapeutic experience with traumatised mothers and their children. These may not be representative, but remarkable conclusions can be drawn from them if one makes use of the theoretical concept of symbiotic trauma and its consequences: (Ruppert 2012, 2014) in contact with their children, mothers are confronted with their own unresolved trauma experiences. This is all the more true the younger the children are and the more they need their mother's closeness and care. The children's symbiotic needs lead the mothers back to their own experiences with their mothers. Were they wanted and accepted? Did they experience care, protection and security? Mothers' experiences with their own symbiotic needs are in my opinion the initial starting point for the way they will manage their own children. Again and again in my practice I come across two fundamental behaviour patterns of traumatised mothers:

- On the one hand there are the over-protective mothers. They want to correct all their own bad experiences. They want to be a better mother to their children than their own mother was to them. Their children are the focus of their lives. They tend not to put their children into childcare and if they do, they watch over them like hawks to make sure nothing happens to them. In this symbiotic entanglement, over-protective mothers confuse their children with their own inner traumatised child parts. The following case history serves to illustrate this.

Eva

Eva's mother sent Eva (now aged 41 years) to a children's home because she didn't fit into her life. Eva's mother hardly ever visited her. Eva decided her son was going to have a much better life: "No, a child minder or a crèche was out of the question for me. I wanted my boy to be with me all the time until he went to school. I gave up everything during this time. I think that's the reason I've only had one child. I didn't want him to feel an outcast and rejected as I had. He was the most important thing in my life – more than my husband or my career, and definitely more than me."

- On the other hand there are also the merciless mothers. They expect their children to put up with exactly the same as they had to. In this way they slip into their mother's shoes. They reject their children in the same way as their mothers rejected them. For example, they give their children away just as they were given away. These mothers entangle their children due to their symbiotic trauma in their perpetrator-victim split. The mothers feel they are the victims of their child's needs, which they experience as threatening and which they have to resist. They become perpetrators towards their children while they experience the children as being perpetrators towards them. They traumatise their children, whilst feeling traumatised by the children. Again, an example:

Pia

Pia (39) came to my group because of her son's school and social problems. Tim (13) is at a private school in year 7. He was diagnosed with ADHD when he was at primary school. He is extremely restless. Tim was not a planned child, but was the result of a one-night-stand. Pia did not consider having an abortion: "I've made my bed, now I have to lie in it." During her pregnancy Pia continued to work as a business consultant. When her mother was diagnosed with a tumour, Pia also looked after her. In order to be able to plan the birth better, Pia decided to have a Caesarean. Shortly after Tim was born Pia's mother died. During this time Pia gave Tim to a child minder. After the funeral Pia concentrated once again on her job. When Tim was six months old she found a crèche place for him.

In the constellation there was an intense hostility between Pia and her 'intention' ("What can I do so that Tim functions normally?"). They accused each other of having completely failed in his upbringing. He should have been treated much more harshly and not so mollycoddled. After a while Pia turned to me and told me that she couldn't bear Tim being so clingy. She said he was extremely whiny and always needed physical contact – "worse than a baby". On hearing that the 'intention' was horrified: "For Heaven's sake! You have to stop that!" Pia said shamefacedly that she couldn't always manage that.

I asked Pia who had spoken to her like that. Her answer came straightaway: "My mother. It was horrible, but I learnt to function with the pitiless way she brought me up." I suggested to Pia that she set up her mother, but she refused. She said she had put her childhood into a safe and thrown the key into the ocean. After that Pia turned to her 'intention': "Tim has to learn to pull himself together, just like I did. It hurts but that's the tough school of life."

12.4 Splitting as a necessary survival mechanism for children

How can children deal with their traumatised mothers? For example, how does Tim cope with his mother's "tough school of life"? Children are totally overwhelmed by their traumatised mothers if their mothers have not worked on their traumas. This also applies to crèche personnel. (Brisch 2009, p. 149) The child is traumatised by contact with the survival parts and traumatised parts of mothers and other caregivers.

Children experience their mothers in two ways: as insensitive perpetrators and also as powerless victims who are themselves seeking help. Despite the child's crying, clinging and protesting, their mothers are unrelenting leaving them in a crèche, a nursery or with a child minder. At the same time the children also feel their mothers' split distress and despair, which the mothers themselves do not feel, but which renders them unable to react appropriately to their children's distress. In this situation all a child can do is split his psyche. (Ruppert 2008) He gradually adapts himself completely to his mother. He splits his distress and despair off, as his mother did, and develops similar survival parts to hers. One part endures the crèche bravely and obediently, while the traumatised part is strongly attacked by the child's survival parts, which protect and excuse the mother and also imitate her.

The psychological split into traumatised and survival parts can be clearly seen in the example of Tim, Pia's son.

Tim

> Tim (13), Pia's son, came to a one-to-one session on his own. He wanted to resolve the problems he was having at school. Tim started by saying that his fellow students laughed at him when he took an active part in the lessons. They turned up their noses at him when he approached them. His best friend also pushed him away and made him look a fool and said he behaved like a lapdog, but Tim said he wanted to be part of things as well. He'd also been to see the liaison teacher at school and his class teacher, but they'd said he had to cope on his own. I then said to him that his mother, Pia, also thought that. Tim nodded sadly: "I have to get through it on my own! That's why I want to be very strong and I don't want to be so stupid anymore!" When I asked him what he meant by 'stupid' he explained: "I start to tremble and cry like a baby!" I suggested to Tim that he choose a cuddly toy for this 'trembling and crying baby'. He selected a sad-looking bear. "I hate this

baby!" He immediately threw the bear out of the door. Then he became more and more restless: he stood up, ran round the room and finally crawled, crying, under the sofa. From there he talked about his immense fear of being alone. I nodded: "Your mother wasn't there when you were a baby." Tim agreed vociferously: "She always had to work and look after granny."

Then he crawled out from his hiding place, fetched the bear and brought it back into the room because it was all alone. He hugged it tightly to his chest. "He's always so afraid and then he cries a lot. He'd really like to lie in bed with Mummy." Then Tim sat the bear on the sofa. "You get into your bed. Mummy's got her room and you've got your room! Always this crying nonsense!"

My conclusion is that the mother is of crucial importance to the child in the case of a using a crèche or a child minder. Depending on her circumstances and her own experiences, the mother will either prefer to look after her child herself or take him at a young age to a child minder. And that decision will have a lasting effect on the child's development.

13

Growing up with grandparents as an early trauma

Andrea Stoffers

Grandparents have an important role to play. They can take the pressure off the parents in difficult situations, but they can also exert a lot of pressure on their children and grandchildren. A whole raft of questions arises: can grandparents replace parents? Can the grandmother fulfil the mother's role? What does it mean if, for example, war-traumatised grandparents look after the newborn baby? What are the consequences if, in the case of divorce, the grandparents interfere in the care of their grandchildren while in their custody?

There are many good examples of supportive grandparents, which I will not list here, but I would like to stress that many grandparents do offer their children and grandchildren support without interference or manipulation, by happily looking after their grandchildren, or picking them up from nursery, taking them on holiday, and much more. However, this book is about early childhood traumatisation, which can be transferred from the grandparents via the mother to the unborn child, or which a child can also suffer in direct contact with his grandparents, as the following case studies will show.

In my practice I quite often experience the effects of the destructive entanglements of children with their parents. Since I have been concentrating more on pre-, peri- and postnatal traumas, I have increasingly noticed such destructive attachments to grandparents. If a mother is traumatised and the grandparents feel called upon to look after the child, it becomes apparent that they are doing it with the best of intentions, but they do not recognise and disregard their own traumatisation. It often transpires that grandparents want to make up for things they failed to do with their own children. Sometimes grandmothers take on the role of 'mother' because they think their own daughter is incapable. The young child is then caught in a conflict if he is pressured to reject his own mother. No strong words are needed for this, and these manipulative strategies work even with very young infants.

Sven

Sven did grow up with his parents but his mother's mother also lived with them. She was domineering and allowed neither Sven nor his mother much leeway. Sven was very much a wanted child – so wanted in fact that, as one of Sven's constellations suggested, he felt sucked into the entanglement while in the womb, feeling at the mercy of the unfulfilled longings and desires of his mother and grandmother.

Repeatedly in my work the image crops up of a helpless, exploited mother and an all-consuming, dominant grandmother who seeks contact with her grandchild. In such cases the child is already beset while in the womb with numerous expectations. Once the child is born he has no chance of bonding with his mother because the grandmother's jealousy and rivalry make a secure attachment impossible. In Sven's case his mother and grandmother vied for his attention from the very beginning. He felt dominated by women, completely overwhelmed and additionally abandoned by his father. Sven's mother was also suffering from the traumatic experience of having given birth to a stillborn girl when she was six months pregnant, about two years before Sven was conceived. She was still emotionally attached to the girl who died, and Sven saw himself as a replacement for this child. So Sven was probably already psychologically split in the womb, at the mercy of the two women's power struggle and not knowing where he belongs.

He comes to my practice with strong feelings of fragmentation and many current relationship problems. He often feels overwhelmed, particularly in situations of stress, and at that point he usually dissociates. The women he has been with are, like him, internally fragmented, neither stable nor reliable. He describes his puberty as lonely; he read a lot and experimented with drugs. Sven still feels caught in a spiral of power and powerlessness that has existed from the beginning of his life. It used to be his grandmother and mother who made him feel 'trained'; today it is his partners. It was only his grandfather who was good for him, and when he died, Sven was deeply sad, but could not show it. He felt betrayed by his father and at his mercy.

This is his own assessment of the situation then and its affect on him up to the present: "My grandmother (who was born in 1905) was traumatised – World War I, orphaned early, had to fend for herself, forsaken by a man with whom she had become involved because he was the son of a brewery owner and a 'good catch'. She then found work as a housekeeper and cook, or as a servant, in wealthy households until she was 'married off' to my grandfather when she was in her thirties, who was looking for a woman to take care of him.

"When he was 19, my grandfather returned from World War I, paralysed down one side, and received a sizeable pension as a disabled veteran. My mother (born 1940) was their only child. I was born in 1965; the stillbirth [the child before him] must have been in 1963. My grandmother looked after my grandfather. After my grandfather's death in 1969 my mother looked after my grandmother who suffered from 'cardiac asthma' and tyrannised the whole family with it. One 'wrong' word and she got herself worked up and had these asthma attacks and heart problems. Until my grandmother's death in 1986 my mother was more daughter than wife. My father was always annoyed about it but with an attitude of self-sacrifice he would declare: "The woman's ill, you can't do anything to hurt her, you have to protect her." Interestingly, both my parents later sought out new 'grandmas', elderly, ailing relations whom they could moan about, but whom they could also mother and look after, so that they didn't have to live their own lives, whatever they might be. My parents always took on a subservient role. The bosses at home were 'grandma and grandpa', and it was their house.

"Care and illness, self-sacrificing oneself for others, not telling things as they are in order to spare the other person, feeling guilty: those are our family issues. I was touched by your sentence: "The grandmother's jealousy made a secure attachment impossible."

Somehow that feels true; grandma was always somewhere in the system, hovering around. My mother was completely under her thumb. My grandma tyrannised everyone with her emotions, which she also showed on a physical level. My grandparents were very strict with my mother. She sacrificed herself to please everybody. And now my mother's just the same as her mother. And my father always tries to placate everyone: Just stay calm! My father kept himself out of everything and wasn't present for me. I had the feeling he left me in the lurch and allowed me to be devoured by the women. That's why I've got good powers of observation and can recognise the needs of my opposite number, because if I wasn't 'good', especially if I didn't explicitly show my love for mama and grandma, then all hell broke loose. I once said: "I love aunt Monika (a neighbour) as much as I love grandma" and my grandma didn't speak to me again until I came to her in repentance and denied it. In the end my parents simply weren't able to do their own thing. The grandparents' energy was too dominant."

Katharina

Katharina spent most of the time with her grandparents. Her father was absent during her entire childhood because he was studying elsewhere. Her mother went back to work a few weeks after Katharina was born and Katharina spent her early childhood with her grandparents. She remembers it as a nice time, but in her constellations it becomes more and more clear that these memories are distorted. From the very beginning, Katharina was there to compensate for her grandparents' traumas, to bring light into their lives and comfort them. Quite soon she was caught in a very caring, grown-up role, which she only became aware of as an adult. In constellations she could feel her grandmother holding onto her tightly as an infant, and realised that the care she thought she could feel was actually her looking after her grandmother and not the other way round. Once as a child her grandmother took her to bed with her and snuggled up to her. Katharina felt as if she were being sucked dry, as if her role as an infant was to support her grandmother. She remembered her grandfather as a loving man, although he had been a Nazi during World War II and had actively supported the Lebensborn Association. She had images in her head of scenes where he was the only person playing with her as a little girl. However, several constellations allowed reasonable doubt to creep in concerning these childhood memories. Katharina seems to have absorbed the split trauma feelings of both her grandparents.

Here is Katharina's own account: "My mother was pregnant with me when she was 22. She wasn't married to my father then and they didn't live together either. She hadn't planned to get pregnant and I expect it was a huge shock for her to discover that she was. Constellations have revealed that there might even have been an attempted abortion using knitting needles. According to my aunt, my mother's sister, my grandma offered her support straightaway. My grandma had left it up to my mother to decide whether to marry my father or not – at any rate, my grandparents didn't insist on a wedding. My parents got married eight months before I was born. My father had started studying in S. before I was born and my grandparents supported him financially. My mother lived with me in my grandparents' home – my father was in S. and only came home occasionally at the weekend. I can hardly remember my father from my childhood. On the weekends when he was at home he would usually be in another room, studying. My mother went back to work full-time eight weeks after I was born, so that it was mostly my grandma who brought me up. I wasn't breastfed. According to my mother I refused to drink. I also don't have many conscious memories of my mother from my childhood. Shortly before I was born, my grandma had suffered from severe depression and had tried to take her own life. She seems to have attempted suicide in the years prior to that as well, but I can't say what the exact cause was. She was 50 years old when I was born. I was her new mission in life.

"My grandpa had a full-time job. He was the person I was most attached to. Every day after work he spent time with me: went to the zoo with me, played 'tennis' or board games with me. Even when I was a child I felt that my world would end if he were to die. I can well remember how extremely sad it made me as a little child, even thinking about the loss of my grandpa. My grandpa was in the SS Division *Totenkopf* [Skull and Crossbones] and probably active in the Lebensborn Association. There is a strong suspicion that he fathered several children during the war. There's a photo album with loads of pictures of women from the Czech Republic, Poland, Hungary, Belgium, etc. who wrote messages on their photos for him. Constellations have shown – and neighbours' accounts have also revealed – that he was a passionate supporter of Nazi ideology. My mother's name and mine are from the Nibelung saga.* The Nazis had a great liking for the ancient Nibelung myths. Unfortunately I know very little about what my grandfather did during the war. He was in the Russian campaign, in France, and in various other places, and also served a sentence in Nuremberg after the war. After my grandfather's death my mother sold and gave away a number of SS 'souvenirs'. There were supposedly even cyanide capsules in the house. My grandma was active in the League of German Girls [Bund Deutscher Mädchen]. She had very bad psoriasis on her legs. During the war she had an administration post in a government office. I don't know what post it was. My grandparents only got married after the war.

"I lived with my grandparents until I was six. My grandma took over my entire upbringing from my mother. According to my mother, my grandpa begged her not to go to S. to join my father. As far back as I can remember, I slept in my grandma's bed and not in my mother's room. At that time my grandpa was already sleeping in a little box-room. It seems to me that I had nightmares every night. My nightmares were always about a 'bad wolf' that wanted to kill me. I never actually saw the bad wolf in my dreams. In time it got so bad that I didn't want to go to sleep – I was afraid I'd dream again. Over the years it was no longer a 'bad wolf' but assassins who wanted to kill me. But I never knew why.

"My parents decided to move out of my grandparents' house when I was six. I can only remember the removals van but not my emotions at the time. As often as I could, I went to my grandparents after school. I never felt comfortable at home with my parents. The feelings I had were of loneliness, being cooped up, completely erratic behaviour, indifference and ignorance – then later in a total struggle for emotional survival and continuously fending off emotional and physical assaults. My father is a manic-depressive and also tried to take his own life. My parents are furious at my grandparents because of their attitude and also because both of them interfered too much in my parents' lives. All the family relationships are strained: my parents' relationship with my grandparents – my mother's with her sister. Looking back I can say that I suffered from depression from when I was a child – at least

---

* The *Nibelungenlied* is the German mythical saga of Norse origin. (English editor)

since the move from my grandparents' house. I told girlfriends that I would kill myself, I felt unloved, melancholic, hardly slept at night. I can well remember the feeling of being under a glass dome – not properly living and not feeling anything. And unfortunately I still have this feeling today. My grandma's death further intensified my psychological symptoms. I felt as if I'd lost my nerve, I was in total shock and suffered for months from dizziness, anxiety and panic attacks. That was when I was 26. A medical consultant suggested that I begin a course of therapy and I have been working on myself since then."

Julia

Julia was planned, but even so not wanted, and when she was three months old her grandparents on her mother's side looked after her during the day, as her parents, both professionals, wanted to carry on with their careers. So the baby was taken to the grandparents first thing in the morning and picked up from there in the afternoon.

Julia is an only child. Two years before she was born her mother had been pregnant with a little boy and had had an abortion; her justification was that he might be disabled because she was pregnant despite taking the pill. Her doctor was of the same opinion. Julia's parents planned the pregnancy with her. In a constellation the mother representative said without warmth: "We're going to make ourselves a child." There was no feeling of warmth and love in other constellations either, not even from the mother's womb. The representative for Julia as an embryo described the womb as an "ice belly". Conceived, developed and born in coldness, Julia was given away when she was just three months old. To this day she has felt unwanted. Her parents 'made' her but didn't really want her. However, they always told her that she was a wanted child. Her parents were obviously not aware of the consequences of having a baby. Julia started going to kinder-garten when she was four, and before that she spent every day with her grandparents who had previously lived their lives just doing what they wanted. That had been things like wandering round the town, shopping and going to restaurants; nothing they could continue to do with a baby. Their lives were changed completely. Julia spent most of her time in her pram on the balcony. Her grandmother says today that she was an easy baby. She was bottle-fed, as she had been with her mother as well. It was only when she went to kindergarten that she met people who accepted her lovingly, but by this time she was already so split that she was mostly caught up in herself and played alone in a corner.

Julia tells me that she has got in touch with her grandmother. She wants to know more about her early life. Her grandma told her that she was 'easily led'. Julia finds these words as fitting as they are alarming, as she always felt manipulated in her life. Her grandma explained to her that she discovered Julia liked to do the opposite of what she was told, so her grandma simply told her to do the opposite of what she really wanted, and that way she avoided any arguments and got the result she wanted. For Julia it's important to take these things seriously. That way she can access the little girl who was all alone, not really wanted by anyone and 'led' like a puppet so that she wasn't any trouble to anyone. Even so, Julia found ways to be a burden to her grandmother. That way she received more attention, and in any event she didn't have any other choice because she always experienced two extremes with her mother: "My pretty, clever little girl" or "You freak".

For Julia's grandmother, looking after Julia not only changed her way of life, it also meant that she was confronted with her own traumas. When Julia tried to gain her grandmother's attention by infuriating her, when, for example, she trashed her room and refused to tidy it up, her grandmother felt exasperation, fear and powerlessness, but also anger, which she didn't show externally. She had been a refugee from Silesia in World War II and had witnessed violence and rape, maybe even having experienced rape herself. She was treated as a 'second-class human being' not only by the Russian soldiers but also by the people who owned the farm in West Germany where her family were accommodated. The fact that as a small child Julia didn't show her respect, triggered exactly these feelings.

Julia is now in her 30s and is completely isolated. She is afraid of social contact, has broken off her university studies and is living on her savings. Her dearest wish is to step out of this isolation into life, but her survival structures are so complex that she finds the first step extremely difficult. Her traumas are still active; she received her mother's traumatising energies while in her womb, and then she suffered from her mother's absence, followed by daily emotional and physical violence from her mother, and sexual abuse by her father. The little girl didn't have a chance to develop trust in anyone; her parents weren't a calming influence, quite the opposite; she continually had to be on her guard. The way out of this, which she has been following for some time, is to face the scars of her earlier traumas. Through therapy she is gaining more and more self-confidence, but her fear of people is still a survival programme that she will only be able to give up when she has completely integrated the little Julia who has remained deeply split off within her.

The same applies to all these case histories: if the grandparents' care does not emanate from healthy structures, but rather from their own needs or their rejection of the child, or if their care is fuelled by destructive bonding energies, the child is in great danger of experiencing an early trauma. The decision to put a child in the care of a grandmother who had just tried to take her own life, as in the case of Katharina, cannot have been a decision from healthy structures. Julia's case history also shows how carelessly the parents behaved in giving their child to the grandparents to be looked after, when the grandparents had planned their lives quite differently and for whom looking after the child was a nuisance. Each of these examples shows that the grandparents cannot be a 'substitute' for parents and that the longing for the parents' love remains, or culminates, for the children, in a 'trauma of love'.

14

Violence instead of love from the very start

Margriet Wentink

14.1 Early violence

My understanding of 'early violence' is of parents, family members, carers and others carrying out, or failing in their attempts to carry out, actions that physically and psychologically harm an unborn or newborn child or young infant, which then lead to short- or long-term physical, psychological and emotional developmental problems.

This definition poses the question: how can we determine whether injuries to babies and young children, and developmental defects that appear in slightly older children, have been caused by early violence? Physical injuries are relatively easy to determine, however there is not always solid evidence of the connection between the behaviour of parents or carers and a child's injury. Even if the injury is clearly visible, the question arises: who is going to explain the real reason for the injury? The child cannot, and the adult concerned probably won't out of fear or shame about his or her actions or because he or she is afraid to be blamed and punished. Often there is no witness. So who can prove whether a child, for example, accidentally fell off the table or whether his bruises are the result of a parent's violence?

If a baby is injured and a doctor is not immediately consulted, who then writes the medical report recording the injury, and the accident or violence that caused it? Then all that remains is a scar, a sensitive spot on the body, a limp or a strangely bent toe that can't be straightened. If, in later life, someone asks where certain scars or certain physical disorders come from, then questions arise that frequently remain unanswered.

If the child was neglected or under-nourished as a baby, perhaps almost died of malnutrition, or if his nappy wasn't regularly changed or he wasn't looked after, cared for and comforted there is often nothing visible externally. This information only exists in the child's deeply rooted memory.

If parents persistently make negative comments about their child over a long period of time, shout at him, verbally humiliate him or deny that he is their child, withholding love, affection and acceptance from him, or if they are violent towards one another and ignore and disregard the effect of this on their child, it is difficult to prove such psychological violence has been used towards a child. If there is some permanent damage to the child's psychological health or development, it is even more difficult over time to determine definitively that this damage was linked to such abuse of the child, especially, if none of the witnesses present at the time is willing to talk about it. For adults who, as a result of being in therapy – for example, constellation therapy – gradually become aware of early violence towards them, this fact is one of the difficulties they have to overcome, in addition to dealing with their actual experiences: how can I know it's true and who is going to believe me?

14.2 Hidden violence

There is a sort of violence meted out to unborn, newborn infants and youngsters that takes place behind closed doors and is kept secret. But there is also a sort of violence that is not recognised as such or acknowledged. I have called this 'hidden violence'. The fact that hidden violence is not recognised or certain violent actions are regarded as legal in society, has to do with adults' trauma survival strategies that prevent them from recognising what is really happening. If a certain form of violence is even legal, then it is an expression of a collective blindness to traumatisation. I would like to use some examples to illustrate this:

- There are subtle forms of neglect where children apparently lack nothing material, and the family seems to function well. However, in reality the façade of a perfect, affluent family can sometimes hide serious, affective neglect, with the children being systematically denied love, attention, security and warmth.
- Parents who, due to limited psychological or physical ability, are not able to assume responsibility for a child or a whole family, and who either do not ask for help, or receive help which is not suitable, sometimes place their families in a situation where their children are treated with violence. Children are traumatised if, as infants, they are neglected, if they are left alone for too long or if they are subjected to their parents' unpredictable emotional outbursts.
- Many publications concerning secure attachment stress the point that adults need to be sensitive and react according to the needs of the individual child. Despite this, many children are taken to a crèche a few weeks after they are born, where sometimes very young staff have to look after what is often too large a group of children for the whole day. Against this background it is not surprising that a national Dutch study has revealed the following: "If a child has a difficult temperament, a relatively early start in a crèche where he also spends a relatively large amount of time, and if this is combined with the crèche not being of the best quality, then these can be possible risk factors in the child's development". (NCKO 2011) [Netherlands Consortium for Research in Child Care]
- Although in the Netherlands, as well as in most other Western European countries, the religious and ritual practice of female circumcision is illegal (although this is deliberately overlooked at times) because it is generally regarded as genital mutilation and violence, this does not apply to the circumcision of boys. In most Western European countries this is (still) legal. Amongst the followers of certain religions and cultural practices, the circumcision is carried out when a boy is seven or eight days old, sometimes without an anaesthetic.

- The stress in our society has consequences for unborn children and young children. The correlation between the expectant mother's stress and the consequences for the child was clearly established in a comprehensive study of more than 9,000 pregnant mothers at the University of Rotterdam (EUMC 2010) [Erasmus University Medical Center]
- A few decades ago, little was known about the consequences for children if their parents suffered from psychological disorders. If such traumatised parents are triggered into their own traumas, their survival strategies can be activated, some of which are dangerous and a threat to children: hate, uncontrolled anger, aggression and sadism, emotions that were originally associated with completely different people, are acted out and vented on the child. Many children who have grown up with unstable and insecure parents who display severe behavioural problems, have never received the understanding and recognition they need in order to understand themselves.

The number of examples of situations in our western society, in which infants and young children or unborn children are subjected, consciously or unconsciously, to violence, with society turning a blind eye or not noticing the traumatic consequences for the child, can be increased by all the other examples described in this book.

14.3 Consequences of early violence for personality development

Violence experienced at an early age is overwhelming for a small child, and accompanied by intense feelings of anxiety and powerlessness, and so we can speak of traumatisation at this early age. (Herman 2003) Ruppert's model (2012, 2014), which is based on trauma causing the person's psyche to split into three parts, applies here. Because this is about power and powerlessness, helplessness and dependence, violence and wounded trust at a young age, this has far-reaching consequences for the later development of a child's personality, and the extent to which he can become autonomous. The split-off, helpless, dependent, traumatised parts might stay very young all his life. The first survival parts, with their very childish and incomplete cognitions, draw confusing and wrong conclusions about himself and others, usually to the child's disadvantage, and to the advantage of others who were perpetrators to them, and who remain as such. Usually the child thinks or feels that *he* is not OK, but that his parents and carers are. That is one of the many examples of the adaptation strategies adopted by young children in order to protect the parent who is traumatising them. The survival parts can also be, for example, hyper-vigilant. They react to every movement and sound, see danger everywhere and trust no one. In addition, the survival parts develop an inner representation of the perpetrator. As this is very important in order to be able to adjust to any approaching danger, these inner representations are frequently very dominant.

The internal dynamic that develops within a person from traumatised victim parts and internalised perpetrator parts, that can only perceive reality from his own limited perspective, is frequently very complex. As a result, this dynamic distorts perception of everyday reality. Problems arise in assessing day-to-day situations, which then lead to new problems such as conflicts with others, lack of concentration or inability to complete work or school tasks. It is in fact the dynamics between the many different internal parts of the person that emerge following a repeated trauma that forms the basis of personality disorders such as, for example, 'Borderline Personality Disorder'. The stress this leads to has to be released repeatedly, usually unconsciously and almost automatically, in a way that is familiar and was learnt in their early childhood from their most important attachment figure. This means that the violence is more likely to be repeated, either against the person themselves or against weaker people such as, for example, dependent children. The assumption that people treat others as they have been treated themselves has all too often been shown to be true, although there is sometimes a difference in the intensity.

Victim and perpetrator parts in one person

The client's intention was to understand why she always treated herself in such a negative way despite knowing that it wasn't necessary and, looked at objectively, wasn't true. The woman she sets up for her 'intention' walks around with quick, short little steps and says she doesn't want to stand still because she's afraid she will feel something. The client confirms that she recognises that in herself. The more she realises that she also has such a part inside her, the calmer the representative of her intention becomes. She describes how this realisation means that she starts to feel more ground under her feet and she finds it easier to remain standing in her place. For a little while they stand silently opposite one another. Then the 'intention' says that she's starting to feel ill, feverish, shivering and cold. She feels as if she wants to be looked after and as if she's very alone and abandoned. The client agrees that it was like that when she was young: neglect, coldness and loneliness, even when she was ill, and she was frequently ill. The 'intention' says she can feel that quite clearly and also that more feelings are hidden underneath, but that she doesn't really dare to allow these through because if she felt them she would rather just let herself fall over backwards: "So ... dead ... finished."

The client says that she would like to set up her mother as well. As we are working in a private session she chooses a stone to represent her mother and places it on the floor. After she has done that, she and the 'intention' no longer feel anything: all feelings have gone. I suggest that she sets up the little, lonely child part. She takes a cushion and clutches it desperately to herself. The representative of the intention starts to get angry. She rants and rails against this child part and wants to kick it. The client says: "My father used to do that; it seems that that's my father." And again she describes a part of her youth. She represents the father with a large wooden block. However, this doesn't make any difference to the 'intention', who says: "I have to say what I feel, it has to be expressed: hate, wanting to destroy, wanting to make others small, wanting to break them." The woman cries and again talks about her father. The 'intention' says: "I really don't feel that this is from the father. It's from you; I would so much like it to be your feeling, that's the feeling in a part of you. I feel as if I'm a part of you who has this hate and this destruction inside, and I would very much like you to know me. I am quite sure and it feels very complex and confusing." She continues: "We know this story already; we've often told it; but we have to know whether we may also feel it."

I suggest to the client that she sets up the part that has such hostile behaviour separately, which she does. The representative of the intention is relieved. She wants to look at it. The client stands next to her. Together they focus on the part with the hostile behaviour. The 'intention' says: "It feels very complex: as if it's a very intelligent part of us." The client recognizes that and says that she's touched by it. Then she says: "It's the part with which I've suppressed my gentleness and my vulnerability." The client and the 'intention' both have goose pimples when those words are spoken. They explore it further emotionally and discover the following: one part of the client wanted to protect them and save them. She wasn't allowed to be vulnerable and weak; that was much too dangerous. The best she could do was to fight it within herself and suppress it, so that her gentleness didn't provoke her father to use any violence. The only way she could do that was to behave the way she had seen him behave. She places the cushion that she is still clutching tightly to herself, next to the part. She feels gentle and amazed and says: "They are now equal. First of all there was a difference: one was good, the other bad; now they're equal. One part of me wanted to save me by destroying my gentleness."

When I meet her again she tells me that this constellation has enabled her to be much kinder to herself and to recognise her own needs better.

14.4 Allow the truth step by step

The method 'Constellation of the Intention' based on multi-generational psychotraumatology' is particularly suitable for revealing and healing traumas caused by early violence, and I see this daily in my practice. Good trauma therapy helps clients name the real perpetrators and the innocent victims, which resolves their childlike confusion as to what is normal and what constitutes violence or behaviour that oversteps boundaries. Good trauma therapy also helps the client grow out of his victim attitude and assume responsibility for his own feelings and his own life. A constellation is a great relief for many people because it makes their early childhood experiences tangible: experiences they internally and unconsciously already know but only seldom have clearly recognised.

During the constellation, the representatives as well as the client experience things that contain information about what the child must have felt in the context in which he grew up. For the client, admitting this information is a gradual process, and the truth that becomes visible cannot always be recognised at once. When clients are able to accept their own experiences, feelings and memories, a healing process can gradually take place, in which they are more connected to themselves and are able increasingly to gain insights into their own personal history. Particularly when processing traumatic experiences accompanied by violence, a person loses trust in other people and in himself. If such a person is not forced to take steps he or she is not ready for, a natural healing process from inside can take place at his own pace. The following example illustrates this.

Good to have it finally confirmed

A female client has been working for some time on her therapeutic process with the help of the method 'Constellation of the Intention'. In a previous constellation she saw that there is a part within her that has a great need for closeness and physical contact. This part gets her into situations that are not good for her. In her daily life she experiences how strong this part is, and the behaviour that emanates from this part makes her feel ashamed. She tries to keep it at a distance but she knows that she cannot escape it. Through the therapeutic process she has discovered that admitting and recognising these parts within her helps her to achieve greater balance, even though she really rejects these inner parts. At the same time she is still afraid of the information and feelings that confront her when she encounters these parts.

For her next constellation she formulates the following intention: "I would like to allow, within me, the feelings of the part that has such a great need for closeness." After setting up the 'intention', a part is revealed within the 'intention' that wants closeness, but not contact. This part is afraid of contact, as is the client. Both have difficulty breathing and feel intense pressure on the chest. The 'intention' says: "I'm afraid that you'll expect things from me. I'm afraid that you'll demand answers from me that I can't give you. I don't know what the matter is with me. I don't want to have to know; it feels like betrayal. I feel tormented." The client's anxiety increases. She feels increasing pressure on her chest and her breathing is more and more difficult. The 'intention' says: "I'm starting to feel as if I'm stuck in a pack of cotton wool and I can feel myself becoming emptier and emptier. Now I don't feel anything any more." The client also feels less and less. She wants to let the part know what that reminds her of. The 'intention' quickly responds with: "Be quiet. I don't want to know what happened. If I don't know I can breathe again and come closer."

A month later the client comes back for another constellation. In the past month profound events have taken place in her life. A girl-friend of hers died suddenly and in her work environment she had several experiences that felt to her like existential threats, although her head told her that they were actually not life threatening at all. She says: "This month feels like a mirror. I have the feeling that I will put myself in mortal danger if I go on running from the truth and using this survival strategy." Again she sets up a constellation. Now she has the courage to allow the truth. The constellation reveals that her mother had tried to suffocate her with a cushion when she was a baby. At the end of the constellation, after she had lain for some time on the floor next to a very young part of herself, crying, she says: "I can't get my head round it; as if my head still can't believe that my mother did something like that. But every fibre of my being knows it's true. I feel deeply sad but at the same time calm and relaxed, strange as that might sound. Lying here like this, the jigsaw of images and memories is completed with things that happened to my sister and me. It's good to be sure at last."

14.5 Explicit and implicit memories

What makes the constellation method, i.e. 'the "Constellation of the Intention" based on multi-generational psychotraumatology', a suitable psychotherapeutic approach for adults traumatised by early violence? In order to answer this question we have to understand something about our memory, which is divided into implicit and explicit memory. (Le Doux 1996, Schacter 1996, Ladan 2003)

Information about certain events and facts is stored in our explicit memory. To enable this sort of information storage, the child's brain needs to have gone through a certain developmental stage and be capable of storing language and images. This is generally not the case before the child has reached his third year of life. For that reason, no information concerning the events experienced in a person's earliest childhood is stored in explicit memory, (Nelson and Carver 1998) and therefore many people cannot remember images of early abuse and violence and do not mention them in their autobiographical details when they come for therapy.

The information stored in implicit memory is completely different. This is information not consciously remembered but unconsciously 'lived'. Behavioural patterns, thoughts, beliefs and feelings that are based on recurring patterns of early experiences become visible in relationships and daily life. A person cannot remember these individual experiences but they are stored as a unity of motor reactions and sensory impressions in a memory system that doesn't use language and images. (Terr 1994) This happens, for example, when a child born prematurely is put into an incubator, and hooked up to machines when it is so delicate and vulnerable that every touch constitutes over-stimulation and increased stress. This person will not later consciously remember things like: "And then hands came and stressed me out, and again on the next day, and again the day after that". However, when this person enters into an intimate relationship, he will experience that, although he desires closeness and physical contact, it scares him and causes feelings of stress. This is also true in a positive sense:

the child who has experienced from his earliest childhood that his individual needs for nourishment, comfort, warmth and security have always been met by someone sensitive to them, will not remember each and every time he was given food or comfort, but he will possess a basic feeling of fulfilment and security with which he encounters the world and his relationships.

That is how we recognise the content of the implicit memory system: by the way a person behaves and enters into relationships. We never consciously remember, with images or thoughts, information from our implicit memory, but rather as an underlying state, a feeling or type of behaviour, that we do not understand by itself, but that others often point out to us or that stands in our way, preventing us from living our life as we want to.

Another difference between these two memory systems is that the information stored in explicit memory can become blurred and is subject to distortion. Time, context and relevance, for example, are factors that influence whether we remember an event or not. The quantity of stress hormones accompanying an experience also influences the extent to which we can store information in explicit memory. Interestingly, this is not true of implicit memory. Stress reactions, fear, pain and anguish are stored in implicit memory and remain in the nervous system. This is why traumatic events leave an indelible mark, even if the individual cannot remember the events themselves. (Le Doux 1996)

When working with constellations we create a particular therapeutic environment. The client formulates his intention, and by doing so he determines the focal point of the therapeutic session for that day. The therapist must be able to see and understand the boundaries set by the client by how he formulates his intention: the client would like to achieve A today, which implies that he does not want to achieve B, C or D. As the client sets up a representative for his intention, there is an immediate interaction between two living people. Information from the client's implicit memory frequently becomes apparent from the very first moment through features of the representation: the temperature of the hand leading the representative to their position, the pressure exerted, or the way the client positions himself in relationship to the representative. Issues emerge the longer the client and the representative of the intention are in contact with one another such as trust, mistrust, security, fixation, anxiety, and physical sensations. The implicit behavioural patterns, of which the client is not consciously aware, become explicit in the constellation. Information from the explicit memory can also be activated by the interaction, the information, the images and the feelings expressed in the work. Phrases frequently used by clients during or shortly after a constellation are: "I suddenly remember . . ." or "I've just realised . . .". The client becomes aware of facts or events that he can relate to situations emerging from the constellation. Sometimes no concrete information arises in the client, but the feelings that both the client and the representatives in the constellation have convey an image of the early trauma that might have taken place in the client's childhood.

Sex addiction and premature birth

A man says he has been aware for a long time that he cannot feel his body. The only time he can is through sexual stimulation, which he seeks frequently. The intention the client formulates for this constellation is that he would "like to have more contact with his body". After a while he says that seems senseless because he is much too afraid and he would rather "know first why he is so afraid of feeling his body".

The representative of the man's intention expresses feelings that the man slowly recognises: fear and accelerated breathing, as if he is drawn up inside his body and then no longer inhabits his body. The stiffness and tension is visible in the client and in the representative. The representative says he has to avoid contact with his body and above all he feels very afraid, he has to sink down inside his body and only then begin to feel it. A representative for the man's mother is set up and she, too, is very afraid. She holds her belly. She says her fear is unbearable and she's afraid her belly will split open. The representative of the intention begins to tremble. The man says afterwards that there were complications during the pregnancy and he was born two weeks too early. He was in an incubator for five weeks. Although he was asked about momentous events in his life before the constellation, he hadn't mentioned this. "I just didn't think about it for a moment" was his comment.

During this process in which more and more information gradually appears, memories from explicit and implicit memory are activated. It is clear that this process can be very confrontational for people who have experienced violence as an unborn or very young child. However, it is remarkable how it always becomes clear that the confrontation with the truth of the person's own life can bring forth intense feelings, but in the end these are seen as a relief and are recognised at the profound level of implicit memory. People who have had the courage to explore their underlying trauma frequently describe their positive feelings as: contentment, relief, connection with themselves, fulfilment, a flowing feeling and easing of tension.

We are regularly asked how reliable the memories are that come to light during constellations. I would like to make the following comments:

First of all it is important that the therapist sticks with what has come to light in the constellation and does not put his own interpretation onto what is visible in the constellation. If, for example, a representative expresses pain, it is pain, and we do not yet know where the pain is coming from. If neither the constellation nor the client supplies any information about the cause of the pain we leave it open until further information is forthcoming from the client. The therapist can use his skill and knowledge to help the client to perceive and understand many occurrences in the constellation. However, if he suggests that he knows the *meaning* of the images in the constellation, he is skating on very thin ice. On the other hand, the therapist should not leave the client too much on his own in his confusion if the latter does not immediately understand what the constellation has revealed. Sometimes being left alone is the defining trauma experience from his childhood. This should not be repeated during the constellation process in case the client is retraumatised.

The ideal way for therapist and client to work together is for the therapist first of all to offer the client the time and space he needs for his inner process to take place at his own pace. No one can determine for anyone else the pace at which this process should happen. For the practised eye, the inner process is evident from the client's non-verbal communication and from the course of the constellation. The literal use of respect (respicere, Latin = care for, look back at, consider) for the process and the client's individual pace is called for here.

It is also the therapist's task, if called for, to make use of his experience and knowledge to help the client connect what he has learned from the constellation with the content-related information already known to him. However, it is only the client who possesses all the information related to his own life experiences, or who can sometimes get hold of this information from members of his family or other sources.

The struggle against being driven away

A female client has set up several consecutive constellations for herself and takes part in a constellation seminar. When it comes to her turn for a constellation she says that she came to the seminar with three questions that were important to her. To begin with she hadn't been able to decide which question was most important at that moment. However, during the seminar she had seen other participants' constellations and had been set up in a representative role in some of these and these experiences have helped her to understand what the issue is. She formulates her intention thus: "I would like to allow the feelings concerning what happened to me as a child." She sets up a woman as representative of her intention, holds her hands and gazes at her. They stand opposite one another in silence. The client's body begins to tremble and she says she feels that everything around her is becoming tense. The tension around her becomes so strong that she says: "I want to go, I want to go!" The representative of her intention nods slightly and continues to hold her hands. She sinks further into herself to escape from the tension and says: "No, it's not that I want to go; I have to go, I'm being pushed away by the tension; I have to go but I'm trying to fight against being driven away because I don't want to go." The woman begins to sob; the sobbing comes from deep within her belly. After a while she says, crying gently: "Shame, too much shame; I can't stay here where everyone can see me; shame that I exist." For this client many events from her youth and experiences from earlier constellations come together in this constellation.

Her mother was an ambitious young woman who wanted to grow and develop, build up her own career and earn her own income: things that were not yet a matter of course in those days and that environment. She fell in love and got engaged and married. A short while later she was pregnant. In those days that meant a woman had to give up her job, which she was pressured into doing. She found being at home with her first child very difficult and her inexperience, insecurity and discontent led to the child being undernourished, which in turn led to more stress. After six months she became pregnant again. When she was three months pregnant and the first child was nine months old, her mother became seriously ill and needed to be looked after. Out of a sense of duty she moved with the oldest child and her husband to her parents' house to care for her ill mother. Living conditions there were hard and she felt totally overburdened, rejected and ashamed.

The pressure, hardship, rejection and feelings of shame were expressed in the constellation. When the client got in touch later, she said: "The constellation had a great effect on me. Many feelings emerged that I recognised from my life. Above all I am very familiar with the feeling that I'm always living 'against oppression': I always generate pressure and stress with deadlines and work-overload. I also know well the feeling that I'm too much and have to go. I've thought about the shame I felt in the constellation. I wonder whether it actually is my shame. It's either my mother's shame, that I don't completely understand yet, or my own shame that developed later on, because, as a child, it's so shameful not to be loved by your mother. You start to think that you're some sort of sickening monster."

Allowing the information within themselves, the feelings and behavioural patterns that are anchored in implicit memory, as well as the images and words that are stored in explicit memory, ensures that people finally understand themselves and are able to remove the blockages within them. They receive access to their complete experiential world that is a part of their biography at a profound level. They rediscover themselves as a person with a coherent whole of meaningful perceptions, thoughts, feelings, memories and actions.

15
Early trauma, adoption and foster parents

Liesel Krüger

Children who are fostered or adopted have one thing in common: they have been separated from their mother and father very early. In most cases this separation takes place some time between birth and their third year. Foster children and adopted children who are separated from their mothers this early experience the separation as traumatic. In her book series *Mit den Augen eines Kindes sehen lernen* [Learning to see through a child's eyes] Bettina Bonus describes early separation from the mother as the "central early traumatisation" (Bonus 2006, p. 52) with severe consequences for the children's development.

Why is separation from the natural mother so momentous for a child? The child grows in the mother's womb and knows her voice, her circulation, her heartbeat, the sounds of her intestines and also her reaction to stress, anxiety, joy, sorrow and anger. The child experiences his natural mother and himself as an inseparable entity. From the child's point of view, the loss of his natural mother is the worst thing that can happen in his life – he loses the basis of his life. "If the mother rejects her child during pregnancy, the child is in a symbiotic trauma situation right from the beginning, and he will be born as a trauma survivor". (Ruppert 2014, p. 249) Ruppert also writes, referring to the work of Eric Breitinger, "If the child is given by the mother to adoptive or foster parents immediately after birth, the psychosomatic bonds between mother and child that have formed during pregnancy and the birth process are abruptly torn apart. The child is powerless because his signals to his mother achieve nothing, and he has to split in order to survive this situation. He can then only use a part of his vitality to develop a new relationship with his adoptive parents ... thereby more easily becoming entangled with the traumas of his adoptive or foster parents". (Ruppert 2014, pp. 248, 249)

The following case histories refer to the early traumatisation of foster children. The adopted children I know of have usually been through one or more instances of foster care before they are adopted. After birth, a foster child can experience several further separation traumas from intermediate homes before a 'final' foster family takes him in. These can be

- a prolonged stay in hospital,
- a short or long stay in his family of origin,
- an eight-week foster care (only for children who become adoptive children),
- short-term care,
- attempted return to the natural mother,
- one or more stays in a home,
- several foster families.

The child tries again and again to have his needs for love, caring, holding and security fulfilled by trying to form an attachment to the new caregiver. The child experiences these multiple severing of care relationships powerlessly, helplessly, desperately, anxiously and angrily. (Brisch 2013) All foster children 'have' at least two 'mothers'; most have three, some even more: their natural mother and further regular caregivers.

As well as recurring separations from attachment figures, many foster children experience further traumatisation, such as

- through the mother's experience of violence during pregnancy,
- through a birth trauma,
- through their own withdrawal from drug addiction as a result of their mother's addiction,
- through violence experienced in the intermediate homes,
- through neglect and lack of compassion or
- through sexual abuse.

Foster parents have different reasons for taking in children, such as

- offering needy children a home,
- compensating for their own childlessness,
- seeking a replacement child for one of theirs who died,
- receiving financial reward,
- because offering a foster home is their profession.

Foster parents are prepared for their task by social services and receive supervision and advice. Frequently, however, everyday life with the children entrusted to their care quickly becomes overwhelming, due to the children's behaviour. 'Family dramas' are caused by the consequences of trauma such as fits of anger, destructive behaviour, anxiety and panic attacks, refusal to make any effort, self-endangerment (e.g. 'kamikaze behaviour' in traffic), injury to other children and adults with no sign of empathy or understanding (e.g. pulling out hair, throwing stones, lashing out, hitting others with objects), difficult group behaviour in kindergarten and school, refusal to do homework, and difficulties with normal tasks like eating, getting dressed, brushing teeth. For the children it is a matter of their very survival. Overstepping every boundary is a trauma survival strategy "as long as there are no healed parts of the early traumatisation". (Bonus 2006, p. 138) It is particularly the poorly developed empathic behaviour of many foster children that leads to social exclusion. When they were babies they lacked a mother's loving mirroring. If foster children have regular contact with their natural mother, they mostly hope to return to her. After such meetings their behaviour towards their foster parents is often confused, particularly aggressive and negative.

Do foster parents at least offer their foster children a trauma-free environment? Unfortunately, based on my experience with foster children and foster parents, in many cases they do not. Sometimes foster parents 'lose it' because they are so overwhelmed and scream, threaten, overreact, hit out even against their own convictions; they are reminded of their own experiences in their childhood and can no longer respond to the child in a calm manner, giving them the bonding support they need. If foster parents have children of their own, these children are frequently jealous and hostile towards the foster children, because their abnormal behaviour means the parents have to pay the foster children more attention. That often leads to situations of unbearable conflict between the children.

The foster parents are often told little about the children's previous experiences and are ill-informed and helpless. It is not only the foster children who need in-depth assistance from outside, but also the foster parents. What traumas can a foster child encounter in a foster family?

15.1 Personal statistics

I have accompanied 11 foster and adoptive children in Clay Field therapy: three girls and eight boys. One of the boys was disabled from birth. Of the 11 children, five were separated from their mother for more than two weeks in hospital following their birth. Of the 11 children, eight were placed into care by social services, four children due to the mothers' drug addiction, three because the mothers were underage and had experienced violence before and during the pregnancy, and one because the mother had been severely disabled by the birth. Three of these children were placed in care 'voluntarily' by their mothers. Of these 11 foster children, six were later adopted, two during their Clay Field therapy. Five children are likely to stay foster children until they are 18. They are in touch with their natural mothers. Of the 11 children, four effectively 'have' three 'mothers' (their natural mother and two foster mothers). Of the 11 children, three were temporarily housed in a home, one child several times for longer periods. Six of the children were diagnosed with ADHD, with five of them being prescribed Ritalin as therapy. Two children were taken off the medication because they lost their appetite. All 11 children display the consequences of trauma, such as avoidant behaviour to suppress their fears, aggressive behaviour, developmental disorders, attachment problems, agitation, refusal to make any effort, learning difficulties, social problems, lack of self-esteem and reduced or little empathy.

15.2 'Work at the Clay Field®'

I was a breech presentation baby born during a bombing raid in World War II. My mother was severely traumatised. I was separated from her and taken to an air raid shelter. My mother had tried in vain to kill herself and me before and after my birth. She was never able to form an attachment relationship with me. I have worked on these traumas mainly with the 'Work at the Clay Field®' and Franz Ruppert's method of the 'Constellation of the Intention'. (Ruppert 2012, 2014)

Before I write about working with foster children and foster parents I would first like to describe the method 'Work at the Clay Field®', which is a Gestalt therapy method developed by Heinz Deuser from 1972 that is being further researched. (Deuser 2004, Brockmann and Geiß 2011, Elbrecht 2013) In my own practice, and in kindergartens and schools, I offer 'Work at the Clay Field®' for children from the age of two and a half, as well as for adolescents and adults. I see the 'Work at the Clay Field®' as a therapeutic method that helps to make up for neglected developmental needs and heal traumas.

The field is a rectangular wooden box filled thumb-deep with soft clay and smoothed over. There are no specific dimensions of the field. The field I use for children is filled with about 15kg of clay; there are about 20kg in the field for adults. A bowl with warm water is ready on the table. Providing these simple things with no stipulations is an invitation to touch and feel the clay spontaneously, to move it about. Children work with their eyes open; adults usually with their eyes closed. With adults we discuss the process of shaping in our concluding dialogue. The field of clay offers the opportunity, supported by the relationship with the therapist, for the individual to establish a relationship with the field of clay with their hands, and thereby to get in touch with their underlying senses, to address developmental blockages and to develop new opportunities in a creative way. When working with Clay Field therapy with fostered and adopted children, I am very aware that these children have experienced many traumas before arriving in their final families. In addition, the extreme behaviour sometimes displayed by these children means they experience new difficulties daily, for example marginalisation at school, through accidents or doctor's visits. For outsiders their reactions are often incomprehensible and intolerable. The children are frequently retraumatised in their everyday life.

The path to healing is long, since every trauma has to be worked on separately. The fact that the children are still dependent on their caregivers means that they are often only able to work therapeutically with their trauma as adults. As a therapist, it is important that I remain open, alert, attentive and present; then it is possible to achieve some contact with the child. The child needs to be able to trust the therapist; he needs to feel accepted, supported, encouraged and helped so that he dares to show and describe his needs, his feelings and his distress. He can then find his own path to solutions. The way his hands move when working at the Clay Field will show the psychological state of the child, his survival structures, his trauma and his healthy structures. It always fills me with joy to be able to support these children when they take hold of their own life history in the Clay Field work, and experience a strengthening of their 'I' through the development of new relationship, competence and skills, and creatively acquire new opportunities for their life in the 'here and now'.

The basis of my work is Franz Ruppert's model of personality splits following traumatisation. The sooner traumatised children receive therapy, the better their chances are of working through their trauma experiences, overcoming the disturbances in their development, and so reducing or eliminating difficulties in their behaviour, and finding new ways of social cooperation. In the main the work is non-verbal. This is particularly helpful for children, as they often have no words for their difficulties, especially when the causes lie in their pre-linguistic period i.e. during pregnancy, at birth and in their very early years.

Children shape their world in the Clay Field. The soft clay invites them to touch, stroke, dig, grab, knead, hit, remove, shape and mess around. While they are working, they describe what they are doing, and may call for the therapist to join in, and are then happy to be working together. Often they bury their hands in the clay, or ask the therapist to cover their hands and parts of their lower arms, and sometimes their feet as well. Being cocooned gives them the feeling of support and security they did not experience in the womb. Some want the therapist to pour warm water through an opening into the cavities in the clay. Pleasurable lip smacking can then be heard. In this way children can nurture their need for warmth and touch.

If children feel overwhelmed by events they remember during the work, they often protect themselves by escaping into magical thinking (witches and sorcerers may be formed in the clay), or the therapist is asked to create bows and arrows or bombs for them, in order to kill enemies. If a child disperses all the clay in water, thereby reflecting a situation they have experienced (e.g. drug withdrawal as a baby), it is important that the therapist offers support and security for the child. Children often secure the field first by filling out the corners with clay, so that then they can dare to tackle their trauma events.

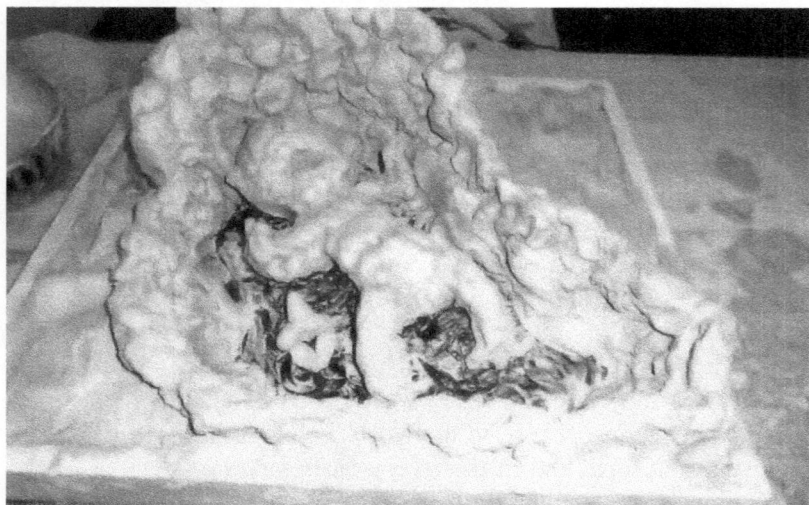

Figure 5: Xaver (5 years) enjoys his hands and arms being cocooned

Elisa

Elisa (nine years old) establishes loving contact with the crying baby within her. She divides the field in the middle of the clay tray into two countries with a riverbed the width of a hand that she calls the 'Isar'. She connects both countries by a bridge with railings and explains to me: "The adults have fallen into the river; they're all dead; there are only babies standing on the bridge". I explain to her that babies can't yet stand and have to be carried by adults. She looks at me briefly, nods, and then purposefully takes clay from the field and, totally immersed and concentrated, she shapes a big baby on the table. Her hands move as if they are driven and knowing. The vital, natural movements of her hands establish contact with healthy parts of herself that enable healing.

The baby seems to grow out of her hands. She lifts it carefully and rocks it for a long while in her arms, humming softly. She calls it Elisa and lovingly lays the baby down gently onto the table, bends over it and explains that it will have to wait a little while because she still has to build it a cradle.

With quick, confident movements she energetically grabs and presses the remainder of the clay, forming a cradle in the field and lovingly lays the baby into it. Then she calls out in agitation: "It's crying" and briefly puts a dummy into its mouth to soothe it. She strokes the baby tenderly, looks at me and says: "It's crying and crying!" Then she spends a longer time soothing it with the dummy and loving caresses. After this work Elisa's behaviour is generally calmer and more attentive at school.

Astrid

Astrid has three 'mothers'. In her first three years Astrid frequently spends long periods in different care homes. This is always when her mother is in a psychiatric clinic or in rehab. When she is three years old she goes to a foster family that has a natural child of her own age, where she stays for three years. She becomes very difficult and she does not develop normally for a child of her age. When she is six, Astrid leaves this foster family because her mother has been sent to an institution in a different part of the country that is too far away for visiting. Immediately after her arrival in the new foster family, Astrid's second foster mother brings her to me at the Clay Field. Astrid has stopped growing, and has noticeably thin hair. She cannot move confidently, keeps falling over, and her gross and fine motor skills are considerably lacking for her age.

In the first periods with the Clay Field she stays close to me and wants me to participate, so that she dares to approach the field and use the clay. After the first few Clay Field sessions, I realise with amazement that Astrid is starting to grow. Her hair is also growing and becoming thicker. Her motor skills improve rapidly and her movements become more confident. The work enables her more and more to feel, and get in contact with herself. Her search for touch, and at the same time resistance to it, shows the depth of her injuries. She creams herself for a long time with clay and water, seeks the touch of my hands, only to pull away suddenly, frightened. She frequently forms families, animal and human, as an expression of her longing for a perfect family. She repeatedly depicts her situation with three mothers: three nests with eggs and mother birds. She builds caves and walls as a sign of her need for protection and volcanoes to express her aggression. For a remarkably long time she creates an environment for animals, for horses, dogs and cats, and imitates their movements and sounds. Then she tries to climb into the clay field as the animal. She ends this game when I tell her several times she isn't an animal, that she's a person.

While working, she often demonstrates 'antisocial behaviour' such as squirting water or throwing lumps of clay. This behaviour has to be seen as an expression of her traumatisation through the frequent relationship terminations. Astrid is always confused and unfocused after she has visited her natural mother. When they meet, her mother promises Astrid that she will be able to come back to her, although her mother knows that that is officially not possible. Astrid expresses her need for protection again and again by building walls.

Astrid also likes to escape into fantasy worlds. In those moments she cannot perceive reality. She often forms the fairy tale of 'Rapunzel in her tower' with long hair, and plays through the rescuer outwitting the witch.

Astrid's conspicuous behaviour (lack of distance, tormenting animals, refusal to make any effort and refusal to work at school, lack of empathy towards foster siblings and animals, and extreme destructive behaviour such as cutting up beds and wreaking havoc in the bathroom) is slowly changing. Her reckless behaviour in traffic is also gradually improving. Astrid is becoming generally calmer and showing greater self-esteem: "Look, I've made that all on my own." She is more in touch with herself and her environment and is generally focused in her work at the Clay Field. Her vocabulary is expanding, she learns new words from the forms she shapes and the stories she tells are livelier and more coherent. It is important for her to have my undivided attention, support and appreciation. She casually mentions that her natural mother beat her with a wooden spoon. That is also reflected in the way she beats the clay with her hands: not rhythmically and animatedly, but her hands stay stuck down. After three years in the second foster family Astrid mentions during a medical examination that her foster parents beat her. She is then immediately taken from the foster family and put in a home. This unfortunately put an end to her work at the Clay Field.

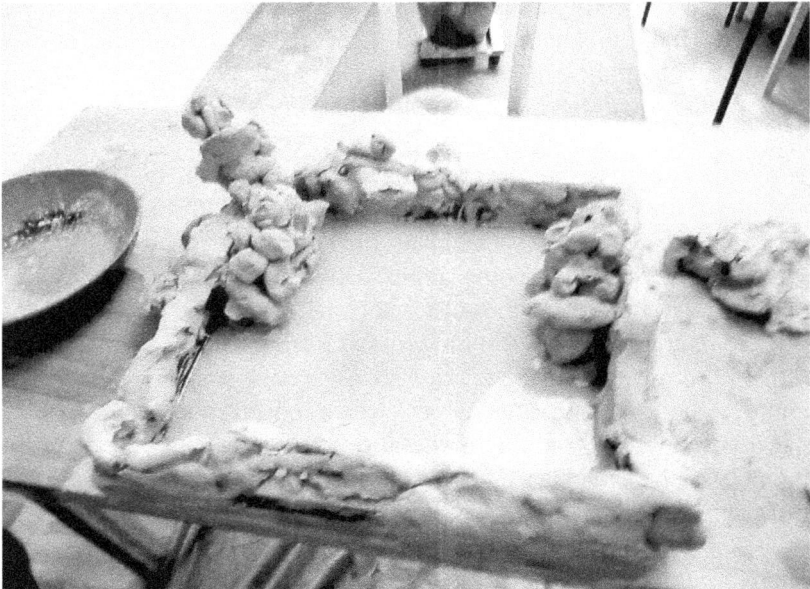

Figure 6: Astrid's protective walls.

15.3 'Work at the Clay Field' with foster parents and adoptive parents

Foster parents often reach the limits of their endurance as they feel helpless in the face of their foster child's rage and destruction. They are afraid of losing control over themselves and using violence. For foster parents who have not worked on their own traumas, it is difficult to maintain the adult role. They encounter the raging foster child with the traumatised child within themselves. The foster child then feels lost, unprotected, helpless, and hopeless, and abandoned, as they were in early childhood.

When I work with foster parents at the Clay Field, I first have a conversation with them, in which they formulate their intention. Mostly this is something like: "I'd like to know why my foster child often upsets me so much – and I'd like to change it." With working in the Clay Field the foster parents use their perception, their own movements and sensory perception, to get in touch with their own early traumatisation and work on it. In our closing discussion they are made aware of the individual steps of their work. I find the feedback that I later receive about the family situation becoming calmer impressive.

In summary

All foster children who were separated early from their mothers and fathers are traumatised by this separation. In addition, most foster children have experienced further traumatisation through violence, neglect and being repeatedly abandoned. When foster parents take a child in, they are confronted with the consequences of early traumatisation, which demand a high tolerance of frustration. Through extreme behavioural disorders such as aggression and refusal to make any effort, foster children can potentially trigger any early trauma in the foster parents and other family members, thereby leading to stressful situations that threaten to break up the family unit.

It is important that the foster children and foster parents receive help and support from outside in order to be able to create an atmosphere of security and loving guidance for the children entrusted to their care. Working in the Clay Field allows children with early traumatisation to get in touch with their fears, their sorrow and their aggression, and to work out new ways of dealing with their personal history. Realising their own competences and experiencing a caring relationship with the therapist in the Clay Field enables them to build up trust in themselves and towards others.

My experiences with extremely difficult foster children have shown that help for the traumatised children alone is not sufficient. The foster parents also need help if the children become an unbearable burden in their daily life together. Astrid's case history clearly shows how foster parents can lose control and use violence out of a sense of helplessness, even though they strongly believe in non-violent education. By doing this they exacerbate the child's trauma. It is important for the welfare services that look after the young to have sufficient numbers of social workers, teachers and therapists at their disposal to support foster families, thereby enabling the children to grow into a life of self-responsibility. Following conversations with them, some foster parents, whose children I have guided at the Clay Field, decided to begin their own course of therapy, through which they got in touch with their own childhood traumas. They worked on these with the 'Constellation of the Intention' and/or with work at the Clay Field or other therapies. They were then able to cope with stressful situations in a more relaxed way and show the child their love so that the child became calmer.

16

Eating disorders as a consequence of early traumatisation

Andrea Stoffers

The feeling of being defenceless against a permanent sense of hunger makes those concerned despair. They describe their symptoms as a longing for food, a strong feeling of hunger, 'food envy', as well as the hope that eating will solve their problems. The supposedly empty stomach is filled, but the emptiness remains. There is growing psychological and physical pressure to satisfy the sense of hunger.

What is stored as a program in the infant, often persists into adulthood if the cause of the hunger cannot be found. Most individuals with an eating disorder provide the explanation that they want to compensate for some lack through eating. At first glance this seems to be true. However, if we look more closely it becomes clear that it is frequently caused by pre- or postnatal traumatisation.

Many of my female clients recognise during their healing process that, to some extent, they received too much food, but their need for closeness, warmth, security, protection and emotional care was not satisfied. Or they almost died of hunger in the womb. These psychological events are caused by the parents, usually mothers, rejecting their child. The mothers are usually severely traumatised themselves, because, for example, they either went hungry during the war, or were subjected to violence, or had to fight for their daily survival. In the following case history, Irena's mother and her whole family had suffered during the war from cold, hunger and continuous existential danger.

Irena

When Irena was 12 she became bulimic. She comes to my practice as a 52-year-old, under great psychological stress. She is not able to like herself. She is under great pressure in her job, which has caused high blood pressure, stomach cramps and diarrhoea. She describes the cause of her mother's behaviour and her own experiences while she was growing up: "I was born in 1959 in L—. My mother was born in 1935 in the same town, which was then part of East Prussia. My father was born in 1939 in L—. My parents married in 1958. I suspect that my mother wanted a child because my cousin had been born two months earlier. She even wanted to give me the same name.

"When I was 10 months old my mother left my father and fled to Germany. I never got to know my father, who died in 1993. In 1960 my mother applied for an exit permit and she fled, just with me, as 'late emigrants' from the then USSR. First of all, we were in a transit camp in S—, and after a few weeks we were moved to G—, where she was assigned a flat. A year later she moved to D—, where she met my stepfather, who was born in 1944. For three generations my family has experienced flight or displacement and deportation. My grandmother had four children when her husband was killed in World War II at the age of 34. In 1942 the fifth child was born as a half-orphan [one parent alive and the other dead]. Before she was married, she had an illegitimate child, a daughter, with her employer; the girl died as a toddler. Later she had another child, a boy, who died at the age of one. My mother spent the first three years of her life with her grandmother on her father's side. This grandmother was a healer in the village and, amongst other things, healed my mother of rickets. This grandmother herself lost several children as infants or toddlers. Four sons died in World War II. When my mother's mother fled from East Prussia to Mecklenburg-Western Pomerania, her remaining children were aged ten, nine (my mother), seven, six, and two. During the three months' flight back to their home country, the family was often in great danger: my grandmother was raped and bore another child which died at birth. Throughout the war the family was hungry. My grandmother couldn't feed the children and abandoned the two boys and my mother and they were picked up by the police. They were in an orphanage for nine months before their mother was able to take them back again. By then she had somewhere to live and had found work for herself and her eldest daughter. I know that my mother had to work for farmers for a while and gave birth to another child when she was still young which did not survive. For decades, this child and the child my grandmother had after she was raped, were kept secret. I suspect that my mother was also raped.

"My mother's survival strategy must have been never to live in destitution or go hungry. So as soon as she arrived in Germany with me, she went out to work and left me with a neighbour or a distant cousin until I was three, when I went to a kindergarten. I know that I was always the first child to arrive there in the morning and the last to be picked up at night. My mother also worked at home and I can't remember her having time for me. I was a fat child and ate to bury my distress.

"I went to two different kindergartens, three different primary schools, and two different secondary schools because we kept moving house. It was 1972 and I was 12 when I left the care facility as my mother had married my alcoholic stepfather, and we were due to move to a different town. This was when I developed bulimia. I had the feeling that my mother's marriage and moving to a new town meant that I was again being uprooted. I was unhappy and wanted to commit suicide. That was the last time that my mother hit me, when she found that out. I still felt her rejection though. Sentences like 'You've no idea what real hunger is!', or 'Work before pleasure!' or 'Go on then, cry; you won't need to go to the toilet so often!' still make me feel pain and sorrow. When I was 17 I couldn't stand it at home any more and I found myself a furnished flat. After having suffered burnout about two years ago and a stay in hospital of several weeks following my mother's sudden death, I knew that I had stepped beyond my limits, and looked for care and appreciation from the outside. Through Professor Dr. Franz Ruppert's books and intensive group work I discovered more about the 'constellation work with the intention'. This work has enabled me to identify many connections and to work on my symbiotic trauma.

"I was able to see and relate to the extent of this trauma in a group constellation with the help of representatives for my prenatal part in my mother's womb. My representative and I felt sick and dizzy and I was overcome with sorrow and profound sympathy when I saw that my representative 'wanted to rip the umbilical cord out'. In the constellation I suddenly said: "As an unborn child I already felt sickened." It used to be normal for my family to drink alcohol at festivities and I suspect my mother must have drunk alcohol without thinking during her pregnancy. My father was already an alcoholic at that time. He could also be aggressive and I think that was the reason my mother left him. My mother couldn't come to terms with her past. Later she continued as an alcoholic and eventually developed dementia. After I was born, my little body was completely and firmly wrapped in linen for about two months – that was common then. I was unable to move or feel myself with my hands or touch myself with my thumb. I don't know whether my mother breastfed me. I have been able to feel in further constellations what it means to be completely wrapped up. I felt helpless and incapable of acting at all. I often experience this feeling in my life today. Now I know where my deficiencies come from. Through the constellation work I have become more sensitive to myself and my actions, and I now know how to separate and protect myself better from others.

"I now know that the traumas of previous generations of my family led to my mother being unable to give me the 'nourishment' I needed while she was pregnant with me. Security, protection and love were simply not there. I looked for these outside and I now know that I can provide these vital things for myself. The constellation work helped me with that. I am now on a good path to myself."

Irena feels better and easier in herself since she has found out how to identify her anxieties, disorientation, sorrow and, as she describes it, her 'deficiencies'. She no longer has to numb herself with alcohol or fill herself with food. The sense of something lacking is slowly giving way to inner harmony, and she is even able to like herself now.

Corinna

Amongst other things, Corinna tells me of her lactose intolerance, which has not been medically confirmed. The intolerance probably doesn't come from the food content, but from the way it was presented to her. She comes to my practice with the diagnosis of fibromyalgia. She suffers from continuous muscle pain, stomach pain, nausea and food intolerance.

During our first therapy sessions she is fasting, only eating alkaline foods. She continually tries out new ideas to gain some relief. Everything revolves around the issue 'eating and pain'. She has been tense for years. Corinna describes it thus: "Hunger and eating was and is a difficult subject for me, as it was for my mother, and I'm getting to be more like her. From my mother's stories I know that I was never able to tolerate lactose. A couple of years ago I had a lactose intolerance test that didn't confirm it, but nevertheless I can't tolerate milk products and haven't been able to since I was tiny. I wasn't breastfed. My mother told me she would have liked to breastfeed me but she didn't have enough milk. So I was bottle-fed. Mummy holds me in her arms, looks lovingly at me, I feel love and warmth and that I'm welcome – all unfortunately just a dream! The truth is: a cushion supports the bottle that is pushed into my mouth. After all, the child just has to drink something. It's one of the three things a baby needs: food, sleep and a clean nappy.

"I didn't feel love or warmth. My mother was and is a block of ice. I couldn't tolerate the food she gave me. I had life-threatening diarrhoea. When I was six weeks old I was taken to hospital. The doctors saved my life. I almost died and in order to survive, I closed down.

"My survival strategy: Take and hold onto everything, absolutely everything, whether good or bad. Hold on, hold on, hold on. Closing down meant not wanting to give back anything that came in, otherwise I'd die. And I didn't want to die. Unlike four of my siblings before me, I didn't die in the womb. I made it; I survived and came into the world. I lived and I wanted to live. And I did everything to ensure that I did. I was nursed back to health in hospital. While I was there I didn't have any diarrhoea. I was discharged from hospital and was back in the care of my mother, and again I had diarrhoea, but it was no longer life threatening as it had been directly after my birth. But I was fed at set times. There was more food than I needed. I had to put on weight and preferably be a little chubbier so that I had 'something in reserve'.

"I still eat at set times, because you have to eat and everyone says that you should eat three times a day. I don't eat when I'm hungry.

Often I'm not hungry at all. If I'm stressed, my portions are very large and I eat what you eat in Germany: bread, bread, bread. Carbohydrates help to add weight, so that I can cope with daily life. But this programme of eating isn't good for me. The more stressed I am, the more demanding daily life is, the more I eat but I don't ever seem to feel full. And I eat food that's high in calories, often totally unhealthy, and I eat indiscriminately. I don't seem to have any control over myself and can't resist the compulsion to eat.

"One thing is for sure: I'm not going to get slim that way. I always have some padding for bad days. Whenever I'm not doing well, I eat, so that I feel better and get healthy. It used to be my mother who stuffed me with food, and I took over from her. If the thought of losing weight ever crosses my mind I almost immediately start to eat. I get a feeling of insatiable hunger and I can't resist this hunger feeling. I can't withstand it and I eat much too much, indiscriminately, and unhealthily too. The main thing is as many calories as I can, in the shortest time. Preferably before I lose weight, put on another one or two kilos. Losing weight still means life-threatening danger. The realisation that I am not allowed to lose weight is new. I wasn't aware until recently of the link between my early childhood experiences and my apparent inability to lose weight. So even if I manage not to eat too much, I hardly lose any weight, or none at all, because I hold on to everything. So that I don't die."

Corinna still does not have a healthy relationship with food and keeps trying out new strategies. Her physical stiffness and pain are almost gone. They reappear when she can't cope with everyday situations that trigger her. She is a slim, pretty woman in her early 40s and no one would think, looking at her, that she had an eating disorder. In her case too, it is not her trying to compensate for something that compels her to eat, but the existential fear she experienced as an infant. Only when she realised the cause of her eating behaviour and weight gain, did she begin to understand and to develop empathy with herself instead of anger. It is now easier for her to experience the hunger and only satisfy it in moderation and with healthy foods, because she can identify it. When she is in touch with herself, she has a healthy feeling for her needs and her body. Corinna wants to do further work on this.

My conclusion from these case histories and many others from my practice is that an eating disorder in the form of over-eating can have many causes. On the face of it, one rewards oneself with food, gives oneself a feeling of warmth, satiety, and a sort of affection and love. Hand in hand with that go abuse of one's own body, harmful treatment of the organism with consequences such as high blood pressure, diabetes, obesity, joint pain, heart disease and many more.

In my experience therapy or counselling in the form of advising new patterns of behaviour either doesn't help at all, or only helps a little. On the one hand, it can convey or confirm the impression of being wrong, and then again the patient could look for loopholes or return to their old ways, if the real cause is not clear.

Traumas cannot be controlled by regulation. Their consequences have to be recognised and understood; only then can the healing process begin. Allowing understanding for oneself and one's own (mis)conduct is a basic requirement of self-love, which can then develop. Anyone struggling with feelings of guilt feels bad about themselves. Anyone who loves themselves and has understanding does not torment themselves by stuffing food into their body beyond their own limits. Instead of the struggle for survival, nourishment can emerge from the healthy psychological structures, becoming a normal issue, sometimes full of fun and pleasure, without feelings of trauma, compulsive control or binge eating.

17
'Anorexia' and early trauma

Franz Ruppert

I would like to follow on from Andrea Stoffers's findings on over-eating as a consequence of early traumatisation, and add my observations on the subject of 'anorexia'. As with most psychiatric diagnoses, this designation, 'anorexia nervosa' or 'anorexia', is meaningless and misleading, because it focuses attention on the superficial. The psychiatric and clinical-psychological viewpoint assumes the real problem to be the symptom of non-eating, and suggests that everything would be fine if the patient took in enough food. In my experience, in my female so-called 'anorexic' clients, the symptom is usually brought on, amongst other things, by a combination of love trauma and sexual trauma, leading them to eat so little that their body is emaciated and becomes practically skeletal and they almost die of starvation. The symptom of refusing to eat is usually associated with a high level of ambition at school or work. Denying themselves food is, in terms of a love trauma, an attempt

- to disappear physically because, as children, they were not wanted,
- and also to struggle for appreciation and their right to exist by achieving exceptional accomplishments and looking after others, in particular their own mothers.

Accordingly, those affected live in a state of a permanent symbiotic entanglement with their mothers, within which there can be neither a coming together nor a healthy release process, (Wardetzki 1996) and into which psychotherapists can easily be drawn.

In terms of a sexual trauma, 'anorexia' is a survival strategy in order:

- to avoid becoming a woman on a physical level,
- to avoid developing a feminine physique, which might encourage the perpetrator to carry out further sexual abuse,
- to control the individual's own neediness and their physical feelings of pleasure arising from the enforced sexual stimulation.

The so-called 'bulimic' vomiting that often occurs in combination with non-eating, can also be a reaction to oral sexual abuse.

Female clients with the symptom 'anorexia' often come from well-off and performance-oriented families, who build up an outward façade of decency and success. The mother is usually also a victim of a trauma of love and of sexual abuse. Those concerned develop this symptom of extreme food refusal secretly. It is a silent rebellion and not an open protest against the traumatising relationships within the individual's own family. It is an attempt to adjust, to endure everything and to go along with the appearance of familial harmony as long as possible. Not eating is a victim attitude that suppresses the individual's own real victimhood, and ruthlessly disregards their own real physical needs. The individual is therefore a perpetrator and a victim at the same time, and is caught up in this irreconcilable contradiction.

I believe that the frequently-quoted assumption in the media and specialised literature, that anorexia has to do with the ideal of a slim body and is encouraged by societal fashion trends and widespread diet mania, is looking in completely the wrong direction. It distracts from, disregards and obscures the disastrous perpetrator-victim dynamic in which those concerned are caught within their family and within themselves. In this respect, psychiatric diagnoses such as 'anorexia' or 'bulimia' dismiss the traumatising circumstances and tend to favour perpetrator protection and stigmatise the traumatised victims.

In the same way, therapy concepts that seek to motivate or even force the 'anorexic' individuals to eat, are of little use and support the 'perpetrator-victim reversal': the victim is looked at as a perpetrator and the perpetrator feels like the victim of an 'eating disorder'. Consequently, in psychosomatic clinics those hidden dynamics degenerate into downright power struggles and hide-and-seek games that continue the perpetrator-victim dynamic within a family in a therapeutic setting. Even if the person concerned gains weight, it does not mean that their traumatisations are resolved. The self-rejection remains and will look for new ways of expressing itself.

In the constellations involving these symptoms that I know and have facilitated, it frequently comes to light that the symptom of not eating or of vomiting is connected directly with the abuser, i.e. that those individuals with the symptoms are emotionally entangled with the perpetrator in their family who offers the love that is not forthcoming from their emotionally-rejecting mother. It is as if the abuser is entrenched in their stomach and guts and, despite their disgust and reluctance, they cannot let him go for fear that they will then be completely without love and all alone. Two things are necessary to resolve the symptoms:

- The individual has to give up their loyalty attachment to their mother, as she is the cause of the love trauma, and she is usually aware of the sexual abuse by, for example, the father, and tolerates it.
- The disastrous entanglement with the abuser, who in many cases is the individual's own father, has to be resolved.

18
Symbiotic trauma in the individual setting

Vivian Broughton

18.1 Trauma and the Individual Setting

The constellations process devised by Franz Ruppert, the 'Constellation of the Intention', is most commonly practised in groups, where participants are available to act as representatives in the constellation. In his most recent publication Franz Ruppert has pointed out that the method is not only suitable for group work, but also opens up completely new opportunities for therapy work in the individual setting if the therapist is able to take on the role of the client's intention. (Ruppert 2014, p. 172) As this sort of therapy work is essentially about the central topic of trauma, (Broughton 2013) the 'Constellation of the Intention' can work very well on a one-to-one basis.

To discuss, or even mention, the word 'trauma' for some people takes them an uncomfortable step closer to their own unaddressed and unconscious trauma. When I originally started to talk of myself as a 'trauma' therapist, many of my psychotherapy colleagues thought that my public and unabashed use of the word 'trauma' would not be helpful in attracting clients. However, many of my clients tell me that they come to see me *because* I use the word 'trauma', because deep down they know that something serious isn't right, and somehow the word 'trauma' encompasses their intuitive sense of the problem. But also, many people come because I make it very obvious that I do work in private consultation sessions.

The reasons a person may opt for a private session are many, and varied. Common reasons are fear of groups, fear of people, fear of revealing oneself in front of others, and shame about one's situation and one's inability to resolve it oneself. For many the idea of doing personal work in front of people that they do not know is too intimidating. Many people tell me that they would never have come to work with me if I hadn't been available to see them privately. Some fear that their issues are too complex to manage in a group, that there will not be sufficient time and that they will have to compete with others for time. For some the idea of being a representative in others' constellations is too frightening, and declining to be a representative, turning someone down, may be just as frightening. The person may not know me, and having to deal with a group of unknown people, and getting to know me all in one go is too much. Understanding trauma as we do when working with Ruppert's theories, we know just how easily people can be projected back into their traumatised self, and for some this danger makes them wary of groups.

In the private session the person knows how much time they are going to have, and they know that this time is theirs and that they do not have to share the time with others. During the session they will have my undivided attention and sufficient time to tell their story in the way that they wish. Although in the group they may get just as much time, prior to working with me they do not know that, and the other people present can be experienced as an added pressure and competition.

Finally, since the underlying trauma for most of us is the symbiotic trauma, the early trauma of attachment, it is a relational trauma and the issue of trust of others is paramount. Trauma seriously damages the person's trust in others, their trust in themselves and their ability to assess the trustworthiness of others. While the trauma constellations practice does not hold the relationship between client and therapist as the crucible for healing and change as in conventional psychotherapy, the issue of trust in the therapist is, even so, pivotal. My experience is that the efficacy of a particular client's constellation will be directly related to the client's current ability to trust the therapist. This more than anything will determine the success of the constellation. In the private session the person has the time to form a relationship with the therapist without having to take others into consideration; over several sessions they can assess the trustworthiness of the therapist. This can be immensely helpful, and in time the person may find the courage to attend a group and profit from that work too.

18.2 The one-to-one Constellation

The private constellation is done with the client and the therapist working directly with one another, using floor markers instead of people as extra representatives. The floor markers I use are simple, a square for males and a circle for females, both markers having a notch in order to know which way they are facing:

Male

Female

Figure 7: The basic floor markers.

The markers are in a variety of colours, which makes it easier to keep track of who the markers are representing. Often the colour has some significance for the client, which may be helpful. Some therapists may use cushions or objects, however in my view it is important to have some way of indicating the direction in which the markers are facing.

The session is the same as for the group in that the person decides on an intention before the constellation starts, and then sets up the beginning constellation as herself and her 'intention' just as she would in a group, but with the therapist taking the role of the 'intention'.

There tends to be a certain pattern in the individual session, which is roughly as follows:

- Establishing the intention.
- Setting up the basic constellation of client and the therapist as the 'intention'.
- 'Intention' and client share experiences.
- The process goes as far as it can go.
- The therapist and client put down markers and sit down to discuss what has happened so far.
- More markers may be added, for clarity (family members, other parts of the self).
- This usually evokes further insight for the client.
- Therapist and client may go back onto their respective markers to see what has changed and speak to each other.

18.3 Challenges and Advantages

The first challenge to both therapist and client in the individual constellation is the therapist's involvement as a representative, and the business of keeping the 'therapist role' and the 'therapist-as-representative' role clear and separate. This requires care and clarity on the part of the therapist, so that the client knows exactly which role the therapist is speaking from at any one time. Particularly in the beginning stages it can be disorienting for the client to have her therapist make such a switch of roles, and the more the therapist can do to keep things clear, the better it will go.

Throughout the process the therapist must maintain a clarity within him or herself as to whether any particular thought, idea or statement comes from his role as a representative or from his role as therapist, and make this obvious to the client, even to the extent of saying if he himself is not clear. Such absolute transparency improves the process for the client and heightens her trust in the therapist and the work.

Another challenge is the seeming absence of a therapist during the constellation process, particularly if the work goes quite deeply into the pre-verbal trauma. The therapist must always maintain a presence as the therapist, and it may be that some of the more intimate and pre-verbal moments cannot occur as they might in a group, particularly in the early sessions. However the therapist can always say, as the therapist, what she has felt in a particular moment, which can be helpful. For example: "when I was being your 'intention' I felt so young I couldn't really speak and I just wanted to be held close by you." This maintains a safety in the relationship between therapist and client, but allows for such intimate moments to be included as part of the process.

If the client is new to the constellations process, and doesn't have very good self-awareness ability, the individual session has major advantages. In the initial constellation set up, the therapist as the client's 'intention' can share his experience first. The therapist is likely to have considerable experience of being a representative in constellations, and have developed a fairly fine-tuned ability to describe his experience. The client has the opportunity to hear such experiences described, sometimes in subtle detail, and can learn from this how to be a representative for herself, how to become more aware of her experiences and how to put this into words. One of the most common phenomena I find in the one-to-one session is that the client hears someone else, the therapist, tell her about her own, often never spoken, subtle internal experiences. Clients are usually profoundly impacted by this in the beginning of their constellations experiences, often more than anything else. For someone whose experience of themselves is confusing and confused, to have another person stand in their shoes, so to speak, and tell them of experiences they know very well, but perhaps have never been able to articulate, is profound.

I had a client recently, Bertha, who is in her late 50s and has suffered from DID (Dissociative Identity Disorder) since a very young child. She has been in therapy of some sort constantly since her teens, and she understands DID often far better than the many of the therapists and psychiatrists she has been with over the years. She said, after about six sessions, that she felt her experience more understood than ever before, just by having me represent her 'intention'.

Another advantage is being able to set up a configuration of several, even many, markers and have time to look at the configuration presented. In the group constellation it is not so easy to see the configuration, and the movements and statements of the representatives, while illuminating and helpful, may also distract one from seeing the basic relationship patterning. Once the markers are down, it is usually fairly easy to see this pattern, which has its own value, as we shall see in the case example below, and the client and therapist can spend time understanding what they see. For example, look at the following picture:

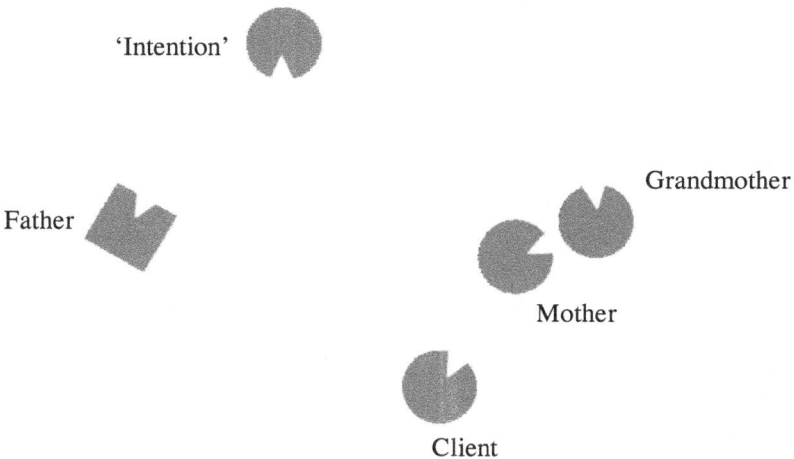

'Intention'

Grandmother

Father

Mother

Client

Figure 8: The basic pattern of a client's constellation

Without any story to this constellation, there are some patterns we can see that are likely to evoke useful questions, for example:

• The mother doesn't look at her child (the client), but instead looks at her mother, which could evoke questions about the mother's relationship to her mother, especially since the grandmother doesn't look at the mother (her child);

- The client looks towards her mother, even though her mother looks away from her. This looks like a potential symbiotic trauma because there is no connection between the client and her mother, since the mother is absorbed by looking at *her* mother.
- The father looks towards the 'intention', which may be a good connection, or may not. It may portray the child as attempting to get a good connection with the father in the absence of a good connection with the mother, or it may show the father having predatory intentions towards the child because he doesn't have any real connection with the mother (his wife).
- The client doesn't look at her 'intention', being more taken up with attempting contact with the mother. This is a clear indication of a split in the client's psyche.

A question this constellation could evoke might be: what happened in the mother's childhood, and what might have happened in the grandmother's background that causes them not to look at their children? The therapist working with trauma constellations according to Ruppert's methods (2011, 2012, 2014) knows when looking at such a patterning that she is looking at a potential symbiotic trauma: the client cannot get into emotional contact with her mother. The marker of the client is at a distance from her mother, and her mother looks away from her ... she is absorbed elsewhere.

Good contact between people is usually represented by the fact that they look at each other at close range or stand close to one another. The sense then is of companionship and collaboration rather than conflict or disconnection, even if they don't look at each other directly.

These kinds of nuances of relationship show well in how the client places the markers. The client usually places the markers with care and attention to detail in terms of distance and direction, and the information gleaned from this can be very helpful.

I am going to give one simple case example here, that shows two different aspects of the individual constellation: one is where insight and perceptual shift come from the patterning of the markers, and the other is where it comes from the 'intention'-client interaction, when the therapist represents the 'intention'.

Alison

It was Alison's first session. She is a woman in her late fifties; she has two daughters and a son. She is particularly worried about one of her daughters, who has been ill for quite some time with anxiety symptoms. Alison finds it hard to talk to this daughter and is vaguely worried that her daughter is suffering because of her. She doesn't quite understand why this would be so, but thinks that perhaps she needs to look at some issues of her life.

She was the first of five children, her mother having got pregnant with her before she was married. In fact Alison's mother never married her father, so that Alison's siblings are actually all half-siblings. As she talks, Alison says that she often feels ashamed, and doesn't really know why, and she has always felt anxious herself. She says she is easily startled, and as she continues talking she starts to cry. She says she doesn't know why she's crying, but eventually she says she has never really felt like she has rights in her life . . . having said that her mother was a good mother and loved her, she then said that in a way she thought her mother always avoided her, preferring her siblings.

Her intention emerged as: "I want to find out why I always feel so anxious, and not make my daughter anxious." When she set up the constellation, as her 'intention' I did immediately feel anxious. My legs felt shaky, and I couldn't look at her. I felt a bit sick, and needed to move close to the wall to have something to lean on. I still couldn't look at Alison. I was very scared, but I didn't know what of.

After a while, when there seemed nothing more to be said, we put markers down:

Alison

'Intention'

Figure 9: Alison and her 'Intention'

We then talked about what had happened so far. During the conversation I asked more about the situation when Alison's mother was pregnant with her... what did she know about how that had been for her mother? Alison said that she knew it hadn't been easy, and that her mother had tried to abort her. I suggested Alison include a marker for the child that her mother tried to abort and a marker for her mother:

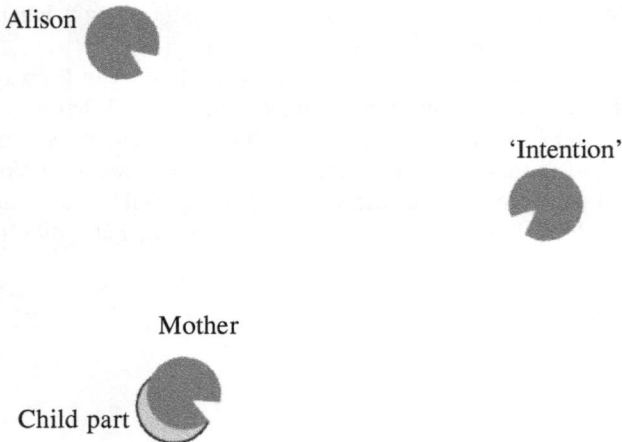

Alison

'Intention'

Mother

Child part

Figure 10: Mother and child part of Alison that was supposed to be aborted

As Alison put down the two markers, she completely covered the child part by the mother marker so that it was not possible to see the child. As she did so, she looked startled and began to cry. She said that as she put the markers down, she realised that the marker for the child part needed to be so obliterated by the mother marker that it couldn't be seen at all. She realised in the subsequent moments that her mother had in fact attempted to kill her, and in that moment experienced some of the split off feelings that were to do with this experience. Over the next twenty minutes Alison started to see that her relationship with her mother had always been affected by this, and she talked about how hard it was for her and her mother to have any kind of relationship. She also understood that the shame she felt was confused with her mother's shame at what she had attempted to do to her daughter, and why her mother had preferred her step-siblings ... and why she felt anxious so much of her life. In this way as Alison put the markers down it graphically showed her relationship to her mother, which she then interpreted herself.

After a while I suggested we go back onto our respective markers, and as I did so I realised I didn't feel scared any more but passionately concerned for the child part, as did Alison, and together we moved to 'rescue' the child part, which Alison then held to her heart as she cried:

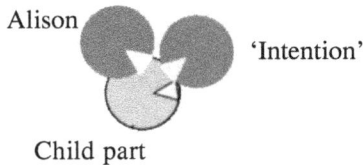

Figure 11: Alison and her 'intention' hold the child part

We can see this ending image as a moment of integration, where the split-off traumatised child part of Alison is taken into her heart, i.e. she experiences love for herself. We ended the constellation there. There is likely to be more work for Alison to do, but this would constitute a good first step.

Attempted abortion is a very real act of perpetration by the mother against her child, and as such is likely to cause the child a trauma if he or she survives it, along with strong split-off feelings of fear and terror. Even the intention by the mother to abort her child may cause an emotional conflict within the mother that is likely to be transmitted to the foetus. If we understand the emotional inseparability of the child from the mother at this early stage of life, we can surmise that the relationship between mother and child from this moment on is likely unconsciously to be confused, involving strong feelings in the mother, perhaps of shame and guilt, that the child may take on as her own, without having a conscious idea of why. The child then has a real life-threatening trauma at the earliest time of life to contend with and survive, along with a confused relationship with her mother that will constitute a symbiotic trauma. We could further hypothesise that this will affect Alison's relationship with her children, since she will relate to them from a split psyche.

There is much to say about the business of facilitating the individual constellations session, but I hope I have shown some of the important issues. It will not do, in my view, to see the group as the only, or even main, environment in which this work can be satisfactorily done. That view will exclude many people from taking the important step towards integrating and resolving their trauma. There is a need therefore for well-trained therapists who are able to offer the 'Constellation of the Intention' in the individual setting.

19

Healing and prevention of early traumas

Franz Ruppert

19.1 Gradual healing processes

Children can be traumatised early by the circumstances of their conception, by the way they are treated from the very beginning, and by the way they are *not* perceived properly with their real needs and vulnerability. This traumatisation can originate from their traumatised parents, a destructive familial system, or societal institutions that show a lack of empathy in dealing with them.

Early traumatisation brings about an early loss of self. The person's whole life becomes a case of survival rather than living out his own potential and making use of his abilities. Early traumatisation leads to the experience of isolation and loneliness. We may remain a stranger to ourselves throughout our life. The lack of connection with our own mother and father results in impersonal behaviour, withdrawal and mistrust in other close and intimate relationships. A deep emotional attachment cannot even be built up with own children. Resolving early traumatisation can therefore permanently alter and improve a person's whole life.

After a year's therapy, Monika writes: "Last year helped me a great deal; above all I got more in touch with my centre. I find it impressive that my family immediately reacts to any changes with me. It's never been so obvious. My son had the umbilical cord around his neck. Now I can understand the connection with my own history. I always had a vague idea, but I could never pin it down and understand it. I can now see it clearly, that the entanglement begins in the womb and the child turns round and round, disoriented, and is occupied with whether it wants to stay, whether it can stay, or not. That's why my son's reaction following my constellation, in which I resolved my entanglement with my father, was totally logical. My son had fallen into a bottomless existential crisis and his self-esteem was deeply hurt. Because I am now clear in myself, he can also accept himself and express it, and understand. I now feel an inner freedom; I no longer have to support my sick Daddy or be responsible for him. Now I realise: as a child, I'm the victim, not him! All this affects me deeply, makes me sad and at the same time it gives me a great sense of freedom."

As humans, we carry the potential within us to be destructive as well as constructive. A well-facilitated trauma therapy is an abundant source of profound feelings and far-reaching insights. One can distinctly feel and clearly understand what makes inter-personal relationships destructive and makes people psychologically ill. As the many case histories in this book have clearly demonstrated, the 'Constellation of the Intention', on the basis of multi-generational psychotraumatology, can even help those people who, early in their lives, have experienced many and extreme traumas. Early traumas can also be brought to light by the 'Constellation of the Intention' and psychologically resolved.

It is a gradual process for a person to admit their own 'trauma of love', to free themselves from symbiotic entanglements with their maternal and paternal ancestors, and to detach themselves from male and female perpetrators within their own families. They then get closer to their own feelings of existential trauma that frequently arose during the period of their incubation within their mother. We humans do not need to be permanently psychologi-cally or physically 'ill' if our symptoms were caused by trauma. We can escape from traumatising perpetrator-victim relationships if we want to, if we receive skilful, therapeutic support and make use of helpful networking in society.

Neither revenge, nor reconciliation and forgiveness enable a split to be permanently resolved. In any case, perpetrators do not usually really understand what they have done to their victims. They continue to justify themselves when they are confronted with their deeds and the far-reaching consequences. They stick to the pattern of accusing the victim, until they have managed to arrive at their own victim feelings through trauma therapy.

Superficially distancing themselves from their parents, who emerged as perpetrators quite early on, is of little use. Extricating themselves from perpetrator-victim relationships is only possible if they have overcome and resolved the perpetrator-victim split within themselves. In other words:

- by consciously recognising their own victim and perpetrator attitudes,
- by recognising that they have not only spent a lifetime fighting with others, but also fighting themselves,
- by resisting their inclination to hold onto their survival strategies,
- by letting in the anxiety, anger, pain and profound sorrow about what has been done to them by others and what they have done to themselves,
- and by finally developing empathy with themselves.

19.2 Prevention is better than cure

As well as healing existing traumas, it is important to work towards preventing new traumas from forming. This is partly the personal responsibility of each and every one of us, and also a joint social task.

In my professional years between 1982 and 1992 I worked in psychological accident and safety research. This field of work had seen encouraging attitudes in the course of its development:

- "Accidents are not accidental!"
- "Every accident is one too many!"
- "A danger foreseen is a danger avoided."
- "Prevention is the best protection."

On the basis of clear entrepreneurial decisions to prioritise safety and the prevention of accidents, the number of accidents and critical situations that might lead to accidents was reduced to a minimum, even in businesses with high-risk potential.

If we apply these points of view and fundamental decisions to the field of psychotraumatology, we can say by analogy:

- "Traumas are not accidental."
- "Every trauma is one too many."
- "A trauma foreseen is a trauma avoided."
- "An ounce of trauma prevention is worth more than a pound of trauma therapy."

So if we interpret the findings concerning the ways in which early traumas can develop as if they were preventative measures, we arrive at a number of precepts that could significantly decrease trauma in interpersonal relationships, and improve the quality of life for all:

- No child should be conceived unwanted.
- Men should not force women to become pregnant against their will.
- Women should not use pregnancy and children to coerce men into establishing a permanent relationship or remaining in a relationship with them
- If women or men make a conscious decision not to have children, based on their own traumas or traumatising relationships in society, this can be a responsible decision from a personal and social viewpoint.
- It is not a good idea to have children without being in a position to be, or wanting to be, parents.
- Women who want children should start to work on their own traumas early so that during pregnancy their child has, if possible, a trauma-free body in which to live and grow.
- The same applies to men: bringing severely traumatised children into the world is not good for them, or for their children.
- Abortion is not to be seen as a method of birth control but as a traumatic experience for a woman and a man. Every

abortion needs to be processed afterwards by trauma therapy in order to prevent further abortions.

- Before couples embark upon conceiving a child with the help of reproductive medicine, they should clear out all psychological blockages that may be preventing them becoming mother or father.
- Couples should thoroughly acquaint themselves with the factors contained in the technical processes of assisted reproduction that could cause traumas, and that, from the very beginning, can massively threaten the child's physical and psychological health and can inflict on them a life full of fear and anxiety instead of joy and happiness.
- The mother should be able to use the duration of her pregnancy to prepare herself psychologically for her child.
- The father of the child can help here, by creating as stress-free an environment as possible for his wife, giving her security and support and connecting with the unborn child himself.
- Expectant mothers should be clearly aware of possible connections between complications in pregnancy and birth and their own unresolved traumas, and female experts in the field of midwifery or obstetrics should make them aware of these.
- Mother and father should connect with the child during pregnancy, take him seriously as a human being with feelings and understanding, and interact lovingly with him in the womb, and also recognise and understand his needs for symbiosis and autonomy.
- It is advisable to keep medical examinations to a minimum during pregnancy. Expectant mothers should not be degraded to mere walk-on parts in medical routines. Their intuitive maternal competence should be strengthened by everyone supporting them during this period, and under no circumstances diminished.
- The unborn child's agreement should be sought in planning the birth and actually giving birth, and communication with him should be intensified during this phase. No child should

be retrieved from his mother's womb with the use of violence or without his agreement.

- Medical measures to induce a birth should be reduced to a necessary minimum. Surgical birth procedures should only be used for emergencies after all other psychosocial measures have been exhausted.

- The birth process should not be subject to pressures of time or cost. Under no circumstances should it be used to maximise profits for a company, nor to raise the professional profile of a medical expert at the expense of mother and child.

- Preparation of the birth process should enable all involved to experience it not as a medical emergency, but as a joyful and indeed pleasurable event.

- After the child is born, he should be given enough time to disconnect from his inner mother, the womb, and to accept his external mother as a person welcoming him lovingly.

- The mother giving birth needs enough time to slowly approach her newborn child and to become accustomed to the smell, sight and sound of him.

- Medical routines must not be allowed to disrupt or interfere with this sensitive attachment and conditioning phase of postnatal mother-child bonding.

- The father can support the birth process if he feels he is able and sufficiently prepared. During the birth process he should remain in the background as a psychological resource for his wife.

- The days and weeks following the birth also belong to the mother and her newborn child. Medical assistance should be limited to what is necessary. The experience of other psychologically healthy mothers is a valuable resource for a mother in the days following the birth, if she is able to access it, and would like to.

- No one whose own traumas could be transferred onto this easily-disrupted mother-child relationship should intrude upon this precious time of regeneration from the stress of giving birth, the formation of secure postnatal mother-child bonding, and orientation towards a common future. An experienced female friend might be able to create a more psychologically beneficial environment than the mother's own mother, whose unresolved traumas may have been triggered by the birth of her grandchild.

- The mother and her newborn child should not be separated for long periods during the first year. It is damaging for children to be given too early into third-party care against their will.
- Economic considerations have to be secondary during this time. The economy has to be there for us; we should not have to be there for the economy. We must not live to work; we must work to live.
- Men also need time to grow psychologically into their role as fathers. They should not be afraid to accept any offers of therapy or counselling if they notice that, following the birth of their child, they are under more stress and their own childhood traumas have possibly been reactivated. (Juul 2011, Garstick 2013)
- Should the mother or her child show signs of psychological abnormalities, the processes of conception, pregnancy and birth should be looked at as soon as possible as potential causes. Symptoms of illness and relationship issues that occur at that time often result from the consequences of earlier causes. Medical and psychological diagnostics cannot disregard the start of conception in their search process. On the contrary: the more quickly the traumatising roots of the immediate problem are recognised, the more clearly and effectively help can be given. In engaging with trauma issues as well, the maxim should be: get to the root of the problem.
- Violence, on whatever grounds, towards unborn children and infants, must not be allowed. Circumcision and mutilation of boys' and girls' genitals should be seen as what they are: acts of raw and cruel violence towards defenceless children. (Terre des Femmes 2003, Franz 2014)

Glossary of special terms

Maternity establishment (*Accouchierhaus*): (from the French *accoucher* to give birth) 18th-century establishments, which were the forerunners of today's maternity clinics.

ADHD: Attention deficit hyperactivity disorder. A group of behavioural symptoms that include inattentiveness, hyperactivity and impulsiveness.

Baby take-home rate (BTHR): A measure of the success of artificial insemination. It indicates the number of treatment attempts on average that lead to taking a baby home.

Chorionic villus sampling: Using ultrasound monitoring, a needle is introduced into the abdominal wall of the expectant mother and advanced further into the placenta. A sample of tissue (chorionic villi) is removed from the placenta for testing.

Cryopreservation: is the process whereby cells (sperm cells or fertilised egg cells) are frozen in liquid nitrogen at a temperature of minus 196°C to preserve their viability.

Extracorporeal fertilisation: Fertilisation that takes place outside the body.

Gamete intra-fallopian transfer (GIFT): A tool of assisted reproductive technology. Eggs are removed from a woman's ovaries, and placed in one of the Fallopian tubes, along with the man's sperm. The technique allows fertilisation to take place inside the woman's uterus.

Intracytoplasmic sperm injection (ICSI): Method of artificial insemination in which sperm is directly injected into the egg cell.

Invasive test: Tissue-damaging medical diagnostic or therapeutic measurements. Invasive tests on pregnant women increase the danger of miscarriage and can lead to injury to the unborn child.

In vitro **fertilisation (IVF)**: Artificial insemination in the test tube, where egg and sperm cells are brought together outside the body and the fertilised egg is later re-inserted into the womb.

Medicalisation: The term for a process of societal change, in which human experiences and spheres of life that used to be outside medicine, become the focus of systematic medical research and responsibility. This process has been observed and described since the mid-18th century and is still apparent today in many areas of society.

Nuchal translucency (NT) scan: Ultrasound scan to measure a collection of fluid under the skin at the back of the baby's neck. An increased value is an indication of a possible chromosomal abnormality.

Osteopathy: Various alternative forms of assessment and treatment of reversible dysfunctions of the active and passive musculoskeletal system. Biodynamic osteopathy: The aim of the treatment is to find health, reflected in the rhythmical balance of the flowing movement between different levels of the fluid organism and the living mechanism.

Polar body diagnostic/treatment: Examination method used in artificial fertilisation to exclude maternal egg cells with chromosomal aberrations **before** completion of fertilisation, so that these unhealthy egg cells are not used.

Pre-implantation diagnostics (PID): Cell-biological or molecular genetic examination method **after** fertilisation to identify genetic diseases and chromosome abnormalities. Selection of gender or certain hereditary characteristics is also possible with PID.

The authors

Assel, Birgit: born 1960; two children; degree in social pedagogy; independent practice since 1998; since 2007 with the focus on multigenerational psychotraumatology according to the approach of Professor Dr Franz Ruppert, and the method of trauma constellations using the 'Constellation of the Intention'. www.igtv.de

Brombach, Doris: born 1950; married to Alexander Brombach, three adult children from her first marriage, and eight grandchildren. Independent joint practice since 1998 in Bergisch Gladbach with Alexander Brombach, alternative practitioner for psychotherapy. Focus on 'Trauma Constellations of the Intention' following the method of Professor Dr Franz Ruppert in the individual setting, facilitating group constellations as well as basic and advanced training, latterly specialising in prenatal work with children and adults. Doris Brombach died on 25.1.2014. www.praxis-brombach.de

Broughton, Vivian: Dip. GPTI, Dip. Metanoia (Gestalt), Dip. Metanoia (Counselling). Gestalt psychotherapist in private practice since 1989. From 2008 has worked with individuals and groups according to theory and practice of Franz Ruppert. Teaches 'trauma constellations' work in UK, Turkey and Singapore, and also works in Holland, Norway, Brazil and Ireland. Editor and publisher of all Franz Ruppert's books translated into English. Has written three books herself, two on the work of Franz Ruppert, and several professional articles. She writes a blog on the topic at www.vivianbroughton.com.

Denk, Annemarie: degree in social pedagogy; therapist for systemic individual, couple and family therapy; health education qualification; medical studies (Ulm/Munich); hypnotherapy according to Milton Erickson; trauma therapy; advanced training in multi-generational psychotraumatology using the method 'Constellation of the Intention' with Franz Ruppert; many years working in medical practices (focus: pain, relaxation, unfulfilled wish to have children, psycho-oncology, healing singing), and in the multimodal pain therapy of the Paracelsus Clinic in Munich. Independent practice with individual consultations, family sculpting and trauma constellations using the method 'Constellation of the Intention', groups and seminars. www.medibalance.com

Freund, Christina: born 1974, degree in social pedagogy; teaching degree in German and history for secondary schools at Regensburg university; social work studies at the University of Applied Sciences, Munich (2001–2006); advanced training in psychotraumatology and trauma counselling at the *zptn* (Centre for Psychotraumatology and Trauma Therapy in Lower Saxony) (2006-2008); advanced training 'Trauma, Bonding and Family Constellations' with Franz Ruppert ; since 2001 analysis of the method of constellations according to Franz Ruppert; since 2009 leadership of group seminars with the 'Constellation of the Intention'; since 2012 trauma counselling in independent practice; since 2012 lectureship at the University of Applied Sciences, Munich. www.bindung-trauma-aufstellung.de

Hoppe, Gabriele: alternative practitioner for psychotherapy: humanistic psychology with a psychoanalytic approach; focus on therapeutic assistance and coaching: art and gestalt therapy, EMDR, multi-generational psychotraumatology, prenatal based psychotherapy; private practice in Aschaffenburg, Germany. www.gabrielehoppe.com

Krüger, Liesel: retired teacher, trained in concentrative movement therapy (CMT) and Work at the Clay Field®. Member of the Association for Gestaltbildung and of the Barbos Foundation. Independent practice offering the method Work at the Clay Field® in kindergartens and schools to children, adolescents and adults to promote their development and work on their traumas. www.tonfeld.de

Lardschneider, Petra: born 1965, married with two daughters. 2001–2003 school for alternative medicine; 2006 qualification in systemic karmic constellations and regression therapy following three-years' training with Erika Schäfer; 2006 training in child development psychology; 2007 further training with Sieglinde Schneider in constellation work with images; 2007 further training in the treatment of trauma and inner-child work; as of 2007 constellations in groups and in the individual setting, as well as talks in kindergartens and schools. Since 2010 working with 'Constellation of the Intention' and since 2011 guest student with Professor Dr Franz Ruppert at the University of Applied Sciences, Munich, as well as regular guest visits in his practice and at his seminars.

Ruppert, Franz: Dr phil., Dipl.-Psych., Professor of Psychology at the University of Applied Sciences in Munich, psychological psychotherapist, founder of multi-generational psychotraumatology (since 2016 called Identity oriented Psychotraumatheory and therapy (IoPT) and the method 'Constellation of the Intention' (since 2016 called Self Encounter by the Sentence of Intention); author of many books about traumawork; leads seminars worldwide and also offers training in his theory and practice. www.franz-ruppert.de

Schulte, Cordula: born 1952; alternative practitioner for psychotherapy in independent practice; independent lecturer and seminar leader at the Paracelsus Schools for Alternative Medicine. Since 1997 training and work as system constellation facilitator with different constellation methods. Training in Neuro-Linguistic Programming (NLP) (Master Practitioner) and Energy Psychotherapy with Dr Fred Gallo. In 2009 training in multi-generational psychotraumatology with Professor Franz Ruppert. Since then work with individuals and groups using this method. www.cordula-schulte.de

Schultze-Kraft, Alice: Independent practice in Kleve/Germany alternative practitioner for psychotherapy. Further training in various body psychotherapeutic methods. Further training in the method 'Constellation of the Intention' according to Professor Dr Franz Ruppert with Doris and Alexander Brombach. Together with her partner, establishment of the Centre for the Development of Potential in Kleve. Facilitating 'Constellations of the Intention' in the individual setting and in groups. www.traumatherapie-aufstellung.de

Specht, Manuela: qualified nurse, training in psychology and psychotherapy, Voice Dialogue and as of 2008 in multi-generational psychotraumatology (Franz Ruppert); independent practice in Bad Tölz working with the 'Constellation of the Intention' in the individual setting and in groups. www.systemische-beratungen-specht.de

Stoffers, Andrea: born 1963; alternative practitioner for psychotherapy with independent practice in the Neuss/Germany; leads constellations seminars and further training based on multi-generational psychotraumatology (Ruppert) and the Attachment Theory of Developmental Psychology (Bowlby). www.hp-stoffers.de

Strauss, Dagmar: born 1962; independent practice since 1991. Married, three grown-up sons, two of whom were born at home and one in her gynaecologist's practice; alternative practitioner trained in Somatic Experiencing according to Peter Levine; since 2010 in further training with Professor Dr Franz Ruppert. Since 2011 regular guest visits at his practice; since 2011 leads 'Constellations of the Intention' in the individual setting and since 2012 also leads group seminars. www.lebenssinn-wandlung.de

Thorsheim, Marta: 1985 MBA in Change Management; 1990 Master in International Management; worked in different international management positions; independent practice as psychotherapist since 1991. Owner of a training institute since 1997; since 2010 implementation of training and further education in the theory and constellation method of Franz Ruppert; organisation of international training with Professor Dr Franz Ruppert in

Oslo. From 2014 also seminars in Singapore. www.konstel-lasjoner.no

Wentink, Margriet: born 1963. Independent practice in Tiel/Netherlands, since 1996. Trained in Neuro-Linguistic Programming (NLP) and hypnotherapy, child therapy and art history. Further training and supervision with Franz Ruppert. Since 2006 working with multi-generational psychotraumatology. Introduced Franz Ruppert's method into the Netherlands in 2006. Has translated several of Franz Ruppert's books into Dutch together with Wim Wassink. Offers individual therapy, group seminars and training in the method 'Constellation of the Intention' in the Netherlands, Belgium and Germany. www.interaktiel.nl

References

Achenbach, T. M., **Dumenci**, L. & **Rescorla**, L. A. (2002). Ten-year comparisons of problems and competencies for national samples of youth: Self, parent, and Teacher reports. *Journal of Emotional and Behavioral Disorders*, 10 (4), 194–203.

Ahnert, L. (2010). *Wie viel Mutter braucht ein Kind? Bindung – Bildung – Betreuung: Öffentlich und privat.*. Spektrum Verlag. Heidelberg.

Ahnert, L., **Kappler**, G. & **Eckstein-Madry**, T. (2012). Eingewöhnung in der Kinderkrippe: Forschungsmethoden zu Bindung, Stress und Coping. In: Vernickel, S., König, A., Hoffmann, H. und Edelmann, D. (Hg.): *Krippenforschung. Methoden – Konzepte – Beispiele* (pp. 74–88). Ernst Reinhard Verlag, München.

Albarelli, F. & **Widhalm**, S. (2012). *Eiertanz. Das Kinderwunschbuch.* mvg-Verlag München.

Alberti, B. (2010). *Seelische Trümmer, geboren in den 50er- und 60er-Jahren: Die Nachkriegsgeneration im Schatten des Kriegstraumas.* München: Kösel Verlag.

Alberti, B. (2012). *Die Seele fühlt von Anfang an. Wie pränatale Erfahrungen unsere Beziehungsfähigkeit prägen.* Kösel Verlag, München.

Allen, J. G., **Fonagy**, P. & **Batemann**, A. (2011). *Mentalisieren in der psychotherapeutischen Praxis.* Klett-Cotta Verlag, Stuttgart.

Allmendinger, J. (2013). *Frauen auf dem Sprung. Wie junge Frauen heute leben wollen.* Pantheon Verlag, München.

Amendt, G. (1992). *Das Leben unerwünschter Kinder.* Fischer Verlag, Frankfurt/M.

Auhagen-Stephanos, U. (2011). Die Bindung beginnt vor der Zeugung – Frauen in der Reproduktionsmedizin. In: Levend, H. und Janus, L. (Hg.): *Bindung beginnt vor der Geburt* (pp. 100–112). Mattes Verlag, Heidelberg.

Baer, U. & **Frick-Baer**, G. (2013). *Wie Traumata in die nächste Generation wirken.* Neukirchen-Vluyn: Semnos Verlag.

Baker, M., **Gruber**, J. & **Milligan**, K. (2008). Universal Child Care, Maternal Labor Supply, and Family Well-Being. *Journal of Political Economy*. University of Chicago Press 116 (4), pp. 709–745.

Bauer, J. (2002). *Das Gedächtnis des Körpers.* Eichborn Verlag, Frankfurt/M.

References

Bauer, J. (2006). *Warum ich fühle, was du fühlst.* Heyne Verlag, München.

Bauer, J. (2011). *Prinzip Menschlichkeit.* Heyne Verlag, München.

Beck, L. (Hg.) (1986). *Zur Geschichte der Gynäkologie und Geburtshilfe.* Springer-Verlag, Berlin.

Beutel, M. (2002). *Der frühe Verlust eines Kindes.* Hogrefe-Verlag, Göttingen.

Birnbaumer, N. & **Schmidt**, R. F. (1996). *Biologische Psychologie.* Springer Verlag, Heidelberg.

Bode, S. (2004). *Die vergessene Generation. Die Kriegskinder brechen ihr Schweigen.* Klett-Cotta Verlag, Stuttgart.

Bode, S. (2009). *Kriegsenkel. Die Erben der vergessenen Generation.* Klett-Cotta Verlag, Stuttgart.

Böhm, R. (2011). Auswirkungen frühkindlicher Gruppenbetreuung auf die Entwicklung und Gesundheit von Kindern. Sozialpädiatrie aktuell 5, pp. 316–321.

Böhm, R. (2013 a). Neurobiologische Aspekte der Kinderbetreuung. In: Dammasch, F. und Teising, M. (Hg.): Das modernisierte Kind (pp. 115–128). Brandes & Apsel Verlag, Frankfurt/M.

Böhm, R. (2013 b). Stress – das unterschätzte Problem frühkindlicher Betreuung. In: Haderthauer, C. und Zehetmair, H. (Hg.): *Bildung braucht Bindung. Argumente und Materialien zum Zeitgeschehen 83*, pp. 27–32. HannsSeidel-Stiftung, München.

Bonus, B. (2006). *Mit den Augen eines Kindes sehen lernen, Band 1: Zur Entstehung einer Frühtraumatisierung bei Pflege- und Adoptivkindern und den möglichen Folgen.* Books on Demand, Norderstedt.

Bonus, B. (2008). *Mit den Augen eines Kindes sehen lernen, Band 2: Die Anstrengungsverweigerung.* Books on Demand, Norderstedt.

Bowlby, J. (1975). *Bindung, eine Analyse der Mutter-Kind-Beziehung.* München: Kindler-Verlag.

Bowlby, J. (1987). *Loss, Sadness & Depression.* Basic Books, New York.

Bräutigam, H.-H. (1981). Fortschritt nach rückwärts? Über die Risiken der sanften Geburt. In: Schreiber, M. (Hg.): *Die schöne Geburt.* Rowohlt Taschenbuch Verlag, Reinbek bei Hamburg.

Brisch, K. H. (2009). Die frühkindliche außerfamiliäre Betreuung von Säuglingen und Kleinstkindern aus der Perspektive der Säuglingsforschung. In: *Analytische Kinder- und Jugendlichen-Psychotherapie (AKJP)*, 142, pp. 143–158.

Brisch, K. H. (2012). Intergenerationale Bindungen. Trauma und

Dissoziation. Ursache, Therapie und Prävention. In: Huber, M. und Plassmann, R. (Hg.): *Transgenerationale Traumatisierung*. Junfermann Verlag, Paderborn.

Brisch, K. H. (2013). *Bindungsstörungen: Von der Bindungstheorie zur Therapie*. Klett-Cotta Verlag, Stuttgart.

Brisch, K. H. (2013). *Schwangerschaft und Geburt*. Klett-Cotta Verlag, Stuttgart.

Brisch, K. H. (2014). *Säuglings- und Kleinkindalter*. Klett-Cotta Verlag, Stuttgart.

Brockmann, A. D. & **Geiß**, M. L. (2011). *Sprechende Hände. Haptik und haptischer Sinn als Entwicklungspotential*. Pro Business Verlag, Berlin.

Broughton, V. (2010). *In the Presence of Many – Reflections on Constellations emphasising the individual context*. Green Balloon Publishing Frome, UK.

Broughton, V. (2013). *The Heart of Things – Understanding Trauma, Working with Constellations*. Green Balloon Publishing, Steyning, UK.

Broughton, V. (2013). *Becoming Your True Self: a handbook for the journey from trauma to healthy autonomy*. Green Balloon Publishing, Steyning, UK.

Brussels (2010) Institute for Family Policies 3.3.2010. Bund-esärztekammer (1998). *Richtlinie zur pränatalen Diagnostik von Krankheiten und Krankheitsdispositionen*. In: Deutsches Ärzteblatt 95 (50).

Bundesausschuss der Ärzte und Krankenkassen (Hg.) (1980). Mutterpass.

Bundeszentrale für gesundheitliche Aufklärung (Hg.) (2006). Schwangerschaftserleben und Pränataldiagnostik. Repräsentative Befragung Schwangerer zum Thema Pränataldiagnostik. Köln.

Castellino, R. (2013). 7. Schweizer Bildungsfestival »Bindung« vom 15. – 18. August 2013. In: Weggis, *Auditorium Netzwerk DVDs Workshop:* »*Die Bindungsphasen des Babys*« 1. DVD 1, pp. 4 ff.

Chamberlain, D. (2010/2013). *Woran Babys sich erinnern: Über die Anfänge unseres Bewusstseins im Mutterleib*. München: Kösel Verlag.

Chamberlain, S. (1997). *Hitler, die deutsche Mutter und ihr erstes Kind*. Über zwei NS-Erziehungsbücher. Gießen: Psychosozial Verlag.

Dattler, W., **Funder**, A., **Hover-Reisner**, N., **Fürstaler**, M. & **Ereky-Stevens**, K. (2012). Eingewöhnung von Krippenkindern: Forschungsmethoden zu Verhalten, Interaktion und Beziehung in der Wiener Krippenstudie. In: Vernickel, S., König, A., Hoffmann, H. und Edelmann, D. (Hg.): *Krippenforschung. Methoden – Konzepte –*

References

Beispiele (pp. 59–73). Ernst Rein-hard Verlag, München.
Deuser, H. (Hg.) (2004). *Bewegung wird Gestalt. Der Handlungsdialog in der Arbeit am Tonfeld.* Edition Doering, Bremen.
Duden, B. (2007). *Der Frauenleib als öffentlicher Ort.* Mabuse-Verlag, Frankfurt/M.
Deneke, F. W. (1999). *Psychische Strukturen und Gehirn: Die Gestaltung subjektiver Wirklichkeiten.* Schattauer Verlag, Stuttgart.
De Jong, T. M. (2002). *Babys aus dem Labor. Segen oder Fluch?* Beltz Verlag, Weinheim.
De Jong, M. T. (2004). *Im Dialog mit dem Ungeborenen.* Verlag Via Nova, Petersberg.
De Jong, T. M. & **Thurmann**, I. M. (2008). *Willkommen im Leben! Kinderwunsch und der bewusste Weg zur Elternschaft.* Patmos Verlag, Düsseldorf.
deMause, L. (Hg.) (1980). *The History of Childhood.* The Psychohistory Press, New York, USA.
Deutsches Ärzteblat 95 (1998). Journal 50, 11.12.1998. A-3241.
Dytrych, Z., **Schüller**, V. & **Matejcek**, Z. (1988). The wantedness-unwantedness continuum and responsible parenthood. In: David, H. P., Dytrych, Z., Matejcek, Z. und Schüller, V. (Hg.): *Born unwanted: Developmental effects of denied abortion* (pp. 30–36). Springer Verlag, New York.
Ehlers, C. (2010). In: *Stillzeit. Die Fachzeitschrift der AFS*, Heft 3.
Eichhorst, W., **Kaiser**, L., **Thode**, E. & **Tobsch**, V. (2007). *Vereinbarkeit von Familie und Beruf im internationalen Vergleich. Zwischen Paradigma und Praxis.* Verlag Bertelsmann Stiftung, Gütersloh.
Elbrecht, C. (2013). *Trauma Healing at the Clay Field. A sensorimotor Art Therapy Approach.* Jessica Kingsley Publishers, London.
Eliacheff, C. (2011). *Das Kind, das eine Katze sein wollte. Psychoanalytische Arbeit mit Säuglingen und Kleinkindern.* dtv Verlag, München.
Elias, N. (1976). *Über den Prozess der Zivilisation.* Suhrkamp Verlag, Frankfurt/M.
Emerson, W. (2012). *Behandlung von Geburtstraumata bei Säuglingen und Kindern.* Mattes Verlag, Heidelberg.
Ensel, A. (2002). *Hebammen im Konflikt der Pränatalen Diagnostik.* Hebammengemeinschaftshilfe e.V., Schriftenreihe 10.
EUMC (2010). Erasmus University Medical Centre, Rotterdam (see Henrichs, J. 2010).
Fergusson, D. M., **Horwood**, L. J. & **Ridder**, E. M. (2006). Abortion in

young women and subsequent mental health. In: *Christchurch Health and Development Study*, Christchurch, New Zealand. Journal of Child Psychology and Psychiatry, 47 (1), pp. 16–24.

Fiedler, P. (Hg.) (2006). *Trauma, Dissoziation, Persönlichkeit – Pierre Janets Beiträge zur modernen Psychiatrie, Psychologie und Psychotherapie.* Papst Verlag, Lengerich.

Fiegl, J. (2012). *Unerfüllter Kinderwunsch. Das Wechselspiel von Körper und Seele.* mvg Verlag, München.

Fischer, G. & **Riedesser**, P. (1998). *Lehrbuch der Psychotraumatologie.* UTB Reinhard Verlag, München.

Franke, T. R. (2007). *Das Schöne wurde mir genommen.* Vortrag auf dem 6. Deutschen Still- und Laktationskongress in Göppingen, November 2007.

Franz, M. (Hg.) (2014). *Die Beschneidung von Jungen. Ein trauriges Vermächtnis.* Vandenhoeck & Ruprecht, Göttingen.

Fritsch, J. & **Sherokee**, I. (2011). *Unendlich ist der Schmerz.* Kösel Verlag, München.

Garstick, E. (2013). *Junge Väter in seelischen Krisen. Wege zur Stärkung der männlichen Identität.* Klett-Cotta Verlag, Stuttgart.

Gemeinsamer Bundesausschuss (2013) (Hg.). *Richtlinien über die ärztliche Betreuung während der Schwangerschaft und nach der Entbindung (»Mutterschafts-Richtlinien«).* Veröffentlicht im Bundesanzeiger AT 19. 9. 2013. Berlin.

Gemeinsamer Bundesausschuss (2012) (Hg.). *Mutterpass.* Dezember 2012. Berlin.

Haderthauer, C. & **Zehetmair**, H. (Hg.). *Bildung braucht Bindung. Argumente und Materialien zum Zeitgeschehen 83.* Hanns-Seidel-Stiftung, München.

Hakemeyer, U. and **Keding**, G. (1986). Zum Aufbau der Hebammenschulen in Deutschland im 18. und frühen 19. Jahrhundert. In: *Zur Geschichte der Gynäkologie und Geburtshilfe* ed. Beck, L. Springer-Verlag, Berlin, Heidelberg.

Harms, T. (2008). *Emotionelle Erste Hilfe.* Leutner Verlag, Berlin.

Harms, T. (2013). 7. Schweizer Bildungsfestival »Bindung« vom 15.–18. August 2013. In: Weggis, *DVDs bei Auditorium Netzwerk; Workshop: »Körper, Emotionen und Bindung«* 1. DVD 1:23 ff.

Häsing, H. & **Janus**, L. (1994). *Ungewollte Kinder. Annäherungen, Beispiele, Hilfen.* Rowohlt Verlag, Frankfurt/M.

Heller, L. & **Lapierre**, A. (2013). *Entwicklungstrauma heilen. Alte Überlebensstrategien lösen, Selbstregulierung und Beziehungs-*

fähigkeit stärken. Kösel Verlag, München.

Hellinger, B. (1994). *Ordnungen der Liebe.* Carl-Auer-Systeme-Verlag, Heidelberg.

Henrichs, J. (2010). Prenatal Determinants of Early Behavioral and Cognitive Development. *The Generation R Study.* EUMC, Rotterdam.

Herman, J. (2003). *Trauma and Recovery: The Aftermath of Violence from Domestic Abuse to Political Terror* Basic Books, New York.

Hey, M. (2012). *Mein gläserner Bauch.* Deutsche Verlagsanstalt, München.

Hildebrandt, S. (2008). *Beziehung und Kommunikation als neue Grundparadigmen in der Geburtshilfe.* Vortrag auf dem XVIII. Internationalen Kongress der Internationalen Studiengemeinschaft für pränatale und perinatale Psychologie Medizin (ISPPM), 10. Oktober 2008. Heidelberg.

Hildebrandt, S. (2008). Spät abnabeln. In: *Deutsche Hebammen-Zeitschrift* 12, p. 26 ff.

Hochaf, R. (2007). *Fruhes Trauma und Strukturdefizit.* Ansanger Verlag, Kröning.

Hochauf, R. (2008). Zur Spezifik pränataler Traumatisierungen und deren Bearbeitung in der Therapie erwachsener Patienten. *Int. J. Prenatal and Perinatal Psychology and Medicine*, Vol. 20, S. 269–282.

Howson, C. P., **Kinney**, M. V. & **Lawn**, J. E. (2012). *Born Too Soon: The Global Action Report on Preterm Birth.* World Health Organization, Geneva.

Huber, M. (2013). *Der Feind im Inneren. Psychotherapie mit Täterintrojekten.* Junfermann Verlag, Paderborn.

Huizink, A. C. (2000). *Prenatal stress and its effect on infant development.* Doktorarbeit, Universität Utrecht.

Hüther, G. (2012). Prä- und perinatale Einflüsse auf die Hirnentwicklung. In: Liem, T., Schleupen, A., Altmeyer, P. und Zweedijk, R. (2012). *Osteopathische Behandlung von Kindern*(pp. 161–164). Haug Verlag, Stuttgart.

Hüther, G. & **Krens**, I. (2013). *Das Geheimnis der ersten neun Monate.* Beltz Verlag, Weinheim.

Hyatt, M. (2012). *Ungestillte Sehnsucht. Wenn der Kinderwunsch uns umtreibt.* Christoph Links Verlag, Berlin.

Janov, A. (2011/2012). *Vorgeburtliches Bewusstsein. Das geheime Drehbuch, das unser Leben bestimmt.* Scorpio Verlag, Berlin.

Janus, L. (1997/2011). *Wie die Seele entsteht. Unser psychisches Leben vor und nach der Geburt.* Mattes Verlag, Heidelberg.

Janus, L. & **Haibach**, S. (Hg.) (1997). *Seelisches Erleben vor und* *während der Geburt*. LinguaMed Verlags-GmbH, Neu-Isenburg.

Janus, L. (2000/2013). *Der Seelenraum des Ungeborenen*. *Pränatale Psychologie und Therapie*. Patmos Verlag, Ostfildern.

Janus, L. (Hg.) (2013). *Die pränatale Dimension in der Psychotherapie*. Mattes Verlag, Heidelberg.

Johnson, A. (2012). *Warum ich keine Abtreibungsklinik mehr leite*. Sankt-Ulrich Verlag, Augsburg.

Jurgelucks, C. (2004). *Kaiserschnitt – Wunsch, Erlösung oder Trauma*. Marbuse Verlag, Frankfurt/M.

Jütte, R. (1993). *Geschichte der Abtreibung. Von der Antike bis zur Gegenwart*. C.H. Beck Verlag, München.

Juul, J. (2011). *Mann & Vater sein*. Kreuz Verlag, München.

Kirkilionis, E. (2008). *Bindung Stärkt*. Kosel-Verlag, München.

Kitzinger, S. (1998). *Schwangerschaft und Geburt*. Kösel Verlag, München.

Klaus, M. H. & Klaus, P. H. (2000). *Das Wunder der ersten Lebenswochen*. Kösel Verlag, München.

Kolip, P., Nolting, H.-D. & Zich, K. (2012). *Kaiserschnitt – Entwicklung und regionale Verteilung*. Erstellt im Auftrag der Bertelsmann Stiftung. Gütersloh.

Krüll, M. (2009). *Die Geburt ist nicht der Anfang. Die ersten Kapitel unseres Lebens – neu erzählt*. Klett-Cotta Verlag, Stuttgart.

Kubicka, L., Roth, Z., Dytrich, Z., Matejcek, Z. & David, H. (2002). The mental health of adults born of unwanted pregnancies, their siblings and matched controls. In: *Journal of Nervous and Mental disease*, 190, p. 653 ff.

Kuhn, W. & Teichmann, A. T. (1986). Zur Entstehung der ältesten Gebärklinik Deutschlands an der Universität Göttingen (1751). In: Beck, L. (Hg.): *Zur Geschichte der Gynäkologie und Geburtshilfe*. Springer-Verlag, Berlin.

Ladan, A. (2003). *Het wandelende hoofd. Over de geheime fantasie een uitzondering te zijn*. Uitgeverij Boom, Amsterdam.

Lang, C. (2009). *Bonding*. Urban und Fischer Verlag, München.

Le Doux, J. (1996). *The emotional brain*. Simon and Schuster, New York.

Levend, H. & Janus, L. (Hg.) (2000). *Drum hab ich kein Gesicht. Kinder aus unerwünschten Schwangerschaften*. Echter Verlag, Würzburg.

Levend, H. & Janus, L. (Hg.) (2011). *Bindung beginnt vor der Geburt*. Mattes Verlag, Heidelberg.

Levine, P. A. (2010). *Sprache ohne Worte. Wie unser Körper Trauma*

References

verarbeitet und uns in die innere Balance zurückführt. Kösel Verlag, München.

Lindner, A. M. (2009). *Geschäft Abtreibung.* Sankt-Ulrich Verlag, Augsburg.

Lothrop, H. (2004): *Gute Hoffnung – Jähes Ende.* Kösel Verlag, München.

Louwen, F. (2012). Kaiserschnitt oder natürliche Geburt – keine schwierige Entscheidung? *DGGG-Kongress 2012*

Lüpke, H. von (2011). Ungewolltes Wunschkind – bedrohtes Traumkind. Die scheinbaren Paradoxien des Kinderwunsches. In: Levend, H. und Janus, L. (Hg.): *Bindung beginnt vor der Geburt* (pp. 40–48). Mattes Verlag, Heidelberg.

Marcovich, M. & **de Jong**, M. T. (2008). *Frühgeborene – zu klein zum Leben?* Kösel Verlag, München.

McCarty, W. A. (2013). *Ich bin Bewusstsein. Ein integratives Modell frühkindlicher Entwicklung.* Innenwelt Verlag, Köln.

Meissner, B. R. (2010). *Kaiserschnitt und Kaiserschnittmütter: Frauen erzählen, was sie erlebten und wie sie ihren Kaiserschnitt verarbeitet haben.* Brigitte Meissner Verlag, Winterthur.

Meissner, B. R. (2011). *Emotionale Narben aus Schwangerschaft und Geburt auflösen: Mutter-Kind-Bindungen heilen oder unterstützen – in jedem Alter.* Brigitte Meissner Verlag, Winterthur.

Metz-Becker, M. (1997). *Der verwaltete Körper.* Campus-Verlag. Frankfurt/M.

Metz-Becker, M. (2012). *Kindsmord und Neonatizid. Kulturwissenschaftliche Perspektiven auf die Geschichte der Kindstötung.* Jonas Verlag, Marburg.

Möbius, P. J. (1903). *Über den physiologischen Schwachsinn des Weibes.* Marhold, Halle.

Mutterschafts-Richtlinien (2013). In: *Buhdesanzeiger* [Federal Gazette] 2013.

NCKO (2011). *Pedagogische kwaliteit van de kinderopvang en de ontwikkeling van jonge kinderen: een longitudinale studie.* NCKO, Amsterdam, The Netherlands.

Neises, M. & **Weidner**, K. (2012). Frauenheilkunde. In: Adler et al. (Hg.): *Psychosomatische Medizin* (pp. 1076–1092). Elsevier Verlag, München.

Nelson, C. A. & **Carver**, L. J. (1998). The effects of stress and trauma on brain and memory: A view from developmental cognitive neuroscience. In: Development and Psychopathology, 10, S. 793–809.

288

NICHD [Early Child Care Network] (1994). Child care and child development: The NICHD study of early child care. In: Friedman, S. & Haywood, H. (Hg.): *Developmental follow-up: Concepts, domains and methods* (pp. 377–396). Academic Press, New York, USA.

Nilson, L. & **Hamberger**, L. (2003). *Ein Kind entsteht*. Mosaik Verlag, München.

Noble, E. (1996). *Primäre Bindungen. Über den Einfluss pränataler Erfahrungen*. Fischer Verlag, Frankfurt/M.

Oblasser, C., **Ebner**, U. & **Wesp**, G. (2008). *Der Kaiserschnitt hat kein Gesicht*. Edition Riedenburg, Salzburg.

Odent, M. (2006). *Geburt und Stillen*. Beck Verlag, München.

Otto, P. & **Wagner**, T. (2013). *Handlungsbedarf Kaiserschnitt. Ursachen der steigenden Kaiserschnittrate in Deutschland – Maßnahmen zur Senkung der Kaiserschnittrate*. Ergebnis der Online-Umfrage und Expertinnen-Interviews 2012/2013 im Auftrag des Arbeitskreises für Frauengesundheit in Medizin, Psychotherapie und Gesellschaft (AKF e.V.).

Piontelli, A. (1996). *Vom Fetus zum Kind. Über die Ursprünge des psychischen Lebens*. Klett-Cotta Verlag, Stuttgart.

Precht, R. D. (2009). *Liebe. Ein unordentliches Gefühl*. Goldmann Verlag, München.

Raffei, J. (2006). *Nabelschnur der Seele*. Psychosozial Verlag, Gießen.

Rakos, E. (2012). *Die vaginale Untersuchung während der Geburt*. Masterthesis 2012, Innsbruck.

Rauwald, M. (Hg.) (2013). *Vererbte Wunden. Transgenerationale Weitergabe traumatischer Erfahrungen*. Beltz Verlag, Weinheim.

Reiter, A. (2011). "Wenn schon ein Kind, dann nur ein Bub"- Erfahrungen aus einer psychoanalytischen Terapie. In: Levend, H. & Janus, L. (Hg.) (2011). *Bindung beginnt vor der Geburt*. Mattes Verlag, Heidelberg.

Renggli, F. (2013). *Das goldene Tor zum Leben. Wie unser Trauma aus Geburt und Schwangerschaft ausheilen kann*. Arkana Verlag, München.

Rockenschaub, A. (2005). *Gebären ohne Aberglauben*. Facultas Universitätsverlag, Vienna, Austria.

Ruppert, F. (2001). *Berufliche Beziehungswelten. Das Aufstellen von Arbeitsbeziehungen in Theorie und Praxis*. Heidelberg: Carl-Auer-Systeme Verlag.

Ruppert, F. (2002). *Verwirrte Seelen. Der verborgene Sinn von Psychosen. Grundzüge einer systemischen Psychotraumatologie*. München: Kösel Verlag.

References

Ruppert, F. (2008). *Trauma, Bonding and Family Constellations: Understanding and Healing Injuries of the Soul*. Green Balloon Publishing, UK.

Ruppert, F. (2011). *Splits in the Soul: Integrating Traumatic Experiences*. Green Balloon Publishing, UK.

Ruppert, F. (2012). *Symbiosis and Autonomy: Symbiotic Trauma and Love Beyond Entanglements*. Green Balloon Publishing, UK.

Ruppert, F. (2014). *Trauma, Fear and Love: How the Constellation of the Intention supports Autonomy*. Green Balloon Publishing, UK.

Schacter, D. L. (1996). *Searching for memory*. Basic Books, New York, USA.

Schindler, P. (Hg.) (2011). *Am Anfang des Lebens. Neue körperpsychotherapeutische Erkenntnisse über unsere frühesten Prägungen durch Schwangerschaft und Geburt*. Schwabe Verlag, Basel.

Schleußner, E. (2013). The prevention, diagnosis and treatment of premature labor. *Deutsches Ärzteblatt Int 110* (13), pp. 227–236.

Schönfeld, K. (2001). *Sexualisierte Gewalt und Geburtshilfe*. Vortrag.

Schreiber, M. (Hg.) (1981). *Die schöne Geburt. Reinbek bei*. Rowohlt Verlag, Hamburg.

Seidler, G. H., **Freyberger**, H. J. & **Maercker**, A. (Hg.) (2011). *Handbuch der Psychotraumatologie*. Klett-Cotta Verlag, Stuttgart.

Singer, W. (2002). *Der Beobachter im Gehirn: Essays zur Hirnforschung*. Suhrkamp Verlag, Frankfurt/M.

Sonne, J. C. (1996). Interpreting the Dread of Being Aborted in Therapy. In: *Internationale Zeitschrift für Pränatale und Perinatale Psychologie und Medizin*, 3, pp. 317–339.

Speckhard, A. C. & **Rue**, V. M. (1992). Postabortion Syndrome: An Emerging Public Health Concern. In: *Journal of Social Issues*, 3, pp. 95–119.

Sprenger, K. (2005). Arztgeschichten – Geburtshilfe und Apparate-Medizin. *Deutsches Ärzteblatt, 102* (30).

Stadelmann, I. (2004). *Die Hebammensprechstunde*. Eigenverlag.

Stening, W. (2007). Die Känguru-Methode. In: *Bundesverband »Das frühgeborene Kind« e.V.* (Hg.): *Frühgeborene und ihre Eltern in der Klinik* (pp. 19–27). Frankfurt/M.

Streeck-Fischer, A. (2011). Traumafolgestörungen bei Kindern und Jugendlichen. In: Seidler, G. H., Freyberger, H. J. und Maercker, A. (Hg.): *Handbuch der Psychotraumatologie* (pp. 450–468). Klett-Cotta Verlag, Stuttgart.

Taschner, U. & **Scheck**, K. (2012). *Meine Wunschgeburt – Selbst-*

bestimmt gebären nach Kaiserschnitt. Edition Riedenburg, Salzburg.

Terr, L. (1994). *Unchained Memories: True Stories of Traumatic Memories Lost And Found.* Basic Books, New York, USA.

Terre des Femmes (Hg.) (2003). *Schnitt in die Seele. Weibliche Genitalverstümmelung – eine fundamentale Menschenechtsverletzung.* Marbuse Verlag, Frankfurt/M.

Terry, K. (2011). Beobachtungen bei der Behandlung von Kindern, die durch künstliche Befruchtung gezeut wurden. In: Schindler, P. (Hg.): *Am Anfang des Lebens. Neue körpertherapeutische Erkenntnisse über unsere frühesten Prägungen durch Schwangerschaft und Geburt.* Schwabe Verlag, Basel.

Tew, M. (2007). *Sichere Geburt? Eine kritische Auseinandersetzung mit der Geschichte der Geburtshilfe.* Marbuse Verlag, Frankfurt/M.

Van der Hart, O., **Nijenhuis**, E. & **Steele**, K. (2006). *The Haunted Self: Structural Dissociation and the Treatment of Chronic Traumatisation.* Norton, New York, USA.

Wardetzki, B. (1996). *»Iß doch endlich mal normal!« Hilfen für Angehörige von essgestörten Mädchen und Frauen.* Kösel Verlag, München.

Woolger, R. (1992). *Die vielen Leben der Seele.* Heinrich Hugendubel Verlag, München.

Wolter, H. (2010). *Meine Folgeschwangerschaft.* Edition Riedenburg, Salzburg.

Zander, J. (1986). Meilensteine in der Gynäkologie und Geburtshilfe – 100 Jahre Deutsche Gesellschaft für Gynäkologie und Geburtshilfe. In: Beck, L. (Hg): *Zur Geschichte der Gynäkologie und Geburtshilfe.* Springer-Verlag, Berlin.

Information from newspapers (daily and weekly)

HAZ (2013) [*Hannoversche Allgemeine Zeitung*] 30.8.2013

Kaiserschnitt bleibt Notausgang. *Hildesheimer Allgemeine Zeitung*, 30. 8. 2013.

Moulin, M. (2013). Liebe auf Distanz. Die Zeit, 13. 9. 2013.

Rögener, W. Geburtshilfe Unfug im Kreißsaal: www.sueddeutsche.de, 19. 5. 2010.

Schreiber, M. Unendliches Vergnügen, unendlicher Schmerz. *Der Spiegel*, 28. 7. 1980.

Internet links

Bundeszentrale für gesundheitliche Aufklärung (Hg). Schwangerschaftserleben und Pränataldiagnostik. Repräsentative Befragung
Schwangerer zum Thema Pränataldiagnostik. Köln 2006.
www.bzga.de
Kaiserschnittgeburten – Entwicklung und regionale Verteilung.
www.bertelsmann-stiftung.de www.faktencheck-gesundheit.de
Schönfeld, K. (2001). Niederschrift eines Vortrages, gehalten in der
interdisziplinären Arbeitsgruppe »sexualisierte Gewalt gegen Frauen
und die Auswirkungen auf Schwangerschaft, Geburt und
Wochenbett«. http://www.geburtskanal.de
http://www.spiegel.de/panorama/gesellschaft/hausgeburten-in-
deutschland a-890023.html, 20. 03. 2013
Schumann. C. Weiblichkeit ist Keine Krankheit-was ist für Frauen
gesund? www.dr-clandia-schumann.de/typo3/index.php?id=29
http://www.zentrum-der-gesundheit.de/hausgeburt-ia.html, 18. 11. 2013
http://www.dggg.de/presse/pressemitteilungen/mitteilung/
dggg-kongress-2012 – kaiserschnitt-oder-natuerliche-geburt-
keine-schwierige-entscheidung
http://www.geburtskanal.de
http://www.charite.de/charite/presse/pressemitteilungen/artikel/detail/
von_generation_zu_generation/, 05. 07. 2012

Index

A

abortion, iii, 27, 29, 42, 55, 64, 72, 89, 95, 108, 125, 146, 151, 190, 206, 213, 215, 266, 271
  attempted, 102
  psychological consequences of, 98
ADD, 150
addiction, 148
ADHD, 114, 150, 206, 237, 274
adoption, iii, viii, 152, 234
adoptive parents, 244
alcohol, 29, 33, 95, 148, 249
anorexia, 253
antisocial behaviour, 242
anxiety, ix, 31, 82, 95, 263, 271
artificial insemination, 38
artificial reproduction
  alternatives, 87
assisted reproduction, 38 (*see also* conception, assisted)
attachment, 16, 27, 30, 38, 48, 103, 189, 199, 255 (*see also* bonding)
  insecure, 181
  secure, 66, 99, 104, 220
  trauma of, 257
attachment disorders, 31, 85

B

birth,
  and sexual violence, 132
  at home, 141
  multiple, 143
  premature, 148
  violence during, 133
birth trauma, 235
birth-houses, 136
bonding, vii, 6, 12, 28, 33, 37, 127, 150, 157, 158, 159, 167, 184, 272
  disorders, 146
  pre-natal, 69
  prenatal, 122
  with father, 161
bonding patterns, 180
breech presentation, 142
bulimia, 247, 254

C

caesarean section, 28, 29, 37, 70, 85, 129
  increase of, 141
  planned, 143
cancer, 4, 108
children
  working with, 114
circumcision, 39, 220
  female, 220
Clay Field therapy, 86, 245, 237
conception, iii, x, 28, 33, 54, 131, 180, 267, 273
  assisted, 77, 82
  from rape, 59
consciousness, 51
Constellation of the Intention, 40, 113, 156, 170, 184, 224, 238, 245, 256, 268
contraception, 55, 77
crèches
  children in, 203

D

depression, iii, ix, 77, 95, 96, 125, 174, 176
  postpartum, 186
  pre-natal, 68
diabetes, 252
Dissociative Indentity Disorder (DID) 260
Down's Syndrome, 123
drug addiction, 235
drugs, 26, 29, 33, 64, 211
dyslexia, 150

E

early trauma, 27
eating disorders, 246
embolism, 90, 144
entanglement

symbiotic, 1, 6, 59, 106, 205, 253, 255
episiotomy, 134

F

fathers
  and early trauma, 35
foeticide, 93
foster parents, viii, 234, 244

G

genital mutilation, 39, 56, 220
grandparents, 209

H

heart disease, 252
hysterectomy, 144

I

incest, 64
infanticide, 186
infertility, 76, 77
insomnia, 4, 9
IVF, 38, 82, 143

K

kangaroo care, 149

L

lactose intolerance, 250
limbic brain, 43
love, 12
  causing illness, 16
  healthy, 14

M

maternal ambivalence, 66, 67
medical obstetrics, 127
  history of, 128
menstruation, 129
midwifery, 125, 130

migraine, 9
miscarriage, 115, 173
mother
  not loving child, 13
  traumatised 32
  as a perpetrator 33
mother-embryo dialogue (M-E-D), 87
multi-generational psychotraumatology, 5, 184, 224
multiple births, 143

O
obesity, 252
oxytocin, 140, 144, 158, 161

P
panic attacks, 31, 58, 116, 215,
  236
perpetrator, 7, 9, 13, 26, 50, 63,
  101, 105, 187, 190, 222, 254
  attitude, 11
  mother as a, 33
  organisations, 39
  traumatisation of, 8
perpetrator-victim, 19, 28, 47, 268
perpetrator-victim dynamics, 131
perpetrator-victim split, 100, 187,
  269
perpetrator-victim systems, 10
personality disorders, ix, 222
placenta, 157
pornography, 23, 39
pregnancy, vii, ix, x, 21–37, 68,
  93, 131, 148, 273
  bonding during, 180
  high risk, 120
  tests and checks, 119
pregnancy management, 37
premature birth, 29, 69, 85, 94,
  148, 150, 159, 175, 229, 290

and symbiotic trauma, 154
  and trauma, 151
prenatal diagnostics, 122
prostitution, 23, 26, 64
psychosis, ix
  postpartum', 186
psychotrauma therapy, 40

R
rape, 28, 33, 54, 92, 248
re-bonding, 172
replacement child, 182
Ritalin, 237

S
self-love, 12
sex addiction, 229
sexual abuse, 23, 26, 35, 39, 64,
  71, 132, 191, 217, 235, 254
sexual liberalism, 56
sexual violence, 25
society
  victims and perpetrators, 11
sperm donation, 84
spirituality
  concepts of, 50
splitting, 8
stillbirth, 115, 173, 175
suicide, 59, 72, 95, 112, 186, 213,
  248
surrogacy, 38, 77, 84
survival strategies, 6, 9, 18, 19,
  25, 26, 29, 46, 48, 147, 181,
  200, 221, 269
symbiotic trauma (*see* trauma,
  symbiotic)

T
thrombosis, 144
trans-generational
  psychotraumatology, ix

trauma
  and obstetrics, 36
  definition of, 5
  existential, 6, 268
  integration of, 45
  natural disaster, 6
  of bonding system, 6, 63, 257
    (*see also* attachment)
  of loss, 6, 173, 174, 179, 184
  of love, 12, 254 (*see also*
    symbiotic trauma)
  of sexuality, 20
  symbiotic, 5, 6, 19, 70, 72, 84,
    154, 156, 161, 169, 170,
    181, 183, 189, 200, 204,
    234, 248, 257, 262, 266
  war trauma, 64
traumatised mothers, 32
twins, 120, 137, 143

U
umbilical cord, 2, 69, 150, 157,
    163, 167
  prolapsed, 128

V
vaginal birth, 138
ventouse suction, 139
victim, 8, 9, 18, 50, 63, 105, 125,
    187, 222, 268
  mother as a, 33
victim attitude, 8, 126, 224, 254
violence
  during pregnancy, 235
  early, 219

W
war trauma, 64
womb, 113

9780955968372